Fire on the Water

TRANSITS:

LITERATURE, THOUGHT & CULTURE 1650–1850

Series Editors
Greg Clingham, Bucknell University
Kathryn Parker, University of Wisconsin—La Crosse
Miriam Wallace, New College of Florida

Transits is a series of scholarly monographs and edited volumes publishing beautiful and surprising work. Without ideological bias the series seeks transformative readings of the literary, artistic, cultural, and historical interconnections between Britain, Europe, the Far East, Oceania, and the Americas during the years 1650 and 1850, and as their implications extend down to the present time. In addition to literature, art and history, such "global" perspectives might entail considerations of time, space, nature, economics, politics, environment, gender, sex, race, bodies, and material culture, and might necessitate the development of new modes of critical imagination. At the same time, the series welcomes considerations of the local and the national, for original new work on particular writers and readers in particular places in time continues to be foundational to the discipline.

Since 2011, sixty-five *Transits* titles have been published or are in production.

Recent Titles in the Series

Fire on the Water: Sailors, Slaves, and Insurrection in Early American Literature, 1789–1886
Lenora Warren

Community and Solitude: New Essays on Johnson's Circle
Anthony W. Lee Ed.

The Global Wordsworth: Romanticism Out of Place
Katherine Bergren

Cultivating Peace: The Virgilian Georgic in English, 1650–1750
Melissa Schoenberger

Intelligent Souls? Feminist Orientalism in Eighteenth-Century English Literature
Samara Anne Cahill

The Printed Reader: Gender, Quixotism, and Textual Bodies in Eighteenth-Century Britain
Amelia Dale

For a full list of *Transits* titles go to https://www.bucknell.edu/script/upress/series.asp?id=33

Fire on the Water

SAILORS, SLAVES, AND INSURRECTION IN EARLY AMERICAN LITERATURE, 1789–1886

LENORA WARREN

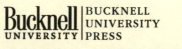

Bucknell UNIVERSITY | BUCKNELL UNIVERSITY PRESS

LEWISBURG, PENNSYLVANIA

Library of Congress Cataloging-in-Publication Data

Names: Warren, Lenora, author.
Title: Fire on the water : sailors, slaves, and insurrection in early
    American literature, 1789–1886 / Lenora Warren.
Other titles: Sailors, slaves, and insurrection in early American
    literature, 1789–1886
Description: Lewisburg, Pennsylvania : Bucknell University Press,
    2018. | Series: Transits: literature, thought & culture 1650–1850 |
    Includes bibliographical references and index.
Identifiers: LCCN 2018025926| ISBN 9781684480180 (hardback) |
    ISBN 9781684480173 (paperback) | ISBN 9781684480197 (epub) |
    ISBN 9781684480210 (Web PDF) | ISBN 9781684480203 (mobi)
Subjects: LCSH: American literature—19th century—History
    and criticism. | Slavery in literature. | Slave insurrections in
    literature. | Antislavery movements in literature. | Abolitionists in
    literature. | English literature—18th century—History and
    criticism. | BISAC: LITERARY CRITICISM / American /
    General. | SOCIAL SCIENCE / Slavery. | LITERARY
    CRITICISM / European / English, Irish, Scottish, Welsh. |
    LITERARY CRITICISM / American / African American.
Classification: LCC PS217.S55 W37 2018 | DDC 810.9/35873—dc23
    LC record available at https://catalog.loc.gov/vwebv/search?
    searchCode=LCCN&searchArg=2018025926&searchType=1&
    permalink=y

A British Cataloging-in-Publication record for this book is available
from the British Library.

♾ The paper used in this publication meets the requirements of the
American National Standard for Information Sciences—Permanence
of Paper for Printed Library Materials, ANSI Z39.48-1992.

www.bucknell.edu/UniversityPress.

Distributed worldwide by Rutgers University Press

Manufactured in the United States of America

To Mom and Dad

CONTENTS

Fire on the Water

Aloft all hands, strike the top-masts and belay;
Yon angry setting sun and fierce-edged clouds
Declare the Typhon's coming.
Before it sweeps your decks, throw overboard
The dead and dying–ne'er heed their chains
Hope, Hope, fallacious Hope!
Where is thy market now?
—J. M. W. Turner, "Fallacies of Hope" (1812)[1]

THIS FRAGMENT OF AN UNFINISHED poem appeared alongside J. M. W. Turner's painting "The Slave Ship (Slavers Throwing Overboard the Dead and Dying, Typhoon Coming On)" at the World Anti Slavery Convention June 12–23, 1840. The famous image depicting the infamous massacre of the slaves aboard the ship *Zong* in 1781 acted as both a commemoration of the hard work of early actors such as Granville Sharp and Thomas Clarkson in abolishing the Atlantic Slave trade, and admonishment to current abolitionists that the work was far from done.[2] Turner's painting simultaneously depicts the grisly aftermath of the massacre by showing the water churning with dismembered bodies and feeding sharks and the fiery destruction of the ship as the storm descends in a dramatic act of divine providence. The accompanying poem fragment retells the story of the massacre as one in which a panicked captain orders the dead and dying slaves thrown overboard before the storm descends. The real story, that of slaves deprived of water and drowned over a period of three days, is transformed into one of moral panic as the crew kills the slaves to hide their sin of slave trading.[3] That the legal outcome of the *Zong* case was not the indictment of captain and crew for mass murder but the denial of an insurance claim for the dead slaves vanishes in the retelling of the story.

As such, Turner's painting presents to us an example of both the power and the problem of narrative as it applies to the history of the slave trade and abolition. Having been placed by scholars such as Ian Baucom as "the single most

famous period meditation on the trans-Atlantic slave trade and a global abolitionist movement's work of sympathetic witness," Turner's "Slave Ship" manages to
reach both backward and forward in time to comment on the whole history of
abolition.[4] In referring to the image in *The Overthrow of Colonial Slavery: 1776–
1848*, Robin Blackburn muses, "It is not, perhaps too farfetched to suggest that
Britain's rulers could have seen in this painting not simply the slave-trader jettison-
ing his cargo but also a symbolic representation of their own sacrifice of slavery, in
order to render the ship of state more seaworthy in a storm."[5] This interpretation of
the image and its reception takes the fifty-nine-year interim between the *Zong*
massacre and the painting's unveiling and reads it as signifying a moral shift in
attitudes about slavery. Likewise, in *The Black Atlantic: Modernity and Double
Consciousness*, Paul Gilroy calls Turner's painting "a useful image . . . for its self-
conscious moral power and the striking way it aims directly for the sublime in its
invocation of racial terror, commerce, and England's ethic-political degenera-
tion."[6] Gilroy's invocation of the violence of the slave trade further ties the
painting's "moral power" to the familiar narrative of the sinning slaver turned
penitent abolitionist in the face of the overwhelming evidence of the horrors
of slavery. The descriptive language used by Baucom, Blackburn, and Gilroy—
"meditation," "sympathetic," "sacrifice," "moral," "sublime"—places "The Slave
Ship" as a work that captures both the imaginative and the moral power of the abolitionist movement.

But while this moral power proved vital to turning the tide against the slave
trade and ultimately slavery as a whole, its place in that history has proved domi-
nant to the point of crowding out other narratives of abolition. Such narratives,
characterized by a history of slave resistance that begins at the moment of the first
encounter between slave trader and African, are necessary not only to give texture
and scope to the history of insurrection but to highlight the way in which abolitionist rhetoric about violence, particularly about slave insurrection, is complicit
in shaping attitudes towards race and violence that still persist into our present
moment. The process by which the preferred image of the enslaved became that of
the slave as perpetual victim while the image of the slave as insurrectionist became
taboo is one that has not sufficiently been addressed by current scholarship.

This book seeks to track some of that moral and imaginative power from a
different source, namely from the perspective of the slave insurrectionist. In
doing so, I hope to shift the focus of the histories of The Middle Passage, abolition, and insurrection from the ship's hold to the ship's deck. Through the stories
of Olaudah Equiano, Denmark Vesey, Joseph Cinqué, and Washington Goode,
four black sailors, I look at how black sailors and insurrectionists are a critical focal
point for recovering a vexed narrative of insurrection in the abolitionist movement.

If, as Hester Blum has argued, "acknowledging the sailor . . . allows us to perceive, analyze, and deploy aspects of the history, literature, and culture of the oceanic world that otherwise might be rendered obscure and abstract," acknowledging the role of black sailors—both free and un-free—as both victims of, witnesses to, and opponents of slavery and its atrocities renders visible the role of slave violence in general, and shipboard insurrection specifically, in shaping abolitionist discourse.[7]

This work will center on four specific moments in which the history of abolition and insurrection intersect using four real life black sailors as points of entry. These moments are the formation of the British Abolitionist movement in the 1780s in the immediate aftermath of the *Zong* massacre; the Denmark Vesey Conspiracy in 1821 and its aftermath; the *Amistad* mutiny of 1839 and the *Creole* mutiny of 1841; and finally, the less well-known case of Washington Goode, a black sailor sentenced to death for murder in 1849. While these moments do not have the kind of larger impact of the St. Domingo uprising in 1791, the passing of the *Fugitive Slave Act* in 1850, and John Brown's 1859 raid on Harper's Ferry, they precipitate crucial and specific rhetorical shifts in debates about the place of violence in the anti-slavery movement. They also reveal the ways in which the gravitational pull of the aforementioned events has, to some extent, obscured and distorted the longer history of insurrection and abolition. Finally, the moments I have chosen are notable, not simply for the events that occurred, but in the ways in which they have gotten transmitted through legal documents and historical and fictional narratives. Sometimes mutineers have been transformed into heroes. Sometimes the reverse has happened. And some figures have been virtually lost from the legal record, only to surface as characters in Romantic fiction. To locate the ways that paintings, stories, novels, newspaper articles, personal narratives, and law construct narratives of heroism and villainy is to reveal the powerful way in which the awareness of and fear of slave violence determines the shape of the history we think we know. Narratives that deal with violence prove both useful and challenging in that the act of narrating violence—or very often failing to narrate violence—reveals anxieties regarding the relationship between race, violence and the very essence of freedom.

While abolitionist rhetoric was arguably successful in creating a climate in which opposition to slavery became more mainstream, the way in which it used the figure of the slave placed African Americans in an untenable position. If we return to the example of Turner's "The Slave Ship," the usefulness of that image and the true story of the *Zong* massacre turns on the position of slaves as perfect victims. To paraphrase Edgar Allan Poe in "The Philosophy of Composition," a slave killed in cold blood is the most perfect political tool to end slavery.[8] Absent

Figure 1. John Greenleaf Whittier (1807–1892). "Am I Not a Man and a Brother" (1837), woodcut on wove paper; 26.7 × 22.8 cm. Library of Congress Rare Book and Special Collections Division, Washington, DC.

a dead slave, the image of the slave as penitent also proved useful in the campaign to abolish the Atlantic slave trade. The famous kneeling slave from the Wedgewood medallion produced in 1787 for the Committee for the Abolition of the Slave Trade is a quintessential example. While the caption "AM I NOT A MAN AND A BROTHER" demands the slave be considered as an equal, the figure is presented in the pose of a supplicant. The political efficacy of these images combined with a growing fear of insurrection both before and after the St. Domingo uprising created within anti-slavery and later abolitionist discourse a growing awareness that any representation of the slave had to be non-threatening.

In *My Bondage and My Freedom* (1855), Frederick Douglass describes feeling like "chattel" and a "thing" when he's urged by the Garrisonians to strip and show his scars at his speaking engagements and to infuse his speech with "more of the plantation."[9] Douglass's frustration with the abolitionists speaks to this problem of representation. Douglass, whose much-vaunted eloquence made him the most famous ex-slave to speak out against slavery, also unnerved his white allies as potentially alienating—as though eloquence would be too disruptive to the image of the abused abject slave. Douglass's choice to embrace a more radical and militant rhetoric can be seen as a reaction against this insistence that he perform the role of the abject slave. But, as I demonstrate in chapter 3, Douglass found that embracing revolutionary rhetoric was only successful in that it created a more palatable narrative of insurrection.

Exploring the effects of this preference for "palatability" is one piece of the intervention this project makes. In order for slave violence to register as a political act it is important to acknowledge that anti-slavery actors had to render such activity unpalatable, which had significant consequences in limiting the emancipatory potential of antislavery representation and rhetoric. These consequences, I argue, have been largely ignored by scholarships in favor of privileging more celebratory narratives that foreground the role of radical abolitionists in ending slavery. Recovering this history is essential to understanding how activists at key moments bowed to political expediency and subsequently became complicit in shaping a racialized view of violence that impacts us today.

The second piece of my intervention shifts the locus of insurrection from plantation abuse (and even the abusive conditions of the Middle Passage) to the moment of capture. Shipboard revolt, unlike plantation revolt, shows us that it is not so much the unrelenting abusive nature of chattel slavery but rather the deprivation of freedom that provokes incitement. Reframing revolt as instantaneous rather than gradual—as the first reaction rather than the last straw—allows us to recover the act of violence as the right to revolt as specified in the case of the *Amistad*

captives discussed in chapter 3, and in doing so argue for slave violence as consti-
tuting a distinctly political act.

The third piece of my intervention is my highlighting the symbolic and historical importance of black sailors. Within the history of slavery, abolition, and
insurrection, black sailors occupy multiple spaces. Slaves served as sailors in the
navy, on merchant ships, and on slavers. They also used skills learned at sea to either
to gain their freedom or to escape slavery. Douglass famously used the disguise of
the sailor when he made his famous escape. Black sailors had mobility and subsequently presented a unique threat to the southern slave power. In short, black sailors
represented both the possibilities of a post-slavery world in providing a challenging
and romantic arena in which to demonstrate their power and, in the imaginations
of slaveholders and fearful white Northerners, the threat of revolt set loose across
the ocean; the terror of St. Domingo under full sail.

The final piece in my intervention is a demonstration of how certain fictions
brush against the historical trajectories that have been shaped by media, legal rhetoric, and political discourse. Fiction, or in the case of Equiano, fictionalized
autobiography, provides us with a useful lens through which to read so-called factual
documents by demanding that we rethink differences between fiction and nonfiction and look at the construction of a particular narrative as a choice to privilege one truth over many possible others. While this point may seem simplistic
and obvious, I believe that scholarship, particularly scholarship on the history of
insurrection, either fixates on one or two historical trajectories that frame insurrection as defined within those parameters, or insists on a reading of insurrection
as always revolutionary. When the threat of revolution was conjured by those who
most feared its consequences, as may have been the case in Denmark Vesey, or in
order to politicize insurrection in service of the abolitionist movement, as was
the case with the *Amistad* mutiny, it is necessary to rethink the question of how
the revolutionary potential of insurrection is being narrated for political purposes.
Recovering the element of fiction in the way in which these events are depicted in
nonfiction texts allows us to see the various agendas at work in creating these
narratives.

To the extent that scholars have addressed these issues—slave insurrection,
the role of sailors, and radical abolition—my work is indebted to the following
scholars even as I question some of their specific conclusions or omissions in
key areas. While John Stauffer's work has done much to draw attention to the
role played by a core of radical abolitionists in the 1840s and 1850s, he does not
sufficiently account for the role played by insurrection in shaping their politics.[10]
Manisha Sinha to date has done some of the most exhaustive and comprehensive
work in looking at the role of African Americans in the abolitionist movement

and looked specifically at the role of insurrection as influential.[11] I depart from her analysis by questioning the larger impact of these figures not only on shaping the movement but also in impacting the how violence shapes how we see race. David Brion Davis describes the energy of abolition as largely fueled by those who found the condition of slavery intolerable in the age of Enlightenment.[12] But that also fails to take into account the reluctance of progressives to embrace insurrection as a legitimate response to slavery. Indeed, as the Terror took hold of France following the revolution there, violence became anathema to those who initially looked optimistically to the French Revolution. Marcus Rediker has done some of the most exhaustive and fine-grained research on the role of seamen in shaping politics in the eighteenth and nineteenth centuries, and while I draw heavily on his research, I also question his conclusions, specifically the failure of moments of interracial cooperation to spread beyond the confines of the ship.[13] Finally, I expand on Saidiya V. Hartman's work by exploring the scene of armed resistance as pre-dating the scene of subjection and as possibly rethinking subjection as erasing the political importance of insurrection.[14] If it is indeed "impossible to imagine the enslaved outside a chain of associations in which the captive dancing in literal or figurative chains, on the deck of the ship, in the marketplace, or before a master does not figure prominently," I wish to show how those images worked to obscure the menace of insurrection just beneath the surface.[15]

The following discussion begins with Olaudah Equiano's very successful *The Interesting Narrative of the Life of Olaudah Equiano*, published in 1789, the same year as the French Revolution and on the eve of the Haitian Revolution.[16] Equiano's narrative was a concerted effort to alleviate British fears that the abolition of the Slave Trade might lead to larger conflagrations by presenting its author as the successful slave turned entrepreneur, a success born of literacy, industry, and piety. I argue that by representing scenes of fighting and near mutiny, Equiano explicitly used depictions of violence to contain readers' fears of slave violence and to redirect their attention to the question of incorporating freed slaves into the polity.

Chapter 2 focuses on the Denmark Vesey conspiracy of 1822. Vesey, a sailor from San Domingo, tried and hung for plotting a large-scale insurrection in Charleston, South Carolina, is believed to have been plotting to set fire to the city and then escape to San Domingo with the aid of Haitian allies. Vesey's plot has been mired in historical controversy with some scholars going so far as to suggest that the conspiracy was purely the invention of paranoid white authorities. I argue that the threat of insurrection functions as a free-floating narrative that made the rumor of rebellion as powerful as an actual plot. This chapter reveals the contours of this narrative by focusing on a little known novella by Scottish travel writer John Howison called "The Florida Pirate." Published in 1821, one year before the Denmark Vesey conspiracy, "The Florida Pirate" attempts to contain the violence of insurrection by chronicling the fall of Manuel, a fugitive slave turned pirate, whose circumstances and possible ties to San Domingo loosely parallel certain features of Denmark Vesey.

Chapter 3 discusses the *Amistad* mutiny of 1839 and the *Creole* mutiny of 1841. While these cases have received ample attention from historians and literary scholars alike, I argue that the role of the *Amistad* case in general, and, more specifically, the reinvention of Joseph Cinqué as revolutionary hero rather than dangerous pirate, both elevated and constrained the concept of black violence to a point where insurrection could be seen as revolutionary but only in the limited framework of American Revolutionary rhetoric. I explore how the failure of the *Amistad* case to extend the "right to revolt" beyond the *Amistad* Africans is reflected in Martin Delany's *Blake, Or, the Huts of America* (1859–1862), and Douglass's "The Heroic Slave" (1853).[17] Their attempts to depict successful slave revolutions using both Joseph Cinqué and Madison Washington as their models illustrate the way in which the spectacle of slave insurrection remains too problematic even for radical abolitionists to fully embrace.

Chapter 4 discusses the little-known 1849 capital punishment case of a black sailor named Washington Goode, for which the presiding judge was Herman Melville's father-in-law, Lemuel Shaw. The Goode case has not figured much in Melville scholarship, but I argue that through the black sailor at the beginning of Herman Melville's posthumously published *Billy Budd, Sailor* (1924), we can recover the story of Goode as having influenced Melville's thinking about race, violence, justice, and freedom, and through which he demands us to consider these same issues. In drawing a comparison between the real life Goode and the fictional Budd, Melville shows us how effectively penalizing violent acts becomes impossible when violence itself is racialized and coopted for political ends. Revolutionary possibility becomes important not because it allows blacks access to the "right to revolt" but because it is a dangerous precedent by which we define violence as either just or unjust.

Taken together these stories problematize the way we narrate the histories of slavery, abolition, revolt, and revolution. These events and narratives, when made into fiction—or in the case of Equiano, novelized biography—raise questions about the manner in which historical facts are narrated or "novelized" by newspaper articles, legal documents, and even by current scholars of literature and history. Black sailors, in occupying states of freedom and un-freedom simultaneously and in being able to at once emblematize the possibilities available to blacks post-slavery and the lawlessness of insurrection, offer a hybrid view of the history of the Middle Passage, insurrection, and abolition.

My use of the word "story" is meant to highlight the blurring between fact and fiction that is apparent when one attempts to piece together cohesive narratives of these historical events. As I have already indicated, this blurring is especially evident in the controversies over the truth of Equiano's origin story and the existence of a conspiracy in the Denmark Vesey case. While I am not especially interested in the outcomes of these debates, because this work engages with the creation of historical fictions, it is more interesting to me to explore the possibility of invention in both cases. The extraordinary power of invention as it relates to both self-fashioning, as in the case of Equiano, and demonization, as in the case of Vesey, is useful in understanding how the process of narration simultaneously conjures and erases violence. Violence itself materializes only to become spectral. At the same time I am leery of treating these matters as fictions absolutely. Whether he was born in Africa or Georgia, Equiano's experience of the Middle Passage does in my estimation count as a firsthand experience. It seems a bit parsimonious to insist on a single definition of what counts as a real lived experience of the slave ship. Moreover, as Cathy N. Davidson notes, the raggedness of the historical record raises as many questions as Vincent Carretta's provocative study answers.[18] By the same token, treating the Vesey conspiracy as full invention does not do justice to the supposed conspirators. Treating them as pawns or scapegoats deprives them of possible revolutionary agency. Whether or not they were unjustly tried and condemned, one must keep alive the idea that revolutionary possibility is always already in the air whether it is seized upon by slaves or prematurely stamped out. In fact it is this very element of invention that creates these competing discourses of slave violence. The same political necessity that produces the free-market friendly Equiano also conjures the Vesey conspiracy. The same pressures that seek to condemn Joseph Cinqué as a pirate reinvent him as a revolutionary hero. And it is only through Herman Melville's story of Billy Budd that one is able to resurrect the significance of the long-dead Washington Goode.

This hybrid view also offers an analysis of the way in which the histories of abolition and slave insurrection are complicated by questions of political efficacy. Walter Johnson has argued that the slave trade and slave rebellion might be seen as confrontations between different temporalities. Slave traders, abolitionists, and enslaved Africans encountered each other through different historical and temporal frames.[19] If for the American colonists to revolt was consistent with "the course of human events," in order to keep hold of this idea and still maintain the slave trade, slave revolt had to be made to be unnatural and therefore separate from Revolutionary time. But it is also through these individual men that those temporal frames overlap and collapse onto each other by exposing the process of rendering slave revolt unnatural as precisely that: a process. Moreover, if, as Michel-Rolph

Trouillot has discussed in *Silencing the Past*, the rendering of slave violence as "unthinkable" was primarily the strategy of the planter and trading class, it would be the abolitionists who, with varying degrees of success, deployed the threat of the violent slave as an attempt to transform the idea of the slave from "savage" to civilized.[20]

WITNESS TO THE ATROCITIES

Olaudah Equiano, Thomas Clarkson,

and the Abolition of the Slave Trade

I N HIS *INTERESTING NARRATIVE*, Olaudah Equiano recalls as his earliest experience in the British Navy being forced to fight another boy for the amusement of the rest of the crew of the *Namur*. It is his first time earning money, his first bloodying, and the first time he felt himself as part of the crew as something other than a slave. He writes:

> On the passage, one day for the diversion of those gentlemen, all the boys were called on the quarter-deck, and were paired proportionably [*sic*], and then made to fight; after which the gentleman gave the combatants from five to nine shillings each. This was the first time I ever fought with a white boy; and I never knew what it was to have a bloody nose before. This made me fight most desperately; I suppose considerably more than an hour; and at last, both of us being very weary, we were parted. I had a great deal of this kind of sport afterwards, in which the captain and the ship's company used very much to encourage me.[1]

In one register the scene presents the community of the ship as one in which the markers of race matter less than physical prowess and the willingness to participate in a hazing ritual meant to induct Equiano into a community of equals. In another less obvious register the fight may stand as a pantomime that acknowledges even as it controls shipboard insurrection. Equiano's prowess at hand-to-hand combat becomes menacing and perhaps an element of his own unexplored potential for violence. The experience of his first bloody nose carries with it both the youthful revelation and a grim sense of satisfaction of not being bested. But the scene passes without further comment as one of the many anecdotes of life at sea that characterize the text. This trace of violence is no more than that, a trace. As Vincent Carretta notes in his book, *Equiano the African: Biography of a Self-made Man*, whatever radical leanings Equiano may have possessed swiftly vanished as his star rose and revolutions broke out in both France and St. Domingo.[2] Yet within the two interpretations of this trace of violence—fighting for liberation versus fighting to assimilate—lie the roots of how the early abolitionists negotiated the presence of slave insurrection in the mid-to-late eighteenth century.

In order to assess more fully the relationship between slave insurrection and the birth of the abolitionist movement, I approach this issue from three angles. First, I locate the origins of insurrection within the history of the transatlantic slave trade, thereby examining the way in which discussions of abolishing the slave trade engaged with the incidence of shipboard insurrection. Second, I reveal that the role of sailor testimony, specifically the testimony collected by Thomas Clarkson in *The Substance of the Evidence of Sundry Persons on the Slave-trade Collected in the Course Of a Tour Made in the Autumn of the Year 1788* (1788), shaped abolitionist rhetoric with regards to the place of insurrection. Third, I show how the slave as victim rather than as freedom fighter became a more compelling trope for early abolitionists.

In 1781 Captain Luke Collingwood of the slaver *Zong* threw 132 slaves overboard, alleging disease and lack of water as having compelled his actions.[3] Through the work of Equiano, Clarkson, and others, the *Zong* case would come to epitomize the evils of the slave trade, dramatizing as it did the corrupt nature of slave ship captains, the maltreatment of sailors, and of course the deplorable conditions for slaves. The slave as victim would become a popular trope both in Great Britain and later in American abolitionist circles. Yet at the same time that slaves were being thrown overboard, beaten, and starved, they were also revolting on ships in great numbers, particularly in the mid-to-late eighteenth century. This latter story, though relatively well documented by historians like David Richardson and Eric Robert Taylor, has not been sufficiently analyzed in terms of how it helped shape abolitionist rhetoric of the late eighteenth century.[4]

The question of how insurrection got written out of the early abolitionist narrative matters because, in the first place, it highlights the way in which abolitionists were conscious of the problem of slave violence in the decades leading up to the St. Domingo revolt. In the second place, writing insurrection out of the narrative also erases these early traces of black revolutionary activity, shielding abolitionists from the more radical dimensions of their opposition to the slave trade. Erasing these early traces ignores a trend of resistance outside of those discourses of abolition couched either in Christian morality or in Enlightenment logic. Revisiting the role of shipboard insurrection in shaping abolitionist rhetoric not only allows us to explore the process through which one narrative prevails over another, but also to see how remnants of the alternative narrative remain in accounts and narratives that otherwise occlude them.

The relative paucity of large-scale slave revolts may in part have led scholars to discount the influence of revolt on abolitionist rhetoric. Indeed, they have been more likely to attribute the rising hysteria of a planter population to a growing awareness that their slaves seriously outnumbered them.[5] But while large-scale revolts were indeed rare, smaller revolts and thwarted revolts combined with an expanding maroon population to create some reality behind the hysteria. Further-more, shipboard insurrections may have played a larger role than previously sup-posed in debates about abolition. In 1764, the year before Tacky's Rebellion, the slave ship *Hope* out of New London, Connecticut, was nearly overcome when the forty-three slaves taken aboard off the coast of Senegal revolted, killing the cap-tain and two of the crew.[6] While the scale of violence pales in comparison to Tacky's rebellion, micro-insurrections of this sort have easily gotten elided in the narra-tive of both the Middle Passage and slave violence. It is perhaps due to the fact that most of these insurrections occurred off the coast of Africa that we do not think about them within the context of the Middle Passage.[7] Yet, despite the fact that at the time that both Clarkson and Equiano were writing and compiling evidence for abolishing the trade, instances of both shipboard and plantation insurrections were in decline, it is clear that early British abolitionists could not help but be aware of the prevalence of insurrection in the Middle Passage.[8] Indeed for Clark-son, the escalating tensions in St. Domingo would necessarily force him to contex-tualize shipboard insurrection carefully to dissociate slave violence from full-scale revolution. How abolitionists used evidence of insurrection in their own printed materials reveals the way in which telling the story of the Middle Passage became a process of garnering sympathy for the slave, coping with the absence of the slave's voice, and ultimately of choosing to highlight the slave as victim rather than as revolutionary.

The question of how to treat these incidents begins with examining why it was necessary to relegate shipboard insurrection to the merely incidental. One rea-son may have derived from political philosophy concerning the conditions under which enslavement could ever be justified. According to John Locke's account of slavery, the enslavement of Africans could not escape the aura of violence. In Locke's words, "the perfect condition of slavery . . . [was] nothing else, but the state of war continued, between a lawful conqueror and a captive." The only way to remove the inherent violence of slavery was via agreement. In Locke's words, "if once compact enter between them, and make an agreement for a limited power on the one side, and obedience on the other, the state of war and slavery ceases, as long as the compact endures."⁹ To include shipboard insurrection within the longer story of slave insurrection is to bring into focus the manner in which African slavery constituted a prolonged state of warfare under the Lockean definition of slavery.¹⁰ Rebellious slaves aboard slaving ships could hardly be described as voluntarily entering a compact. Accordingly if one thinks about slavery as "the state of war continued," it becomes clear that reducing the slave from "captive" to chattel dehumanizes blacks and takes African slaves outside of the context of the political. By this I mean that the efforts on the part of slave traders and planters to downplay slave violence was not simply about maintaining the fictions that slavery was both benign and sustainable, but also about reducing the sense that the Africans were in any way political actors in their own fate.

British abolitionists were willing to use the high incidence of shipboard insurrection to show that traders and planters were trying to conceal the extent to which they violated Locke's own rules regarding the condition of slavery. Clarkson's work seems to have revolved around insisting on the "unlawful" kidnapping of innocents versus the "lawful" trade of prisoners of war.¹¹ This insistence is an interesting strategy because it depends on the idea that even under a system of slavery, the enslaved never lose their agency as political actors. By demonstrating that traders were operating outside the "rules" as established by Locke, Clarkson lends credence to the idea that if there is such a thing as "just" slavery, then it is not to be found in the Atlantic Slave Trade. Showing the high incidence of shipboard insurrection, therefore, provides him with an opportunity to reintroduce the notion of slavery as a "state of war" into the discourse. But as we will also see, Clarkson's embrace of this "state of war" account could also only be partial. His argument against the slave trade would depend ultimately not on the idea of the enslaved as combatant but as victim.

Equiano's place in this discursive process matters because his story of the Middle Passage is told while negotiating the question of how the slave experience figures in the shaping of abolitionist rhetoric. In occupying a dual position of sailor and slave, Equiano is able to act as both plaintiff and witness in what could be read as a narrative case against the slave trade. What is interesting is the way he, too, sidesteps the question of shipboard insurrection and instead favors a position either as victim of the slave trade or as witness to the atrocities. In occupying these specific positions, Equiano, in his *Interesting Narrative*, attempts to bridge the gap between first- and second-hand accounts of the slave trade while also avoiding political missteps.

This attempt may also help us to think beyond the vexed question of Equiano's origins. As scholars know, Carretta has brought to light documentation that suggests Equiano was in fact born in South Carolina. Other scholars still hold that there is also ample reason to doubt such documentation given the sketchy recordkeeping of the era.[12] Whether or not Carretta is right about Equiano's nativity, those who disagree with him have to acknowledge that in the narrative, Equiano's experience as a sailor dramatically overshadows his recounting of his captivity. There is a way in which the anxiety of the current debate about Equiano's nativity mirrors exactly Clarkson's own misgivings regarding shipboard insurrection and his preference for foregrounding the horror of the ship's hold, as if the validity of Equiano's protest depends entirely on his status as a victim and not at all on the soundness of his account of the various dimensions of the trade. But if it is Equiano's hybrid identity as both sailor and slave that shapes his criticisms of the Middle Passage then his narrative does not lose its force if in fact it is true that he was born in South Carolina. Instead Equiano highlights the role enslaved sailors may have played in shaping both the transatlantic slave trade and its downfall.[13]

My analysis both departs from and synthesizes the work of historians Robin Blackburn, David Brion Davis, Seymour Drescher, and Claudius K. Fergus by arguing that shipboard insurrection significantly shaped the early rhetoric of the abolitionists.[14] This approach provides insight into how slave violence affected the economic interests as well as the political world of Great Britain at that moment. I also look specifically at the way Clarkson's sailor testimonies explicitly engage the potential role of shipboard insurrection as a means of shaping an argument to present before Parliament against continuing the slave trade. Bringing Clarkson's work into dialogue with Equiano's *Interesting Narrative* reveals more explicitly the role Equiano's maritime experiences played in shaping his own evolution as an abolitionist.

TACKY'S REBELLION

As I have already suggested above, one reason that scholars have underestimated the effect of early slave insurrections on the emerging abolitionist movement is that reaction to slave violence was always out of proportion to the actual incidence of large-scale revolts. In Jamaica, Tacky's Rebellion in 1760–61 was remarkable both for the length of time it took to put it down and for having resulted in the deaths of approximately sixty whites. Indeed, the years immediately before and after Tacky's Rebellion witnessed some of the bloodiest incidents in the history of shipboard insurrection. In the spring of 1750 a group of Africans succeeded in taking the *King David*, killing fourteen crewmembers including the captain. The ship was eventually retaken off the coast of Guadalupe nearly two weeks later.[15] Additionally, in December of 1764, immediately off the coast of Africa, captured slaves aboard another ship successfully revolted, killing the entire crew, and escaping to freedom.[16] Altogether, sixty-nine shipboard insurrections were documented between 1760 and 1771.

Over the next twenty or so years slave rebellions became less frequent until the St. Domingo revolt in 1791.[17] However, while the period of Tacky's Rebellion was the exception rather than the rule, it set the stage for a debate regarding how to deal with slave violence for the next three decades.[18] Proslavery advocates such as Edward Long used it to argue that the Atlantic Slave Trade should be phased out in favor of augmenting the slave population by natural increase, pointing out that abolishing the slave trade could be seen as solving the problem of slave insurrection while safeguarding the institution.[19] And while antislavery advocates would point to the cruelty of slavery as the primary culprit behind insurrection, they too would cite the ending of slave violence as a primary benefit of the abolition of the Atlantic Slave Trade.[20]

In Long's analysis of Tacky's rebellion in *The History of Jamaica*, he argued that the fact that the ringleaders were native born Africans was indicative of the natural propensity of Africans, specifically Cormantees, towards violence.[21]

> The Negroes, who have been the chief actors in the seditions and muti-nies, which different times have broke out here were the *imported Africans*; and considering the numbers of them who were banished [from] their home country for atrocious misdeeds, and familiarized to blood, mas-sacre, and the most detestable vices, we should not be astonished at the impatient spirit of such an abandoned herd, upon being introduced to a life of labour and regularity.[22]

Long's logic is based on two truisms that persisted throughout the eighteenth century, the first being that different African tribes were either more or less likely to revolt depending on their country of origin. The second was that native slaves, hav-ing acclimated to a life in bondage, were less likely to revolt and, given decent treatment, could be brought to love their masters and their land. According to Long, decent treatment would not soften imported slaves, as evidenced by the fact that none of the ringleaders of Tacky's rebellion had been poorly treated. He writes:

> It is worthy our remark, that the ringleaders of the St. Mary's rebel-lion, belonged to a gentleman distinguished for his humanity and exces-sive indulgence towards his slaves in general, and those in particular; his lenity so far influenced him, that upon their complaint, he never failed to discharge their overseer, and employ another more agreeable to them. No pretence [sic] of ill usage was alledged [sic] by any of the prisoners, in any of these insurrections, by way of extenuating their misconduct; the

sole ground, and object of their taking up arms as they *unanimously* con-
curred in acknowledging, was a vain-glorious desire of subduing the country, and they wanted neither ambition nor self-confidence to doubt their
ability or success, in accomplishing this project.[23]

Long's words both here and above reflect a compelling paradox within proslavery
thinking of this moment. The fear of insurrection contained within it not only
the absolute certainty of the savage nature of the African but also the frank
acknowledgment that insurrections were potential coups in the making rather than
just eruptions of destructive violence. Likewise, while Long's emphasis on the kind-
ness of the planter in question ostensibly bolsters his argument that insurrection
occurs regardless of the treatment of the slaves, it also tacitly acknowledges that the
problem of slave violence goes beyond slave conditions. The second quotation is
particularly telling in that despite framing the ringleaders' "ambition" and "self-
confidence" as "vain-glorious," Long allows for a glimmer of political agency on the
part of the insurrectionists and their followers. This is made even more apparent
later when, addressing possible solutions to the insurrection issue, Long proposes that creolizing the slave population will have the effect of making the slaves
take pride in the land they work, which further acknowledges the necessity of
giving them a stake in Caribbean colonization. If we cannot allow them to be free,
Long implies, we must make them believe that investing in their own bondage is
within their best interests: "Since Negroes are the sinews of West-India property,
too much care cannot be taken of them; and it becomes a Christian legislature, at
the same time that it conforms its policy to what respects their health, and ability
to soften by every reasonable means the obduracy of their servitude, so as to make
them *forget the very idea of slavery*."[24] In this breathtaking statement, Long exposes
both the moral bankruptcy at the center of most proslavery calls for amelioration
and the real threat imposed by insurrection. Alleviating the burdens of slavery to
the point where slaves forget they are slaves reveals the deeply cynical nature of
these early calls for the abolition of the slave trade. By advocating a stop to the
importation of newly enslaved Africans, Long is attempting to shift the narrative of
slavery from one of kidnapping and abuse to one of benign paternalism. But in
proposing this narrative, Long also admits that such a state of affairs is not, in
fact, the case. The so-called benign slaveholder is in fact incidental and not the
status quo. Long's argument for the benefits of creolizing the slave population
through "natural increase" would help to fix the already widespread notion that
slave violence was the result of a natural African pathology, and would also prove
to be a boon to politically savvy early British abolitionists looking for parliamentary support.

One can see how Clarkson and other abolitionists saw an opportunity in Long's arguments. If planters such as Long were willing to go so far as to acknowledge that the only way to make slavery sustainable was to make it feel less like slavery, it would only be a matter of time before they could be cajoled into doing away with the practice altogether.[25] And, indeed, Clarkson was not squeamish about using Long's arguments before parliament. In his *An Essay On the Impolicy of the African Slave Trade in Two Parts* (1788), he details the successes of planters who have adopted Long's amelioration suggestions by emphasizing both the manner in which "natural increase" has benefitted them in terms of providing more slaves through childbirth, and in showing how fewer slaves run away or destroy themselves due to savage treatment.[26] But the consequences of such an approach were that it maneuvered abolitionists into couching their objection to the slave trade explicitly in the language of productivity. Slaves that were brutalized and slaves who rose up in protest became indistinguishable from each other because neither was "useful" to the planter.

Clarkson's true thoughts on the subject are difficult to parse. While he proves all too willing to disavow any ambitions to the total destruction of slavery both in his published works and private correspondence, he also acknowledges both skepticism at the idea that insurrection can be fully contained and an unmixed admiration for slaves who rise up. For example, in a letter dated 1 December, 1789 to Auguste Jean Baptiste Bouvet de Cressé, Clarkson reassures his correspondent that British abolitionists have no intention of ending the practice of slavery wholesale but rather only the Atlantic Slave Trade. "We are of the opinion," he says, "that Emancipation of the Slaves would be of no benefit to them at present, would ruin some of their Proprietors, would endanger the Revenue for a time, and would be an Evil rather than a Good."[27] However, in another letter written to Count Mirabeau that very same month, he relates a story allegedly told by a slave who at one point in his narrative speaks of the rape of his wife and the feelings of vengeance he suffers as a result:

> I went to pour my complaints to my faithful wife, but to my distraction she was nowhere to be found. I knew not what to do or where to look for her.—I was ruminating when a Creole informed that she was seized in my absence by the overseer, and that she is to yield to his embraces this very night. O my friend, never more shall I sleep, till I have satisfied my revenge. Adieu, I will invoke all my country's Gods to strengthen my arm for the deed, and my soul to bear all the tortures that will succeed it, for tomorrow I will number the inhuman monsters with the dead.[28]

The identity of the slave is never revealed and Clarkson is somewhat unclear about the source of this story, whether it came firsthand to him or secondhand through a sailor. It is entirely possible that he made it up entirely or at least filled in the details from a rough sketch. The use of the apostrophe indicates a certain amount of editorializing in the translation. Whether this specific story is true, loosely based on real events, or fiction, Clarkson's deployment of it as a tool for convincing the French to join the British abolitionists reveals both that he understands the power of this story is twofold, lying in the threat conveyed by the slave's words of vengeance and in the specific articulation of that vengeance as eloquent rather than merely reactive. Clarkson, in ventriloquizing the slave voice, insists on positioning this would-be insurrectionist as a tragic hero rather than potential villain. If this story was gleaned from his many interviews with former sailors, it is indicative of how the process of collecting testimony shaped Clarkson's thinking regarding slave violence. The evidence gathered provided both an opportunity and a dilemma for abolitionists. Read in one way, shipboard insurrection could be proof of the Africans' humanity. Read another, and it is evidence of the obdurately violent nature of the African.

At the heart of this dilemma, or at least where Clarkson stands in this dilemma, is his utter conviction for the better part of three decades that ending the slave trade by any means necessary was paramount. This might in part, if not excuse, than at least provide some insight into his disparate thoughts on the subject. In his writings, political expediency is constantly at odds with glimmers of revolutionary sympathy, and political expediency wins out, both because it initially is seen as the best way to sway moderate planters to their cause, but more importantly because of Clarkson's secondhand experience of the pain and suffering experienced by slave ship sailors. It is therefore necessary to examine the manner in which for Clarkson and other early abolitionists, sailors provided the best evidence for ending the slave trade at the same time their testimony also served to efface the slave experience of the Middle Passage. What is more, recovering the testimony also reveals that evidence of insurrection was originally a highly visible element of the argument for abolition, and was subsequently downplayed, erased, or otherwise elided in favor for foregrounding slave victimization. Analyzing the manner in which this happens provides insight into the longer history of transatlantic abolition as well as the specific political context in which Equiano constructed his *Narrative*.

CLARKSON AND VIOLENCE

In a letter to Honoré Riquetti, Comte de Mirabeau dated 9, December 1789, Clarkson devotes the main portion of the text to the description of a slave revolt at sea that resulted in the deaths of 100 out of 190 slaves. Before launching into the narrative, he observes to the Comte how their tragic end is made even more tragic by the fact that their heroism will in all likelihood go unrecognized. He writes,

> The wonderful Patience and Perseverance of those poor People in releasing themselves from their irons, and the intrepidity of two or three of them, after they have released themselves, against a multitude of foes, are not easily to be described. Scenes of the brightest Heroism happen repeatedly in the Holds or on the Deck of the Slave-vessels. The authors of them often eclipsed by the splendour [sic] of their actions the celebrated characters both of Greece and home. But how different is the fate of the one and of the other. The actions for the former are considered as so many acts of Baseness, and are punished with Torture or with Death, while those of the latter have been honoured with publick rewards: The actions of the former again are industriously consigned to oblivion, that not a trace, if possible can be found, while those of the latter have been industriously recorded as Examples for future times.[29]

It is unclear precisely when this incident happened. Clarkson only tells us it occurred on a "certain vessel from Bristol." The letter itself is one of a series addressed to the Comte in which he devotes each letter to a single horrific event of the slave trade in the hopes of helping to facilitate the creation of a more robust French abolitionist movement. The letter is noteworthy because the unmixed admiration Clarkson shows for the insurrectionists goes against other writings in which he either avoids describing insurrection altogether, or takes great pains to frame it as a byproduct of abuse. For example, in *An Essay On the Impolicy Of the Slave Trade (1788)* Clarkson frames marronage as a byproduct of plantation brutality thusly: "several of the slaves whose lives become a burthen [sic] to them, destroy themselves. Others fly into the woods, where exposed to the cold of the night, attacked by pangs of hunger and thirst, and lacerated in their bodies by the prickly teeth with which every shrub is armed in that country, they soon perish."[30] Maroon communities are reduced to traumatized and abused populations. But here, aboard the slave ship, insurrection becomes evidence of the heroic mettle of the African; for only a Homeric warrior would have the wherewithal to rise up in such a way.

Clarkson, of all his compatriots in the Society for the Abolition of the Slave Trade, probably did the most in terms of educating himself on the ins and outs of the Atlantic Slave Trade. He interviewed sailors and traders, examined slave ships in the ports of Bristol, Liverpool, and Manchester.[31] He gathered specimens of African produce and workmanship to argue for a more equal trade relationship with the continent.[32] He was instrumental in establishing the colony of Sierra

Leone for repatriated freed slaves.[33] In short, his contributions were the result of near exhaustive study and activism. Yet Clarkson, in many ways is also representative of a persistent blind spot that characterized much of abolition, particularly as it applied to white abolitionists, in that he could not recognize the legitimacy of slave violence without also calling into question the whole of the British colonial project. In agreeing to such an approach, abolitionists all too easily fell into using racist rhetoric promoted by slaveholding opponents of the slave trade. In promoting a system of natural increase they both lent credence to the racist notion of the African's violent pathology and tied the notion of the humane treatment of slaves to increased productivity and revenue. As such, Clarkson's work at times reveals simultaneously a committed activist, a calculating politician, and a confused and despairing humanist. His awareness of the high incidence of slave insurrection in the Middle Passage threads through his work in such a way as to raise questions about the impossibility of his fully suppressing that knowledge in the wake of political pressure.

Clarkson's transfixion with, and antipathy towards, the slave ship as an object of evil is important to understanding both the obsessive way in which he set out to gather evidence and what proved to be a limited approach to wholesale abolition. The ship *is* slavery for Clarkson, and his description of his feelings when first boarding one in 1789 allows us some access into the kind of mindset that produced the evidence later gathered. He observes, "The sight of the rooms below and of the gratings above, and of the barricado across the deck, and the explanation of the uses of all these, filled me both with melancholy and horror. I found soon afterward a fire of indignation kindling within me. I had now scarce patience to talk with those on board. I had not the coolness this first time to go leisurely over the places that were open to me. I got away quickly."[34] The horror that Clarkson describes echoes some of Equiano's language in describing his feelings upon first sighting the slave ship. He writes in his *Narrative*:

> The first object which saluted my eyes when I arrived on the coast was the sea, and a slave ship, which was then riding at anchor, and waiting for its cargo. These filled me with astonishment, which was soon converted to terror, which I am yet at a loss to describe, nor the then feelings of my mind . . . Indeed, such were the horrors of my views and fears at the moment, that, if ten thousand worlds had been my own, I would have freely parted with them all to have exchanged my condition with that of the meanest slave of my country.[35]

Equiano, in trying to convey to the reader both the incomprehensibility of the situation to his child self and the sense of foreboding no doubt put there by hindsight, does not have the luxury of righteous anger at this stage in the *Narrative*. Moreover, in reverting to the language of indescribability when speaking of the slave ship, Equiano seems more interested in dwelling on the horror of the moment than mining it for its revolutionary possibilities. The righteous anger comes later when he demands of these "nominal Christians" if they "learned this from their God" which manifests as less a threat of revolt than a condemnation from the pulpit.[36] Clarkson's feelings of horror, however, are overlaid with "indignation," a feeling that the child Equiano has yet to discover within himself in his description. This moment is worth noting because it speaks to what I perceive as Clarkson's instinctive understanding of the role of shipboard insurrection, an understanding that he appears purposely to stifle as it becomes increasingly clear that the place of violence in the debate over the slave trade is too vexed to be addressed honestly. For Clarkson, translating his feelings about the slave ship to the public and to other would-be allies becomes an exercise in emphasizing certain horrors and deemphasizing others.

In order to understand fully how this dynamic of violence works within the framework both of influencing Equiano's *Interesting Narrative* and in shaping the discourse of the abolitionist movement, it helps to review the manner in which Clarkson built his case against the trade. In 1786 Clarkson, upon founding the Society for Abolition of the Slave Trade along with Sharp and William Dillwyn, conceived of the idea of turning the tide of public opinion against the transatlantic trade by collecting testimony from sailors who had served aboard slave ships in order to reveal the true nature of slave trading. Accordingly, Clarkson published his findings in *The Substance of the Evidence of Sundry Persons on the Slave-trade Collected in the Course Of a Tour Made in the Autumn of the Year 1788* (1789).[37] This collection revealed, not only a clear pattern of abuse and depredations, but also confirmed that shipboard insurrection was a common occurrence aboard slave ships. Clarkson collected testimony from twenty-two former sailors who reported fourteen instances of insurrection. What happens to these instances of insurrection is the subject of the next section of this chapter. In some ways the story of this evidence is also the story of the suppression of evidence and the manner in which the narrative of the Middle Passage became one of abjection rather than resistance and defiance. However, in focusing on Clarkson's shifting vision regarding abolition, I want to emphasize how, despite the manner in which political necessity dictated the suppression of this evidence, the power of these events escapes the larger narrative in small but crucial ways.

In gathering testimony from sailors who had served aboard slave ships, Clarkson shifted the focus from the practice of slavery in the colonies, and the questions and potential obstacles surrounding the wholesale abolition of the institution of slavery, to the space of the slave ship. Furthermore, whereas in his 1785 *Essay on the Slavery and Commerce of the Human Species, Particularly the African* Clarkson manufactured fictional representations of slavery to induce his reader to "witness" the atrocities of slavery ("By asking the reader to stand 'witness' to the truth of a scene he or she 'may have' seen") in order to build a more robust case in *Substance of the Evidence*, Clarkson sought to supplement his narrative of the slave trade with hard evidence.[38] The dysfunctional culture aboard the slave ship provided Clarkson and his colleagues with a microcosm of the practice of slavery in the Atlantic world. Forcing, as it did, slaves, sailors, and captains into close contact with each other, the slave ship threw the tensions inherent in slavery into sharp relief in a way the diffuse plantation system did not.[39] Clarkson was able to draw a bright line beneath the abuses suffered by slaves and sailors by presenting such abuse as a common feature aboard many ships.

By undertaking such an exhaustive project, Clarkson also seems to have been intent on making his case as fact-based and airtight as possible. In an attempt to counter the misinformation being presented to Parliament by Caribbean planters and their sympathizers, Clarkson devised a system of questions that he arranged into six tables folded into a "small almanac":

> The first related to the productions of Africa, and the disposition and manners of the natives. The second, to the methods of reducing them to slavery. The third to the manner of bringing them to the ships, their value, the medium of exchange, and other circumstances. The fourth, to their transportation, the fifth, to their treatment in the colonies. The sixth, to the seamen employed in the trade. These tables contained together one hundred and forty-five questions.[40]

This methodology of fact-finding reveals a mind intent not on working on the sympathies of his listeners, but rather on their intellect by concerning itself with facts and details, data rather than narrative. No single element of the slave trade goes ignored. In referring to the pamphlets as almanacs, Clarkson also grants them the signification of truth telling for the general reader. This is not to suggest that Clarkson is opposed to working on the emotions of both Parliament and the general public, but rather that his work reveals faith in data over narrative at least in these early stages of building a case against the Atlantic Slave Trade. His main sources for these facts were the sailors who served aboard these slave ships.

Writing over twenty years later in *The History of the Rise, Progress and Accomplishment of the Abolition of the African Slave Trade* (1808), Clarkson would say that the committee's approach divided the problem of slavery into two evils: the Atlantic Trade, and the practice of slavery in the colonies. Clarkson writes that after some deliberation, "it appeared soon to be the sense of the committee, that to aim at the removal of both would be to aim at too much, and that by doing this we might lose all. . . . For, by aiming at the abolition of the Slave Trade, they [the committee] were laying the axe at the very root."[41] In 1787, Clarkson proposed that the best way to begin their campaign against the slave trade was for one of them "to undertake a journey to Bristol, Liverpool, and Lancaster, where he should reside there for a time to collect further light upon this subject."[42] Clarkson, in particular, was bent on the collection of evidence in clandestine fashion as he feared that "many avenues of information [would be] closed" to them should they not proceed quickly and quietly.[43] In the interest of keeping things relatively quiet and also ensuring that the testimony he collected would be seen in the best possible light should a parliamentary inquiry ensue as a result of his work, Clarkson interviewed only those sailors whose service aboard slavers was long past and who were currently serving in the British navy with sterling records.[44]

The first seaman he met in the port of Bristol, through the aid of an unnamed informant, was a free black sailor called John Dean, who Clarkson had reason to believe would help his case. "The report was, that for a trifling circumstance, for which he [Dean] was in no-wise to blame, the captain had fastened him with his belly to the deck, and that, in this situation, he had poured hot pitch upon his back, and made incisions in it with hot tongs."[45] Further investigation including an interview with Dean, who showed him the scars on his back, and corroboration by other sailors and the attorney representing Dean in the case against his former captain revealed the account to be true and set Clarkson on the track of uncovering more accounts of sailor abuse aboard slave ships.

Each interview has roughly the same structure: The sailor describes the ways in which slaves are acquired in Africa, then goes on to describe the conditions for the slaves aboard the ship. The testimony is written in the third person, implying a degree of interpretation on the part of the recorder, Clarkson himself. This third-person reportage makes *The Substance of the Evidence of Sundry Persons* less of a collection of first-person accounts than a co-authored document in which Clarkson constructs a distinct narrative of the Atlantic Trade. The narrative begins with the illegal acquisition of slaves, who, once on board, attempt to revolt and are severely punished for their actions.[46] The Middle Passage manifests itself in a series of abuses towards the sailors and slaves. The slaves arrive in the West Indian colonies, ill and their numbers greatly reduced, while the sailors are often cheated of their wages and left to die. By constructing a narrative in this way Clarkson puts sailors and slaves on equal footing. Combating the assertion that the slave trade provided useful early training for British sailors in the empire's race for maritime dominance over the French, Clarkson pursued these stories to reveal explicitly how this so-called "nursery for British seamen" was, in fact, their grave.[47] "It appeared that more seamen died in that trade in one year than in the whole remaining trade of the country in two," he writes. "Out of nine hundred and ten sailors in it, two hundred and sixteen died in the year, while upon a fair average of the same number employed in the trades to the East and West Indies, Petersburgh [*sic*], Newfoundland, and Greenland, no more than eighty-seven died."[48] The difference in numbers of sailor deaths in the slave trade versus other trades served to draw attention to the distinct and brutal character of the slave trade.

The testimonies also suggest that Clarkson specifically addressed the issue of shipboard insurrection in his questions. The witnesses, more often than not, attested to the high incidence of revolt or attempted revolt. According to one informant, "Many of them [slaves] are unable to bear the loss of liberty, and try every means to regain it on the day before the ____ arrived at Barbados, the slaves by means of a hacked knife and the bar of the men's gratings, had freed themselves from their irons and, just before day light in the morning, forced themselves upon the deck. . . . These insurrections are not unfrequent [*sic*]."[49] Responses of this sort, which indicate the sailors' experience with shipboard insurrections, points to Clarkson's awareness of the possibility of using the high incidence of violence aboard slave ships as a political tool. *The Substance of Evidence* does not spell out where slave violence fits into the plans of Clarkson and his colleagues. But what seems clear is that Clarkson was looking at the violence in the slave trade as something ever-present and not simply a result of harsh treatment by overseers on the Caribbean plantations.

Focusing on the trade rather than the practice of slavery in the colonies allowed Clarkson to point to these shipboard insurrections as evidence that the brutality of slavery began at the moment of kidnapping and was not something that could be ameliorated by implementing legislation on the care and treatment of slaves. Furthermore, by drawing the treatment of sailors into the discussion, Clarkson could also claim that he was not just looking at slavery as a moral wrong but taking a holistic view of the slave trade and the mistreatment of sailors, revealing a symbiotic relationship between British seamen and African slaves.

In one account, the sailor first describes the treatment of the slaves upon being kidnapped as follows: "The slaves that are brought on board have their arms generally pinioned behind their backs with grass ropes. They are made to lie down in the bottom frequently, of a wet canoe, and if they stir, get only hard blows from the rowers or the guard."[50] Later, in the same account, he describes similar treatment of the sailors. "The seamen are used worse in point of corporal punishment, in this than in any other trade. They are beaten on every trivial occasion. Mr. _____ has seen them knocked down with handspikes and stamped upon until the strength and passion of their tyrants has been exhausted."[51] Presenting the brutality acted on the slave, and then again on the sailor, Clarkson describes the slave ship—and thus the whole of the Atlantic Slave Trade—as steeped in violence. In the wake of the *Zong* massacre, the depiction of slave ships as lawless vessels was essential to building a case against the slave trade. The violence visited upon sailors and slaves, as well as the shipboard insurrections, become bound up in the myriad evils of slavery, so that a view of violence as dehumanizing to both slave and enslaver became one of the cornerstones of moral suasionist arguments against slavery in the United States.

Each interview concludes with a description of the conditions for sailors aboard each slave ship. Sailors are typically lured away from the ports of Bristol and Liverpool with drink and promises of wealth, made to endure near-starvation, exposure, and physical abuse at the hands of their captains, and left destitute once they arrive in the West Indies. One interview reads:

> Mr. _____ has frequently seen in the island of Jamaica the sailors of Guinea-men in great distress, from their having been imprudently discharged or obliged to desert in so bad a state of health that no other vessel would take them in. He has seen them lying about the wharfs at Kingston in a dying state. They are generally distinguished by the name of wharfingers. They appear to be ulcerated all over, but particularly in their legs, and their ulcers are covered with musquitoes [*sic*]. In this dreadful situation they are left to perish, for no merchantman will take them in and no King's ships will receive them for fear of infection. Mr._____ when he has been attending a negro holiday at Spring Path which is the cemetery of the negroes, has often seen the bodies of these wharfingers brought there, and interred in an adjoining spot.[52]

The image of sick sailors abandoned to die in the Caribbean ports appears calculated to disabuse the public that the slave trade was anything resembling a "nursery" for British seamen, while the final image of their bodies interred next to a Negro cemetery seems meant to blur the line between the fate of the sailors and the slaves. However, the blurring of this line, designed to use the plight of the sailors to also incite sympathy for the slaves, in this particular context is limited. What comes through is not the full horror of the trade as it affected both sailors and slaves, but the indignity that white Britons, mistreated and abandoned, were buried amongst blacks. Sympathy for the sailors in this instance takes over at the expense of any kind of sympathy for the slave.

Clarkson also inadvertently illustrates the limited nature of first-hand accounts in his methods. On the one hand, he prized them as the most direct means to turn the public against the slave trade. On the other hand, he appears to be aware that firsthand accounts were, in their own way, suspect. As I mentioned earlier, Clarkson was at some pains to vet the character of his witnesses so as to preemptively deflect criticism of the veracity of their statements. Faulty or inaccurate evidence could potentially compromise his project, inviting questions regarding bias and personal grievance. The act of witnessing becomes as essential as claims to have experienced abuse in the rhetoric of abolition, creating a dual-voiced approach of "I am" and "I saw." In the Clarkson project, however, the voice of the slave, despite this method, remains absent.

What is more, sailor testimony also proves problematic in terms of how it often positions the suffering of sailors at the expense of the suffering of slaves. In presenting his findings to Parliament, Clarkson cited shipboard insurrection but in such a way as to frame it as either a suicide impulse on the part of the slaves, or to make its real import the potential harm done to the sailors. In the *Abstract*, Clarkson notes "It is evident that insurrection and contagious disorders from the slaves must be natural causes of the mortality to seamen in slave ships, which could not exist in the ships in other trade."[53] Writing later in *The History of the Rise and Fall of the Slave Trade*, he also describes an incident in which a scuffle between a ship's steward by the name of Peter Green and a slave woman called Rodney, who belonged to the owners and acted as interpreter aboard the ship, resulted in Green being beaten by the captain. Clarkson writes:

> About five in the evening . . . the captain as was his custom went on shore. In his absence, Rodney, the black woman, asked Green for the keys of the pantry; which he refused her, alleging that the captain had already beaten him for having given them to her on a former occasion, when she drank the wine. The woman, being passionate, struck him, and a scuffle ensued out of which Green extricated himself as well as he could. When the scuffle was over the woman retired to the cabin, and appeared pensive. Between eight and nine in the evening, the captain, who was attended by the captain of the Alfred, came on board. Rodney immediately ran to him, and informed him that Green made an assault on her. The captain, without any inquiry, beat him severely, and ordered his hands to be made fast to some bolts on the starboard side of the ship and under the half deck, and then flogged him himself, using the lashes of the cat-of-nine-tails on his back one at a time, and the double-walled knot at the end of it upon his head at another; and stopping to rest at intervals.[54]

This incident, while ostensibly meant to illustrate the brutal nature of many slave ship captains, depicts the sailor's position as below that of the slaves, thereby suggesting that slaves had more recourse to justice aboard slave ships than sailors. The question of the sailor's abuse of the slave does not appear to figure greatly in the reportage of this incident. The sailors' suffering risks painting the slaves as irredeemably violent rather than humans whom slavery has made into the enemy.

Contrast this moment with another in Equiano's *Interesting Narrative* where Equiano describes a scuffle he has with another slave shortly after being emancipated, in which he makes a similar point but with far more context. When his adversary's owner demands that his captain deliver him for flogging, Equiano discovers that, having been emancipated, his captain can no longer protect him. "He [the captain] said he knew nothing of the matter, I was a free man."[55] Here Equiano is able to frame the powerlessness of sailors in context with the absence of rights for free blacks in the Caribbean. The "freedom" to be a sailor proves empty and dangerous here when a slave appears to have more protection than a free black. As we begin to see, the absence of the slave voice in the sailor testimonies proves consequential in these small but significant moments.

The consequence of Clarkson's methodology and the use to which his collected testimonies were put was that abolitionists came to view violence as simply further evidence of the evil of slavery rather than as organized activity among the enslaved to liberate themselves from their oppression. In highlighting the violence and brutality of the trade, Clarkson begins a process that later becomes a defining feature of the abolitionist rhetoric, namely insisting that the chief sin of the slave trade was the perpetuation of violence. Yet in doing this, Clarkson and his colleagues also place violence firmly outside the idea that in resisting bondage, slaves were asserting innate rights to their freedom. Slave violence, rather than being seen as a form of viable resistance, was interpreted as merely reactive: simply the consequence of the violence of slavery in which enslaved Africans were passive actors within the theater of the Atlantic Slave Trade. Africans appear to lack any kind of political agency without slavery to react against.

What makes this process of interpretation notable is that, as we have seen, Clarkson, like many other players in the slave trade, was intimately acquainted with slave violence. Most of Clarkson's testimonies contain accounts of shipboard revolts, indicating a specific interest on his part in the role that slave violence played in the slave trade itself; and while it is true that plantation insurrection at this period was at a low-point, the number of shipboard revolts, as I have already stated, was at the highest it had been in the history of the trade. Whatever the reason, the rise in shipboard revolts coincides precisely with both Equiano's career as a sailor, and the time when Clarkson's sailor witnesses would have been most likely to serve aboard slave ships.[56]

Clarkson's testimonies therefore, appearing as they do in the aftermath of the height of shipboard and plantation insurrections and on the eve of the

St. Domingo rebellion, needed the evidence of violence in order to use it as a reason for abolition. But the testimonies themselves had to be managed carefully because they also reveal the slave more as autonomous actor rather than innocent victim. In pointing to the past sins of the Atlantic Slave trade Clarkson risked reigniting fears of insurrection. The testimonies, in sympathetically representing shipboard insurrection, presented a possible alternative to the trope of slave as victim, namely the slave as revolutionary. As I have already touched on, and note further below, Clarkson could acknowledge the political dimension of slave resistance, but he could not fully embrace it. This momentary recognition of the natural right to revolt would not be seen again within abolitionist rhetoric until the *Amistad* case in the nineteenth century.

There is no more telling moment than his description of his meeting with the Deputies of Color from St. Domingo during his time in Paris with the Friends of the Negro at the Marquis de Lafayette's house in 1789. At this moment the deputies are requesting representation on the National Assembly. Throughout his own time there, also smarting from his failure to rally support for his own cause, Clarkson witnesses the fruitless attempts on their part to gain access to the National Assembly. He recalls:

> At this, my last conference with them, I recommended moderation and forbearance, as the best gifts I could leave them. . . . I found, however, notwithstanding all I said, that nothing but a redress of their grievances could subdue; and that, if the planters could persevere in their intrigues, and the National Assembly in delay, a fire would be lighted up in St. Domingo, which could not easily be extinguished. This was afterwards realized: for Ogé, in about three months from this time, left his companions to report to his constituents in St. Domingo the state of their mission; when hearing, on his arrival in that island, of the outrageous conduct of the whites of the committee of Aquin, who had begun a persecution of the people of color, for no other reason than that they had dared to seek the common privileges of citizens; and of the murder of Ferrand and Labadie, he imprudently armed his slaves. With a small but faithful band he rushed upon superior numbers, and was defeated. Taking refuge at length in the Spanish part of St. Domingo, he was given up; and his enemies, to strike terror into the people of color, broke him upon the wheel. From this time, reconciliation between the parties became impossible. A bloody war commenced, and with it all those horrors which it has been our lot so frequently to deplore. It must be remembered, however, that the Slave-trade, by means of the cruel distinctions it occasioned, was the original cause and though the revolution in France afforded the occasion; it was an occasion which would have been prevented, if it had not been for the intrigues and injustice of the whites.[57]

This section, at first glance, seems written to absolve Clarkson of warmongering regarding the Haitian Revolution. He makes it clear that he cautioned them against action and laments the "horrors" unleashed by the war. Nevertheless, his admiration for the deputy called Ogé and his sympathy for the outraged dignity of the black creoles echoes the sentiments set forth in the description of the shipboard revolt mentioned above. In trying to straddle the line between acknowledging the political dimension of their demands and rooting the problem in the abuses of the slave trade, Clarkson reveals himself to be simultaneously aware of, and oblivious to, what it is the delegation is actually demanding. As C. L. R. James writes in *The Black Jacobins*, the mulattoes claim was not explicitly about slavery, but about claiming the Rights of Man for themselves, even going so far as to offer their considerable wealth for the National Debt.[58] And while slavery is, indeed, at the root of the St. Domingo revolt, for Clarkson to relocate the problem with the slave trade and not the more complicated question of black political recognition categorizes the revolution there as merely reactive.

In the same letter written to de Cressé, in which he claims that total abolition is not the aim of British abolitionists, he warns that the failure to end the slave trade would be the ruin of France and a mark against the ideals of the French Revolution.

> The French Revolution can never be kept from the Negroes. The efforts of good men, who are hourly increasing in their Favour throughout all Europe, must unavoidably reach their ears. These two circumstances combined cannot fail to have their Influence in the Islands, and sooner or later very serious Revolutions (if they have not already happened) will take place there. And suppose, Sir, that they do. Is the French Revolution wrong? I reply no—It is an Honor to those, who have brought it on. So also would a Revolution of the Negroes be honorable? Would it not be criminal in any nation to attack France in the present moment engaged as she is in a virtuous and noble cause? I answer yes.[59]

Clarkson, in first reassuring the Frenchman that abolitionists have no intention of depriving planters of their slaves, only to turn around and warn him that failing to abolish the trade will result in insurrection, reveals a willingness to exploit fears of insurrection to his own ends even as he also appears to be conceding the necessity of slavery itself to preserving economic stability. But what is most intriguing about this turn is not simply the way in which Clarkson manages to accurately predict the conflagration in St. Domingo five years later, but that he also acknowledges that any uprising in St. Domingo would only be the natural outgrowth of the French Revolution.

The danger of presenting slave insurrection as in any way positive was that those who opposed the abolition of the Atlantic Slave Trade often cited insurrection as the consequence of abolition. Clarkson acknowledged such criticism, writing, "The abolition it was said, would produce insurrections among the slaves," adding, "But insurrections would produce the massacre of their masters; and, if any of these should happily escape their butchery, they would be reserved only for ruin."[60] Additionally, according to the planters, the laws passed to ensure the ethical care of slaves in Jamaica and Grenada made abolition unnecessary.[61] Accordingly, as he made his case against the trade, Clarkson recognized that for the collected testimonies to be effective, the perception of slave violence necessarily had to characterize it as a consequence of the unavoidably abusive slave trade rather than a product of African savagery or revolutionary ideals. As for the condition of the slaves, it would not be evidence of their desire for freedom that would be the most effective means of arousing the British public against the slave trade, but rather evidence of the brutality acted against them. Not surprisingly, then, the circulation of the broadside, "Plan and Sections of a Slave Ship," and its shockingly mundane approach to packing people into the ship, would arguably become the most iconic image of the Atlantic Slave Trade.[62]

Clarkson's discovery and use of the diagram of the slave ship *Brookes* sets the stage for how anti-slavery rhetoric would evolve over the next several decades. The diagram, an actual tool used by slave-traders to dictate how slaves were to be stowed, becomes almost talismanic for Clarkson in illustrating starkly the dehumanizing nature of the trade. In his *History of the Rise, Progress etc.* and at least one other volume, *The Cries of Africa to the Inhabitants of Europe, Or, a Survey of That Bloody Commerce Called the Slave Trade* (1822), Clarkson included folio-sized foldouts of the diagram. Indeed, after Clarkson's presentation of the diagram to the Friends of the Negroes in Paris, Mirabeau was so impressed with the image, "that he ordered a mechanic to make a model of it in wood, at a considerable expense. This model he kept afterwards in his dining room. It was a ship in miniature, about a yard long, and little wooden men, which were painted black to represent the slaves, were seen stowed in their proper places."[63] The effectiveness of this image is indisputable, but the actions of Mirabeau also reveal problems in the way the image of the *Brookes* ship was received. The image powerfully dramatizes the reduction of humanity to cargo. The unapologetic nature of the image exposes slave-traders as being aware of the process of dehumanization slave trading enacts. But the image is also reductive and easily fetishized. The lack of humanity in the tiny humanoid engravings is in danger of becoming the entire story of the slave ship and not just one part of it. The abused slave becomes a vehicle for white redemption. Witnessing became an effective tool for ending the slave trade but it also augmented the silence surrounding the slave experience. The language of resistance is subsumed, or nearly subsumed, by these other voices that contextualize resistance in these narrow ways. The net effect flattens the possibilities of the ways in which white readers experience, secondhand, the Middle Passage. The language of abolition is objectifying even at its most humane.

It is within this context that Equiano's *Interesting Narrative* was conceived, written, and received. If Clarkson's testimonies established the sailor as a surrogate for the slave, Equiano's biography fuses the two personae together. In doing so, Equiano appears to be reclaiming autonomy from the white abolitionists by adding his apparently firsthand account of the slave's experience in the Middle Passage. Most intriguing, though, is the way in which Equiano uses his experiences as a sailor to construct his own identity as British, specifically his years in the British navy during the Seven Years' War.

EQUIANO: SLAVE VERSUS SAILOR

Olaudah Equiano published the first edition of his autobiography *The Interesting Narrative of the Life of Gustavus Vassa, or Olaudah Equiano, the African* in 1789, one year after the publication of Clarkson's testimonies and the same year that the French Revolution would break out. While Equiano, himself, does not address directly the role of slave insurrection in the Middle Passage, his text takes up where accounts like Clarkson's leave off. Ostensibly, Equiano's account adds a firsthand illustration of the Middle Passage, bolstering secondhand testimony from Clarkson's sailors. But in taking its cue from Clarkson, *Interesting Narrative* reveals Equiano to be more the sailor than the slave with regards to his experience at sea. When he does address slave insurrection directly, his language echoes the sentiments of those such as Edward Long who saw ending the slave trade as a means of controlling slave violence.

During the Seven Years' War Equiano was both a witness to, and potential victim of, the British navy's draconian impressment practices. At this moment in his youth, we see a different Equiano from the sailor-merchant of his post-war years, diligently earning enough money to buy his freedom, and different from the Christian abolitionist, making political connections and writing anti-slavery tracts under a pseudonym. This Equiano celebrates naval victories alongside his masters and participates in the social world of the ship. When he gains his freedom he serves aboard merchant ships and slave traders, which I will address at length later in the chapter. Later he takes part in expeditions to the North Pole and travels to Turkey.

And finally, he attempts to help a black sailor called John Annis, who is threatened with kidnapping, which brings him to the doorstep of Granville Sharp, and touches off his later career as an abolitionist.[64] For Equiano, these experiences facilitate his transformation into a Briton. He represents himself at this moment as a burgeoning patriot, but also as a brutalized crewmember alongside white sailors. Equiano's emphasis on his role aboard ship plays into Clarkson's campaign of turning public sympathy against the slave trade through the testimony of sailors. This early part of the text is Equiano's own testimony, if not on the slave trade, then on the undeserved treatment of sailors who, in turn, also serve their country.

Rather than confining itself to retelling the story of the Middle Passage strictly from the hold of the slave ship, the text focuses on the experience of the sailor. About half of the narrative is devoted to his life after Equiano succeeds in buying his freedom, and even the moments before are often less about the experience of slave life and more about the details of battle, his friendships, and the sights he sees. In telling the story primarily from the perspective of the sailor, Equiano creates a sort of dual narrative. The outrages visited upon Equiano as a slave blend with those afflicting him as a sailor, making the argument about the treatment of slaves synonymous with the treatment of sailors. In doing this, he is able to negotiate the terms of evoking his readers' sympathies, at one time directing them to imagine the trauma of kidnapping, at another appealing to their sense of fair play in terms of his being cheated of rightly earned wages.

In the eighteenth century, a small but significant number of British ships made use of slaves as sailors, and during both the Seven Years' War and the American Revolution, the British navy impressed black sailors alongside white sailors into service. Historian Charles R. Foy's recently assembled Colored Mariners' Database "demonstrates that eighteenth-century colored mariners shared many of Equiano's experiences. Almost all were young healthy men. Like Equiano, scores of colored mariners traveled across the Atlantic. And those who did not travel long distances still often worked on a variety of different vessels. However, although mobile, relatively few colored mariners appear to have had as extended a maritime career as did Equiano."[65] Small numbers notwithstanding, a common feature shared by some of these mariners is that those who eventually found their way to Britain and freedom also became active within the abolitionist community. Equiano's friend and fellow black abolitionist, Ottobah Cugoano, had also served in the British navy and changed his name from John Mill. Given the spotty records, it is difficult to argue definitively that the story of black sailors during the Middle Passage holds the same kind of significance as the story of slaves in the holds of slave ships, on plantations, and engaged in insurrections in both locales. Yet the story of black sailors, specifically as it applies to the evolution of the abolitionist movement, is significant to understanding how the movement evolved.

Equiano's own rhetoric regarding the horrors of the slave trade and the abuse he experiences as a sailor who is also a slave centers on the moral outrage at violence done to both slaves and sailors rather than on a view of slave violence as reflecting political agency on the part of the slaves. His language emphasizes the dehumanizing nature of the slave trade, implying heavily that if slavery makes monsters, it is no wonder violent retaliation happens. Furthermore, he follows Clarkson's lead in exposing how that savagery lands on the backs of white sailors as well as slaves. Shortly after he is brought aboard the slave ships, Equiano writes, "on my refusing to eat, one of [the white men] held me fast by the hands, and laid me across, I think, the windlass, and tied my feet while the other flogged me severely."[66] The very next flogging he witnesses is that of a white sailor who dies of his injuries, and whose body is thrown overboard. He writes, "they tossed him over the side like they would have done a brute. This made me fear these people the more; and I expected nothing less than to be treated in the same manner."[67] By tying his experience with flogging with that of witnessing the flogging and subsequent death of a sailor, Equiano paints a picture of the slave ship as a space of total brutality. As a slave witnessing violence against the sailor, Equiano subtly upends the structure of Clarkson's interviews and becomes the speaker on behalf of himself as well as the sailor. Moreover, the tossing of a sailor overboard evokes images of slaves drowning, and was particularly poignant at a moment when the *Zong* atrocities were becoming more widely known. Equiano, who brought the case of the *Zong* to the attention of Sharp, would no doubt have been aware of resonances of this image and ties the image of the drowning slaves to drowning sailors. While poignant and almost certainly effective, this strategy also mirrors the problematic politics at work in Clarkson's writing. By drawing too strong a parallel between the slave and experiences of the slave trade, Equiano risks erasing the distinction between the two. Moreover, drawing the sailor into that same discourse of slave as victim allows the sailor some access to the potential reservoir of sympathy, but by working on the horror of being treated *like a slave*.

This strategy of tying his own experience as a slave to that sailor is made clear later when he serves in the British navy alongside a boy called Richard Baker from the American colonies. Early on in his navy career he describes a conversation he had with his master and Dick over dinner. "He [my master] used to often tell him jocularly that he would kill and eat me. Sometimes he would say to me— the black people were not good to eat, and would ask me if we did not eat people in my country. I said, No: then he said he would kill Dick (as he always called him) first, and afterwards me. Though this hearing relieved my mind a little to myself,

I was alarmed for Dick."[68] This moment, evoking as it does the distance between Equiano's naïve child self and his cosmopolitan author self, also implies an early affinity with sailors. That Baker was also his first good friend, possessing "a mind superior to prejudice," further suggests that in having such a friend to model himself after shaped Equiano's identity as a sailor, specifically a navy-man in these early moments. This, coupled with the hazing mentioned at the beginning of the chapter, along with the accounts of being rescued by press gangs by fellow members of the crew, and descriptions of battle, all serve to paint an image, not of simply of a slave, but of a slave whose life as a sailor complicates and in some ways interrupts his experience of slavery by allowing him to enjoy both his work and his life.[69]

It is a canny move on Equiano's part to emphasize his experience as a sailor in that doing so suggests a career path for slaves outside of the plantation by pointing to the potential usefulness of Africans. But the very invocation of "usefulness" calls to mind Long's argument in favor of amelioration and the potential "value" of slaves who are well-treated. Equiano, in embracing for himself the title of sailor and offering himself as a model for future freed blacks, also distances himself from those other blacks who rise up and revolt. As the outcome of his "usefulness," Equiano's value, whether slave or free, depends upon his continued good behavior. This contingency is made apparent in the moment shortly before Equiano earns enough to buy his freedom. Having gotten wind that Equiano means to take advantage of an upcoming trip to Philadelphia to run away, his master threatens to sell him. "'You cost me a great deal of money, no less than forty pounds sterling; and it will not do to lose so much. You are a valuable fellow . . . and I can get any day for you one hundred guineas, from many gentlemen in this island [Montserrat]' . . . When I asked what work he would put me to, he would make me a captain of one of his rice vessels."[70] Equiano, whose diligence and prowess as a sailor were initially meant as a means both to earn the trust of his masters and to equip himself with the tools to escape, now finds himself trapped by his own skillset. As sailor and a slave, his superior knowledge does little to transform him in the eyes of his master. This moment could be revelatory as it illustrates to Equiano that the signifiers of civilized man—literacy, loyalty, and piety—are but useful characteristics in a slave, rendering him more "valuable." But Equiano does not treat it as an epiphany that might launch him onto a more revolutionary path. Rather he takes it as a sign that he should focus his energies on buying his own freedom rather than attempting to escape. This missed opportunity suggests that Equiano is explicitly smothering anything too suggestive of potential revolutionary thinking.

This commitment to buying his freedom could be seen as an attempt to paint himself in the best possible light. However, this strategy for distancing his narrative from revolutionary sentiments is also notable for how it also deflects attention away from the all-too-real conflagrations occurring within the time frame of the narrative. Having been on the island of Montserrat from approximately 1763 to 1767, Equiano would have no doubt been privy to the aftermath of Tacky's Rebellion in Jamaica. Likewise, the foiled St. Patrick's Day revolt on Montserrat in 1768, the year after his departure would, in all likelihood, have reached his ears. We can only speculate why Equiano chose not to remark on these events, but what he chooses to document, and how his position as a sailor influenced those choices, reveal the degree of politicking in his moves.

The appearance of disavowal becomes even thinner later in the *Narrative* when he finds himself forced to confront both his history as a slave in the Middle Passage and his present position as a free sailor of color participating in the Slave Trade. This particular element of his career plays an interesting role in the *Narrative*. While he never hides the fact that he periodically serves aboard slave ships, the information is slipped into the narrative as almost an afterthought. He mentions having "had some of these slaves on board my master's vessels to carry them to other islands or to America," and taking "a load of slaves new for Georgia and Charles Town."[71] This reflects the problematic position Equiano finds himself in representing the slave voice as a sailor. As a slave, his position aboard slave ships could be finessed as not being his choice. In the latter part of the book, serving aboard slave ships as a freeman calls into question the very nature of freedom itself.

For the most part, Equiano uses this part of the text to comment on the atrocities he witnesses in different parts of the American colonies and the Caribbean. He laments his powerlessness when witnessing the assault of a female slave by white sailors.[72] He describes a slave who was "half hanged, and then burnt, for attempting to poison a cruel overseer."[73] He observes, "It was very common in several islands . . . for the slaves to be branded with the initials of their master's name, and a load of heavy iron hooks hung around their necks."[74] This mimics the role of the sailors in Clarkson's interviews who testified to the atrocities they witnessed as well as their own brutalization. They, too, note the practice of branding using "marking irons" fired with flaming rum as well as incidents of flogging for punishment.[75] If Equiano were merely a sailor, his decision to describe what happens to others without reference to himself as both slaver and victim would be unremarkable. But as a former slave, his silence about his own experience is noteworthy. This tension is more felt than seen. Equiano does not explicitly reference this tension at all. As a good member of the eighteenth-century marketplace, he can condemn slavery on moral grounds but must remain silent about his own complicity.

Is it therefore impossible to locate any trace of insurrectionist impulse in *Interesting Narrative*? In his introduction to the Penguin Classics edition of the text, Carretta points to the few moments of revolutionary potential within Equiano as evidence of a more complex abolitionist than otherwise supposed.[76] According to Carretta, Equiano's receptiveness to violence alongside his support of interracial marriage and his marriage to a white British woman have radical potential. Carretta also notes that the lines from Milton that Equiano places at the end of a catalogue of abuses witnessed while in Montserrat explicitly cite insurrection as a possible outcome of abuse. Equiano asks, rhetorically:

> Why do you use those instruments of torture? Are they fit to be applied by one rational being to another? And are ye not struck with shame and mortification, to see the partakers for your nature reduced so low? But above all, are there no dangers attending this mode of treatment? Are you not hourly in dread of insurrection? Nor would it be surprising; for when
>> No peace is given
>> To us enslav'd, but custody severe;
>> And stripes and arbitrary punishment
>> Inflicted—What peace can we return?
>> But to our power, hostility and hate;
>> Untam'd reluctance, and revenge, tho' slow,
>> Yet ever plotting how the conqueror least
>> May reap this conquest, and may least rejoice
>> In doing what we most in suff'ring feel.
> But, by changing your conduct, and treating your slaves as men every cause of fear would be banished. They would be faithful, honest, intelligent and vigorous; and peace, prosperity, and happiness would attend you.[77]

The first part and the Milton quotation appear to cast Equiano in a radical light, citing brutality as inciting retaliatory violence. The Milton quote is particularly ominous in that it does not merely speak of violence but of festering "hostility and hate." Through Milton, Equiano uncannily predicts the equal measure of brutality that the participants in the St. Domingo uprising visited upon their former masters. But the final suggestion that in changing their conduct, slave owners might avoid violence—that the absence of brutality would lead to the wholesale transformation of the slave from a vengeful insurrectionist to a peaceful and productive member of society—implies a less radical, less resistant ideology at work and something more ameliorative and conservative. To view violent slaves as only violent when incited by ill treatment indicates a certain essential goodness within Africans, something Equiano is at great pains to emphasize. But the use of the Milton quote recalls the reader to *Paradise Lost* and the compelling nature of Satan, the speaker. Insurrection remains alluring even as Equiano appears to disavow it.

There is one final moment where Equiano exposes a glimpse of possible revolutionary thinking towards the end of his seafaring career. In the winter of 1767, he finds himself serving aboard a slave ship under Captain William Phillips, an old acquaintance who has taken over the ship *Nancy* in the wake of the previous captain's death.[78] Phillips plots a new course that appears to Equiano "very extraordinary" implying certain misgivings with his level of competence. Shortly after they embark, Equiano describes the following dream: "On the 4th of February which was soon after we had got into our new course, I dreamt the ship was wrecked amidst the surfs and rocks and I was the means of saving every one on board; and on the night following I dreamed the very same dream."[79] This dream is in keeping with typological narrative at play in the book, in which Equiano ties himself to figures from the Old Testament such as Jacob and, in this instance, Joseph.[80] Having, albeit self-deprecatingly, repeatedly made reference to his own chosenness through multiple instances of divine intervention, he has also insulated himself against possible accusations of hubris and fanaticism. This allows him to portray his defiance to the captain as an act of conscience rather than menace.

When the storm does come, Equiano does not treat the moment at sea as an epiphany regarding his place within the Atlantic Slave Trade. Rather he attributes the storm as punishment for having, quite literally, cursed the ship out of weariness over pumping duty. "I began to express my impatience, and I uttered with an oath, 'Damn the vessel's bottom's out.' But my conscience instantly smote me for the expression. When I left the deck I went to bed, and had scarcely fallen asleep when I dreamed the same dream again."[81] This moment is odd. Having already established his uneasiness with the captain, the nature of the dream seems self-evident. Adding this rather innocuous sin seems a superfluous way of demonstrating Equiano's piety. It is placed there deliberately to set up what comes next, which is the captain's order to nail down the hold in which twenty slaves were kept. In this moment, one forgets about the "sin" of the curse and is struck by the suggestion of guilt regarding Equiano's place in the slave trade. "When he desired the men to nail down the hatches I thought that my sin was the cause of this, and that God would charge me with these people's blood. This thought rushed upon my mind in that instant with such violence, that it quite overpowered me and I fainted."[82] In fainting he relives his first experience aboard a slave ship in which, overcome by the horror of what he is about to endure, he faints on the deck of the ship. "When I looked round the ship too, and saw a large furnace of copper boiling, and a multitude of black people of every description chained together, every one of their countenance expressing dejection and sorrow, I no longer doubted my fate and, quite overpowered with horror and anguish, I fell motionless on the deck and fainted."[83] If one reads this scene as an echo of the earlier fainting, one could argue that Equiano is framing his defiance in a manner that mirrors Clarkson's strategy of interpreting slave insurrection as a reaction to trauma. This moment allows

Equiano to escape momentarily the guise of the pious, free, entrepreneurial sailor and remind us of the traumatized child from the beginning of the *Narrative*. But such a reading, I think, does not fully capture the revolutionary possibility of this scene. The moment that he revives and confronts the captain reveals a more interesting dynamic at play than merely the return of trauma.

> I recovered just as the people were about to nail down the hatches; perceiving which, I desired them to stop. The captain then said it must be done; I asked him why? He said, that every one would endeavour to get into the boat, which was but small, and thereby we should be drowned; for it would not have carried above ten at the most. I could no longer restrain my emotion, and I told him he deserved drowning for not knowing how to navigate the vessel; and I believe the people would have tossed him overboard if I had given them the least hint of it. However, the hatches were not nailed down.[84]

At this moment Equiano, as a free sailor, embraces for himself the agency to defy the captain on behalf of both the slaves in the hold, and the fainting child he once was. In doing so, he rejects that past trauma as ultimately defining his slave experience, transforming the Middle Passage experience from one of pure abjection to self-actualization. The threat to the captain's life and the confidence he has that the rest of the crew would have followed him, reveal a potentially more militant Equiano than he's permitted us to see at other moments in the text. But the moment passes primarily because, at the end of the day, Equiano refuses to unpack the full political implications of his experience for his readers. Rather he redirects our attention away from the glimpse of revolutionary possibility so tantalizingly put before us, to the evidence of his own competence and piety in the face of disaster.

> My dream now returned upon my mind with all its force; it was fulfilled in every part; for our danger was the same I had dreamt of; and I could not help looking on myself as the principal instrument of effecting our deliverance: for, owing to some of our people getting drunk, the rest of us were obliged to double our exertions . . . and though I warned the people who were drinking, and entreated them to embrace the moment of deliverance, nevertheless they persisted, as if not possessed of the least spark of reason. I could not help thinking, that if any of these people had been lost, God would have charged me with their lives.[85]

The intemperate behavior of his fellow sailors allows him some cover from his brush with insurrection and a moment to reflect on the dream as evidence of the influence of Divine Providence in his life. Implicit in the description of drinking and indolence is the argument that had Equiano been forced to take charge of the ship away from his Captain, not only would he have been the best man for the job, it would have been in keeping with God's plan for him.

In the end, as was the case with the larger abolitionist movement in Britain, Equiano lets evidence of his "usefulness" override the glimmer of revolutionary possibility exposed by this moment. In offering himself as evidence of the potential usefulness of freed slaves, he does not do away with the earlier rhetoric of Long's arguments for good treatment in the name of "natural increase" and investment in property, so much as he transmutes it into the emergence of a self-reliant black British population and new trade partners in Africa. The useful, free black is analogous to the well-treated sugar plantation slave, whereas the insurrectionist has no counterpart within the rhetoric of abolition.

CONCLUSION

By the end of the narrative, Equiano reiterates the savagery of the slave trade as being one of its primary features. "Tortures, murder, and every other imaginable barbarity and iniquity are practiced upon the poor slaves with impunity. I hope the slave-trade will be abolished. I pray it may be an event at hand. The great body of manufacturers, uniting in the cause will considerably facilitate it and expedite it."[86] In referring to the "poor slaves" Equiano separates his current free British self from the plight of those still in bondage. This reflects the way that Equiano's experience has separated him entirely from the kind of slave experience that creates an insurrectionist. In becoming British, he has also eradicated any early traces of insurrectionist impulse.

In one respect, one might read this moment as evidence of a larger shift within the Anglo-American World. As W. Jeffery Bolster notes in *Black Jacks,* the years in the wake of the American Revolution saw free blacks flocking to the sea for work in unprecedented numbers as "few other workplaces welcomed them so readily."[87] As many as 24 percent of free black men in Philadelphia were employed in maritime industries by 1803.[88] By 1811 the famous former captain and shipbuilder, Paul Cuffe, was probably the wealthiest African American in the country.[89] And, as I will touch on in later chapters, there are examples of the interracial shipboard community producing tantalizing moments of cross-racial revolutionary possibility. But the problem of the image of the productive black seaman is that, in the wake of the St. Domingo uprising, this image must also compete with the more menacing image of the insurrectionist. In this way, the mobility, competence, and cosmopolitanism learned by black sailors in the late eighteenth and early nineteenth centuries amplifies the threat they present to the slaveholding world.

In the case of Equiano's *Interesting Narrative,* whatever revolutionary possibility evoked in the fight scene aboard the *Namur* vanishes. By characterizing the slaves as victims of a brutal trade—and characterizing slave violence as a product of the slave trade—Clarkson and Equiano were instrumental in creating a discourse that disavowed insurrection as a viable means of emancipation. Slave violence would remain a conundrum for the abolitionists by displaying evidence of the slaves' innate savagery, and bolstering proslavery arguments against emancipation. But in reexamining the works within the context of shipboard insurrection, a more complete picture of the slave resistance emerges.

DENMARK VESEY, JOHN HOWISON,

AND REVOLUTIONARY POSSIBILITY

THE SIGHTING OF A SUSPICIOUSLY moored ship that turns out to be a pirate vessel touches off the action of John Howison's 1821 short story, "The Florida Pirate."[1] The narrator, after reflecting upon his misfortunes while strolling along the seashore, spies the ship.

> I knew that vessels did not usually moor in such a situation, and inquired of a fisherman, whom I met on the beach, if he could tell me what the schooner did there. "I'm not quite sure," returned he, "but I rather suspect she is a pirate. Those on board of her are mostly blacks, and they seem very anxious to keep out of sight. Had she been a fair trader, she would have come into the harbor at once."[2]

The fisherman's suspicions prove correct, and the narrator finds himself the reluctant passenger aboard a ship helmed by fugitive slaves. But, before discussing this fictional ship, I would like to first turn to the sighting of another suspicious ship which appeared in Charleston Harbor in May 1822 and became the first sign for slave-owning South Carolinians of a possible slave conspiracy.

In the testimony that supposedly revealed the existence of what has become known as the Denmark Vesey conspiracy, an informant tells the court that spotting this ship in the harbor was the key to breaking open the heretofore undetected plot. A slave called Devany testifies that William, a slave belonging to a Mr. Paul, accosted him on the wharf to discuss the import of the ship in question.

> On Saturday afternoon last (my master being out of town) I went to market; finishing my business I strolled down the wharf below the fish market from which I observed a small vessel in the stream with a singular flag; whilst looking at this object, a black man, (Mr. Paul's William) came up to me and remarking on the subject which engaged my attention said,

I have often seen a flag with the number 76 on it, but never with 96 before. After some trifling conversation on this point, he remarked with considerable earnestness to me. Do you know that something serious is about to take place? To which I replied no. Well, said he, there is, and many of us are determined to right ourselves! I asked him to explain himself—when he remarked, why we are determined to shake off our bondage, and for this purpose we stand on a good foundation, many have joined, and if you will go with me, I will show you the man, who has the list of names who will take yours down.[3]

The way in which Howison's short story and witness testimony treat the relationship between mysterious ships and slave insurrection speaks to both the facts of the Denmark Vesey conspiracy and the widespread paranoia of slave insurrection. Vesey, as a free sailor with ties to St. Domingo, is the figure who appears to encapsulate slaveholders' worst fears of freed blacks being agents of a possible hemispheric race war. Howison's work, a mix of travel narratives and gothic fiction about the Caribbean world, written both before and after the conspiracy, seizes upon this fear by creating fictions that, at first glance, seem to be cautionary tales designed to warn readers of the possible dangers of refusing to address the threat of insurrection represented both by free blacks and the pernicious influence of St. Domingo. However, a closer look at "The Florida Pirate" reveals a more complicated picture of insurrection, one that seems at odds with the prevailing thinking of the moment. Moreover, reading the short story alongside the "official accounts" raises questions about the ways in which the city officials documented the history of insurrection. The necessity of narrating the events after the fact, particularly when key facts remain unknown, brings these ostensibly disparate texts into dialogue with one another.

The fact that both the fictional text and the account of the insurrection begin with the sighting of suspicious ships might be of no consequence were it not for the specific ways in which maritime history intersects with the histories of abolition and insurrection. That the Vesey conspiracy led directly to the adoption of the *Negro Seamen Acts* (1822–1848) and possibly inspired David Walker to write his *Appeal to the Coloured Citizens of the World* (1829) shows us that the relationship between maritime life and the concerns surrounding land-based insurrection was more inextricably linked than one might suppose. Moreover, the argument that the slave trade itself was responsible for the insurrections of the eighteenth century, as I discussed in the previous chapter, is also true of the period immediately following the abolition of the Atlantic slave trade in 1807.

The abolition of the trade, coinciding as it did with the conclusion of the Haitian Revolution, was accompanied by widespread anxiety over the possibility

of a diasporic slave revolt, as refugees from Haiti brought stories to the States of
the horrors they had seen.[4] Despite the United States' refusal to officially acknowledge Haiti as a sovereign nation, the bonds of trade between the two nations
remained strong, necessitating frequent traffic between Haiti and major southern
ports including Charleston and New Orleans.[5] The years between 1808 and 1819
also saw an uptick in illegal slave trafficking that brought pirates of all nationalities and races into the country via Florida. And finally, the 1807 ban revitalized
northern opposition to slavery, putting the question of emancipation on the table
with regards to westward expansion. Northern opposition to the *Missouri Compromise* and the emergence of the African Colonization Society all pointed to a
growing awareness of the untenability of keeping slavery alive in perpetuity.[6] While
moral arguments against slavery were very much in circulation at this moment,
the threat of slave insurrections engulfing the South was also behind the emerging
calls for abolition.

The Gabriel Prosser conspiracy of 1800 and the Louisiana uprising of
1811 are noteworthy examples in the period. Prosser, allegedly inspired by the
St. Domingo uprising, amassed a sizeable army in Virginia before being betrayed.[7]
In Louisiana, Charles Deslondes led nearly 500 slaves in a rampage across
St. Charles Parish just South of New Orleans.[8] And in 1818 the all-black crew of
the ship the *Holkar* killed their captain and first mate and made for St. Domingo.[9]
But the Vesey conspiracy stands out for three reasons. Firstly, Denmark Vesey, as a
free black sailor with ties to San Domingo, embodied fears of insurrectionist contamination from abroad. Secondly, the facts of the conspiracy are, to this day, subject to much debate and conjecture. As an event that may have existed only within
the imaginations of slaveholding authorities, the Vesey conspiracy reveals the structure of slaveholder fears about violence. The Vesey conspiracy both produces and is
produced by a narrative that illustrates the uncontainable nature of insurrection
even as the narrative itself operates as a method of containment.

In making the crew a band of fugitive slaves and not a crew of disaffected
black seamen, Howison adds a layer of menace onto the story by asking the reader
to imagine the possibilities the ocean offers would-be insurrectionists on land.
Howison's short story, "The Florida Pirate," appeared in the August 21st issue of
Blackwood's Edinburgh Magazine.[10] That same year it was reprinted by a New
Hampshire printer as the "Life and Adventures of Manuel, the Florida Pirate." It
next appeared through a New York printer who produced three separate editions
in 1827 and again in 1828.[11] One final edition would appear in 1834 in Pittsburgh.[12]
To those who know the history of insurrection in this country, the sudden surge in
popularity for this story written by a Scottish expatriate should come as no surprise.
While it is difficult to ascertain whether or not the story was received positively in

Charleston, notices, and reviews of "The Florida Pirate" as well as Howison's other work, appeared in other papers throughout the U.S. A review in the *Washington Gazette* in 1821 takes a dim view of the story, accusing it of being "designed to excite in Great Britain the utmost odium against the whites of our Southern States."[13] One might speculate that Charleston readers would have been similarly indignant.

Howison's story ostensibly appears to invoke St. Domingo in a manner meant to inspire fear. Yet, the story, in creating sympathy for the title character, also seems to suggest that St. Domingo simultaneously occupies a space of hope for the fugitive slaves. Howison's story is not so much prescient as it is vulnerable to the same kind of paranoid speculation that produced the media reportage surrounding the Vesey conspiracy, namely these two texts: *An account of the late intended insurrection among a portion of the blacks of this city* (1822) and *An Official Report of the Trials of Sundry Negroes Charged with an Attempt to Raise An Insurrection in the State of South Carolina: Preceded by an Introduction and Narrative; And in an Appendix A Report of the Trials of Four White Persons, On Indictments For Attempting to Excite the Slaves to Insurrection* (1822). This paranoid speculation results in the creation of what scholar Carrie Hyde calls "possibilistic history" which, I believe, carries with it revolutionary possibilities, even as it appears to be intended as a cautionary tale.[14]

The Vesey conspiracy is uniquely useful for this because of its timing and the spectral nature of the case facts. The only true knowns are the outcomes of the trial. After a summary trial, Denmark Vesey was one of thirty-five blacks hung for conspiracy to revolt in the summer of 1822. An additional thirty-seven were sent into exile.[15] We know the names of the major actors and what they are alleged to have said regarding both Vesey and the conspiracy. We know how the conspirators were betrayed. But Vesey himself remains something of a mystery. He is believed to have been born in Africa some time in the 1760s, purchased in St. Thomas in the 1780s, and brought to South Carolina where he purchased his freedom with winnings from the East Bay lottery in 1799. Beyond that is conjecture, hearsay, and perhaps fantasy.[16]

Aside from these points, concrete facts remain elusive. The trial transcripts themselves obscure more than they reveal. The silences are greater than the things said. For example, Vesey's testimony is never recorded directly. Both the *Account* and *The Trial Record* narrate Vesey's words and reactions but rarely quote him directly:

> When Vesey was tried, he folded his arms and seemed to pay a great attention to the testimony given against him, but with his eyes fixed on the floor. In this situation he remained immovable, until the witnesses had been examined by the Court and cross-examined by his counsel;

when he requested permission to examine the witnesses themselves. He at first questioned them in the dictatorial, despotic manner, in which he was probably accustomed to address them but this not producing the desired effect, he questioned them with affected surprise and concern for bearing false testimony against him; still failing in his purpose, he then examined them strictly as to dates, but could not make them contradict themselves. The evidence being closed, he addressed the Court at considerable length, in which his principle endeavor was to impress them with the idea, that as his situation in life had been such that he could have had no inducement to join in such an attempt, the charge against him must be false; and he attributed it to the great hatred which he alleged that blacks had against him; but his allegations were unsupported by proof. When he received his sentence, the tears trickled down his cheeks.[17]

The lack of direct quotations and hard evidence of his alleged correspondence with San Domingo allows for Charleston city officials to create a version of Vesey that suited their purposes, one who is by turns defiant, arrogant, conniving and persuasive.[18] Indeed, according to a controversial Michael P. Johnson article questioning the reality of the plot, part of the problem with the account is the silence of the accused. "Of the forty-six men on trial during July who did not confess, only two testified in court, according to the transcript. The most frequent exceptions to the silence of the accused in the July transcript and the strongest evidence of their presence in court are their pleas. . . . The July transcript records a plea of not guilty for forty-five of the forty-six defendants who did not confess."[19] This absence of confession points to more than just the high probability of a kangaroo court scenario. It speaks to the potential irrelevancy of first-person accounts of the conspiracy. The debate on whether or not a conspiracy existed was originally opened by Richard C. Wade in 1964, and then resurrected by historian Michael Johnson in a sixty-plus page piece in the January 2002 volume of *William And Mary Quarterly*. Johnson argued that prominent historians of the Vesey case had misrepresented the court documents and he suggested instead that the Vesey conspiracy was a fabrication on the part of the Charleston authorities who wanted to implement restrictions against slave gatherings and black sailors. The firestorm ignited by Johnson's article has mostly subsided, but while the consensus seems to weigh more against Johnson's theory than not, the question of what *really* happened is yet to be satisfactorily resolved.[20]

The controversy surrounding the Vesey case is not without precedence. Indeed it shares many features with an earlier revolt, the New York conspiracy of 1741. During the spring and summer of that year, a string of thirteen fires plagued the city. Eventually rumors of a mass insurrection of slaves began to circulate. "In the end, the colony of New York executed 30 slaves and 4 white ringleaders, publicly flogged 50 slaves, and transported over 70 more to the Caribbean slave markets, never to return."[21] As with the Vesey conspiracy, questions persist as to whether or not any conspiracy actually existed, though there was considerably more contemporaneous outrage particularly as it related to New York party politics of the preceding decade.[22] And while the slave population was the primary target of New York City law enforcement, it was their relationship to local and foreign sailors that gave rise to much of the alarm. John Hughson, owner of the bar near Trinity Church where slaves and sailors often gathered, was among those executed, as his bar was believed to be the site of the plotting.[23] But while the question of the Vesey conspiracy's veracity went mostly unchallenged until the twentieth century, the New York conspiracy became a scandal almost immediately. I mention it here to point to the dual stigma of race and the occupation of seaman as being part of the matrix of factors in the Vesey conspiracy. When one adds the widespread fear of insurrection and the specter of the Haitian Revolution, one can see the heavy incentive on the part of Charleston to press the advantage at any whiff of conspiracy. As Edlie L. Wong writes, "Rather than acknowledge the 'domestic' origins of slave unrest, southern legislators and officials had begun to represent 'the rank and file of the conspiracy as the victims of *foreign* seduction' in the concerted effort to redirect the source of revolutionary black agency elsewhere beyond the boundaries of the state."[24]

This absence of consensus is also more than just the product of racism-induced paranoia. I argue that confession and fact are beside the point within the narratives of this conspiracy. "The Florida Pirate" provides not simply an example of the ways in which fears of a St. Domingo-inspired insurrection were always already circulating in the years before the alleged conspiracy, but also the impossibility of fully exorcising those fears through the use of fiction as a cautionary tale. I use the term "alleged" not because I endorse Michael Johnson's theory that the conspiracy was completely the invention of the Charleston authorities, but to highlight the manner in which the conduct of this particular trial and the narratives produced in the wake of the trial, function in the same way as fiction. The creation of a narrative absent the concrete facts of the case creates gaps even as it tries to fill them in. In attempting to gloss over the absence of concrete testimony, Charleston city officials augmented the menace of insurrection. In turn, Howison's short story produces a speculative scenario that appears designed to foreclose the possibility of a transnational slave revolution but, instead, gives it new life and power. This new life and power is specifically a function of setting the bulk of the story at sea and creating a scenario of partial success on the part of the fugitives.

THE DENMARK VESEY CONSPIRACY

The insurrection is believed to have been planned for July 14, 1822, which was a Sunday and also Bastille Day and therefore an ideal day to catch the city off guard. The case turned on alleged evidence that Vesey had both been discussing ongoing congressional debates regarding the *Missouri Compromise* of 1820 and corresponded with sympathizers in St. Domingo for aid. Beyond these facts and what appears in court documents, there is little else to assist in ascertaining what happened in the courthouse during these proceedings. Slave codes meant that the trial was closed, attorneys were not permitted to discuss the case with their clients, and slaves whose masters were not willing to pay for counsel received no legal defense. Carolina law denied blacks the right to appeal or challenge rulings.[25] What we do know is that Lionel Henry Kennedy, one of the presiding magistrates, who also provided the official account, insisted that no slave would be tried without his masters' presence and that counsel would be allowed, masters permitting.[26] The trials started on June 19 and ended August 22. In all, thirty-five people were executed for conspiracy. Given the coercive nature of the trial, the lack of firsthand accounts, and indeed the intentional silence maintained by several of the ringleaders, it is little wonder that speculation over whether or not there was a conspiracy persists. It is not my intention to reopen this question for real debate, but rather to make a case for the very debate itself as being instructive in how to "read" the fear of insurrection.

Michael Johnson's contention that the conduct of the Charleston authorities points to evidence of a concerted effort to eradicate potential troublemakers rather than mete out justice to actual insurrectionists is, at heart, a well-meaning one.[27] Philip Morgan, siding with Johnson, cites the many conspiracy scares preceding the Vesey trial as evidence of the prevalence of such fabrications on the part of city officials seeking to cow would-be insurrectionists before they thought to organize. Conversely, Robert S. Levine faults Johnson for speculating too freely on the motives and feelings of the black witnesses. Douglas R. Egerton, in countering Johnson's argument, marshals the value of the legacy in his argument, asserting, "Activist Frederick Douglass, like abolitionists Martin Delany and William Lloyd Garrison, who sat beside Robert Vesey at the April 14, 1865, flag-raising ceremony at Fort Sumter, well knew the old carpenter was no passive victim, just as he understood the folly in forgetting Vesey's legacy of black activism."[28] This vehemence is noteworthy because, as was the case with the debate over Equiano's origins in the previous chapter, the value placed on the Vesey conspiracy depends entirely on the way the legacy has been interpreted over the last century and a half.

Indeed, the urgency attending the question of whether or not there was a conspiracy to revolt in Charleston in 1822 in the years following the publication of Michael Johnson's piece in 2001, in some ways, replays nineteenth-century arguments over the character and shape of slave insurrection. By trying to determine what counts as an actual conspiracy versus mere "talk," these scholars inadvertently employ a template of organized insurrection that mirrors the methods Charleston city officials used in figuring out what counts as evidence of a plot. Levine's use of the trial transcript as a container for the seeds of David Walker's work is instructive; it points to the scholarly impulse to locate within these fragmented documents signs of revolutionary activity. Levine writes:

> if, as Johnson alleges, white South Carolinian elites deliberately put Vesey and his supposed accomplices on trial in order to reinforce their power, this was an act of surpassing stupidity. For the result of their actions was to create in the widely circulated published version of the trial transcript the figure of a heroic black revolutionary whose "cunning," as described by one of the black witnesses, continued to inspire blacks long after the authorities put him to death. In this respect, I would argue, contra Johnson, that those like myself who detect in the trial transcript the voices of a black revolutionary and his co-conspirators are colluding not with the South Carolina authorities of the early 1820s but rather with the many African Americans, including David Walker, who were inspired by Vesey.[29]

I do not wish to suggest that Levine's reading of the transcript as a coded message to future black revolutionaries is wishful thinking. Indeed, his analysis of the text against Walker's *Appeal* is both sharp and persuasive.[30] However, his assertion that this whiff of radicalism contradicts Michael Johnson's thesis assumes a canniness on the part of the Charleston authorities that it is not clear that they possessed. In the first place, there is the problem of ascertaining the nature of the audience for the transcripts. For a nervous slave-owning public, the image of a "cunning" Vesey would read very differently than it would for a free and enslaved black audience. In the second place, if the Vesey Conspiracy and its outcome prove anything, it is that there is nothing really needed to "inspire" an insurrection. Those who agree with Johnson, and assume that the threat of insurrection was more southern paranoia than anything else, do not give proper consideration to the myriad ways in which the history of slave resistance has been subsumed and distorted by documents like the Vesey trial transcripts. In both cases the stakes of proving the conspiracy to be real involve the elevation of the actors from mere slaves to either heroes, as in the case of Egerton, Pearson, and Levine; innocent victims of racism, as in the case of Johnson; or villains, as in the case of Charleston magistrates in 1822. I mention this because the similarity of the impulses points to a problem with the way in which contemporary scholarship relies too much on the specifics of the individual instances of insurrection. In fixating on the presence or absence of individual conspiracies, one insists that the coherence of a single insurrection emblematize the entire spectrum of insurrection. This fixation produces a historical narrative of insurrection that is "incidental" rather than comprehensive, which is precisely the problem with this debate. As Hyde has stated, "The polarizing terms of the Vesey controversy have put critics in the over-determined position of choosing between enslaved insurrectionary agency and manipulative white fictions."[31]

Reading the Vesey documents alongside Howison's "The Florida Pirate" highlights the slippery nature of words like "evidence" and the unbound nature of revolutionary possibility. Speculative or "possibilistic history" proves to be in itself revolutionary despite the intentions of the author. The resonance of the sighting of the suspicious ship I mentioned at the beginning of the chapter speaks to the way in which ships in these texts obliterate the line between real events and speculative fictions. The coincidental nature of the way in which these stories open with the inciting moment of the discovery of the conspiracy calls into question the nature of "coincidence" or "foresight" in the relationship between fact and fiction. The ship in all cases is presented as evidence, both in the concreteness of what kind of trouble each ship engages in and as representative of the possibility of contamination from without. This is also precisely how these stories, both of the legal accounts and the novella, escape their cautionary frameworks. The possibility of ships from St. Domingo landing in Charleston to offer assistance in a wide-scale insurrection and to spirit escapees away to the sanctuary of St. Domingo speaks so clearly to the wishes of the slaves that it threatens to undermine both righteous assertions of the Charleston city officials and the larger justifications behind the slave system as a whole.

The aforementioned court documents produced in the aftermath of the trial were *An Account of the Late Intended Insurrection Among a Portion of the Blacks of this City*, by James Hamilton (1822), and *An Official Report of the Trials of Sundry Negroes Charged with an Attempt to Raise An Insurrection in the State of South Carolina &tc.* written by Lionel Kennedy and Thomas Parker (1822). Hamilton was the city official who first investigated the conspiracy and Parker and Thomas were the presiding magistrates. The accounts in question were requested by the governor and subsequently used as evidentiary support in passing the *Negro Seamen Acts*. The accounts, therefore, are bracketed within a larger narrative in which local and national politics are playing a part in containing black violence from within and without. It is important to read both accounts not simply regarding what truth claims they make about the conspiracy, but also regarding the way they use speculation to sidestep issues of truth and to bolster ongoing arguments regarding containment. More to the point, looking at the way in which each account highlights the role of St. Domingo in the conspiracy reveals that part of using speculation as a substitute for fact invokes the specter of something already achieved. St. Domingo offers itself as "proof" because of its position as a successful slave revolt.

In a footnote of the *Account*, Vesey's biography is told like this:

> As Denmark Vesey has occupied so large a place in the conspiracy, a brief notice will, perhaps, not be devoid of interest. . . . During the Revolutionary War, Captain Vesey, not an old resident of this city, commanded a ship that traded between St. Thomas' and Cape Francais (San Domingo). He was engaged in supplying the French of that Island with Slaves. In the year, 1781, he took on board at St. Thomas' 390 slaves and sailed for the Cape; on the passage, he and his officers were struck by the beauty, alertness and intelligence of a boy about 14 years of age, whom they made a pet of, by taking him into the cabin, changing his apparel and calling him by way of *Telemaque*, (which appellation has since, by gradual corruption, among the negroes, been changed to *Denmark*, or sometimes *Telmak*). . . . Among his colour he was always looked up to with awe and respect. . . . All his passions were ungovernable and savage. . . . If the party had been one moment later, he would, in all probability, have effected his escape the next day in some outward bound vessel.[32]

Relegating Vesey's biography to a footnote that takes up most of the space on the page makes Vesey's life both beside the point to the facts of the case and the very thing that matters most. The salient details regarding his sojourn in St. Domingo, the position of favor he found with his former master, the way he allegedly dominated his peers, all reflect a preoccupation with the idea that Vesey is both the center of this trial but also incidental to it. The absence of hard evidence pointing directly, either to the presence of a conspiracy or Vesey's leadership role in said conspiracy, forces Hamilton to find within the details of Vesey's biography "evidence" of his propensity to revolt.

In the introduction of *The Trial Record of Denmark Vesey*, Kennedy and Parker indicate that evidence of real collusion with agents from St. Domingo was lacking and therefore not a large feature of the trial. They write:

> In addition to the foregoing circumstances, it was proved and subsequently acknowledged by Monday, that Vesey had written two letters to Santo Domingo on the subject of this plot; but of the character, extent, and importances of this correspondence, no satisfactory information has been obtained, and perhaps by no other person but Vesey could this have

been given. . . . One or two of the insurgents said, that Vesey, after robbing the banks of specie, and plundering the city of all that was most valuable, intended to sail for Santo Domingo with his principal adherents; but the informants themselves spoke of it more as a suggestion, than a fixed plan.[33]

However, the instances in which St. Domingo was directly referenced indicate a line of questioning that was preoccupied with ferreting out such a conspiracy. It comes up as testimony in the trials of the chief conspiritors, Rolla, Peter, Jesse, Jack, Smart, Bacchus, and Saby Gaillard. While it is true that none of the testimony points to anything concrete, in so far as evidence is concerned, the "suggestiveness" of references to St. Domingo indicates an awareness on the part of the court that repeating the name St. Domingo could work on the imaginations of the hearers regardless of the facts of the case. For example, in his testimony against Rolla, an unnamed slave said:

> There are said he [Rolla], who have come from far off, and who say that Santo Domingo and Africa will assist us to get our liberty if we only make the motion first. . . . He told me that at the first meeting it was said that *some white men said Congress had set us free, and that our white people here would not us be so,* and that Santo Domingo and Africa would come over and cut up the white people, if we only made the motion here first.[34]

Over and over the witnesses claim such knowledge of "talk" of St. Domingo. "Monday was writing a letter to Santo Domingo to go by a vessel lying at Gibb's and Harper's Wharf—the letter was about the sufferings of the blacks, and to know if the people of Santo Domingo would help them if they made an effort to free themselves." "Vesey told me that a large army from Santo Domingo and Africa were coming to help us, and we must not stand with our hands in our pockets; he was bitter towards the whites," and so on.[35]

The focus on St. Domingo's place in the alleged conspiracy matters within the construction of the Vesey narrative because it creates, for Charleston City officials, the proper bogeyman required to justify both the swiftness with which the conspirators were tried and executed and the passing of subsequent laws against literacy and congregation, and the infamous *Negro Seamen Acts.* The question of what constitutes overreaction versus a measured and logical response relies on the nature of the conspiracy being vast. St. Domingo, as a potential ally, does more than simply provide the possibility of invasion. It creates the sense of an insurrection already achieved. The success of the Haitian revolution proves useful in proving the

Vesey conspiracy true because, as a successful revolution, it invokes success without having to achieve anything.

This dynamic between real and possible conspiracies creates an interesting paradox concerning the political usefulness of slave insurrection and St. Domingo. For slaveholding states like South Carolina, the threat of slave insurrection would prove politically advantageous in providing them leverage against antislavery northern legislators in the elections of the 1830s, as well as in stifling discussion of slavery with the institution of the Gag Rule in 1836.[36] It also effectively stymied the burgeoning abolitionist movement, particularly by attributing insurrection to the influence of anti-slavery pamphlets in the north. The full effect of this latter charge would not be felt until the years following the Nat Turner Rebellion.

It is here, however, that the trial records and account are also complicit in creating the very problem that they are trying to repress. The repeated invocations of St. Domingo reinforces its iconic position as a space of freedom and safety even as the recorded testimony seems designed to bolster the city's case against Vesey. Early in their account, Kennedy and Parker assert that the collective testimony is enough to prove that Vesey was, indeed, in conversation with St. Domingo despite the lack of hard evidence. In disregarding the need for concrete evidence even as they admit that the endgame regarding St. Domingo was more or less speculative, Kennedy and Parker tacitly admit that real evidence is less important than speculative evidence. Moreover, in failing either to confirm or deny the existence of a link between Vesey and St. Domingo, they invite even wilder speculation regarding what might have been in those alleged letters. Inviting speculation is not tantamount to creating fiction, but in creating narrative in the absence of evidence, Kennedy and Parker blur the line between fact and fiction. Finally, despite their best efforts to soften the language of the Negro Act, their having closed the case itself and having stripped the defendants of all but the feeblest pretenses of legal protection, betrays the court case as being more pretense than policy. It is here where their narrative threatens to escape the confines of its legal framing. The mentioning of the "suffering of blacks," the focus on the feelings of bitterness, anger, revenge, the reports of boastful speculation on how a fight might go down, all of these serve, if not to justify the reasons for insurrection, to give voice to the humanity of the conspirators. Finding evidence of a conspiracy forces Charleston city officials to give a platform to the revolutionary slave voice.[37]

Reading these documents alongside Howison's "The Florida Pirate" reveals the way in which the revolutionary slave voice is, at its heart, "fictional" not in its unrealness but in that its mere narration evokes power even without materializing the event in fact. Howison, no friend to the as-yet fledgling abolitionist movement, still cannot help but ventriloquize the revolutionary slave voice in the same way that the two accounts cannot help but give it a platform. Without the legal framing, the story cannot contain that voice even as the plot attempts figuratively to put down the possibility of maritime-based slave revolution.

"THE FLORIDA PIRATE"

Howison was a doctor and writer who made a name for himself through his travel writing. He arrived in Canada in 1818 and left in 1820, visiting the United States, the West Indies, and Cuba along the way. Later he was posted in Bombay for twenty years and used his leave time to travel to Africa as well as other parts of India. His famous *Sketches of Upper Canada* (1821) was the most celebrated of contemporary accounts of the area. "The Florida Pirate" was Howison's first piece of published fiction, and as such, it is both typical and atypical of his later writing. The plot centers on an unnamed white narrator who, at the story's opening, is marooned on a Caribbean Island, destitute and in debt. He falls in with a band of fugitive slave pirates captained by a one-handed man named Manuel and reluctantly agrees to serve as ship's doctor in exchange for a berth. While on board, the narrator is drawn into an uneasy friendship with Manuel after learning that the fugitive's current circumstances are due to maltreatment at the hands of an abusive master and the death of his sweetheart. The pirates are captured after a failed attempt at securing another ship, and the story ends with Manuel bequeathing the narrator his share of the pirate spoils before he is executed.

In imagining a fictional fugitive slave pirate and his crew, Howison uses the setting of the ocean to both highlight the spectral nature of insurrection and draw attention to the diasporic possibilities of widespread insurrection. In one register, "The Florida Pirate" reads as a cautionary tale of the dangers of allowing slaves to learn how to read. The slave Manuel's literacy stands as the reason behind his coming to hate slavery. The ocean setting acts as a physical obstacle that distances the threat of the Haitian revolution from the plantation system. However, in another register, the story, in giving voice to the grievances and hopes of slaves, allows a thin thread of revolutionary possibility to escape. The cautionary tale points not simply to the dangers of educating slaves but also to the dangers inherent in slavery itself. The geographical distancing of the threat from land to the ocean literalizes the slaveholders' denial of the real danger of insurrection.

The plot of "The Florida Pirate" fuses fantasy and history by tying piracy to slavery in a way that makes the ex-slave the pirate. Piracy and slavery have been linked since the implementation of The Treaty of Utrecht following the War of Spanish succession in 1713. In one fell swoop, the treaty ended the war, leaving hundreds of privateers without work, which allowed the British Empire to supply the Spanish colonies with unlimited numbers of slaves. As a result, when these privateers turned pirate, they preyed heavily on ships transporting goods, silver, gold, and slaves from the western coast of Africa. The damage done to the Atlantic Slave Trade was immense. As Marcus Rediker writes in *Villains of All Nations: Atlantic Pirates of the Golden Age*, the slave ships made ideal pirate ships in that they "would be stiffer and go better."[38] Sailors serving aboard slave ships were often so poorly treated that seizure by pirates was at times met with relief rather than terror. But, although recent histories of piracy in the early eighteenth century emphasize pirates' egalitarian ideology, pirate attacks on slave ships and slave fortresses had less to do with feelings against slavery and slave traders than with the silver and gold that often accompanied the human cargo and the ships themselves.[39] According to W. Jeffrey Bolster, despite Rediker's claims of pirates holding more cosmopolitan views towards slaves, the formerly enslaved, and free blacks, pirates were just as likely to sell plundered slaves as they were to free them or offer them places aboard their ships.[40] "As welcoming as most white pirates were to skilled black sailors . . . sea robbers were not race-blind. None of the renowned pirate captains at the turn of the eighteenth century was a black man, and pirates generally sold captured slaves with the rest of the plunder. Many kept slaves aboard ship for pumping and other work disdained by sailors who wished to impersonate gentlemen." Within the context of nineteenth-century piracy, there is not much evidence regarding the makeup of the few American pirate ships in existence.[41]

This history makes "The Florida Pirate" particularly unique in that it features an ex-slave as the captain. Black pirates made up a substantial portion of the pirate population in the early part of the eighteenth century, but there is no evidence that there ever existed a black pirate captain.[42] This complicates an analysis that casts Manuel and his crew as embodying the fears and consoling visions of whites regarding both slave insurrection and the spread of St. Domingo violence. For at the same time that "The Florida Pirate" embodies the most prevalent fears of both the pro- and anti-slavery white populations of Great Britain and the United States, it also contains a kernel of radical fantasy.

The position of whites on both sides of the Atlantic is embodied in the unnamed narrator, a doctor who finds himself in serious debt in the Bahamas and approaches Manuel's ship, the *Esperanza*, in the hopes of offering his medical services in exchange for a berth on the ship. The narrator, whose past remains somewhat shadowy, offers the readers two perspectives from which to view the ensuing action. On the one hand, his position in the Bahamas, broke and desperate, casts him as an adventurer, possibly an unsavory one. As we see later, Howison's Caribbean tales tend to take a dim view of Britons seeking their fortunes in the colonies. On the other hand, if his ambition repels them, his fear of the fugitives might speak to readers by aligning him with their anxieties. As such, the narrator offers for us a study in Howison's own possible ambivalence about the place of slavery in 1821. Rather than having him coerced or kidnapped by Manuel and his crew, Howison has the narrator, after a period of reflection, choose to fall in with the pirates in order to escape his creditors. The narrator's questionable character is never fully addressed although his willingness to negotiate with pirates suggests moral flexibility. His distaste for piracy, his complicated sympathy towards Manuel, and his heroics and marriage to Mr. R__'s daughter serve as the narrator's evolution from debtor to hero and his reentry into civilized society. The narrator's personal course intersects with Manuel's narrative, the tragic fall of a would-be honorable man, at their meeting aboard the *Esperanza*. Though the reader receives the story of the narrator's past, the reader can infer an abolitionist allegory in which the thing to be feared is not violence against former masters from emancipated slaves, but violent insurrection if slaves are not emancipated. The narrator, redeemed through his interaction with Manuel, becomes an avatar for the misguided British planter. The name of the ship, "hope" in Spanish, is made doubly ironic both by the hopelessness of the narrator's situation and the ultimate failure of Manuel. This dual irony makes the text's politics difficult to track. In one register, it seems to mock Manuel's foolhardiness and warn the reader against feeling too much sympathy for him. In another, it reinforces the tragedy of Manuel's end and acknowledges the feelings behind insurrection.

The narrator's uneasy contract with Manuel and his crew reflects the necessity of confronting the consequences of slavery in the form of violent and abused slaves. The uprisings of 1816, 1823, and 1831 in Barbados, Demerara, and Jamaica respectively disabused Britons of the notion that slave violence could be controlled merely through restricting importation.[43] Howison makes this explicit in describing the scene that confronts the narrator when he first boards the ship. He notes upon first meeting Manuel that, "He wanted a right hand." Later, upon more closely observing the crew, he notes the marks of abuse on their bodies. "A number of the negroes lay around the fire, roasting ears of Indian corn, which were eagerly snatched off the embers the moment they were ready. I could distinguish the marks of the whip on the shoulders of some of them. The limbs of others had been distorted by the weight and galling of fetters, as was evident from the indentations exhibited by their flesh."[44] In noting their scars and injuries, the narrator seems to be providing a context for their later depravity. This observation does not necessarily lead to sympathy. The narrator's descriptions of the crew are all negative:

"disgusting," "insolent," and as "wretches."[45] But it does call into question any reading of this text as pro-slavery. Drawing attention to their injuries allows the narrator to express simultaneously his revulsion for both the dehumanizing nature of slavery as well as his fear of the monsters slavery has made. Manuel's story of how he came to be a pirate, as I will demonstrate, makes more explicit the way in which violence becomes the means of corrupting otherwise "good" slaves.

This "good slave" motif reveals itself elsewhere in Howison's work, and he explicitly deploys it to illustrating the effects of slavery and colonization on the colonist. In both his travel writing and his fiction, Howison exhibits a preoccupation with race, slavery, the character of colonists, and the role of wealth in shaping individuals. His maritime fiction tends to punish those white characters who seem overly driven by greed while it rewards those who display some moderation. Slavery operates within these texts as a test of the protagonists' judgment and compassion. The rewards involve acquiring wealth in a way that both avoids the exploitation of slavery and is impossible without it. While the bad actors may, indeed, be guilty of poor treatment of the slaves, slavery itself is not up for critique. Conversely, the hero's distaste for slavery speaks less to the institution itself than it does to the character of the hero. If slavery is represented as evil here, the fault lies with the mishandling of slaves more than it does with the institution of slavery.

This view is consistent with Howison's thinking on abolitionism, race, and colonialism. In his two-volume work *European Colonies, in Various Parts of the World: Viewed In Their Social, Moral, and Physical Condition* (1834), he devotes sections to the land, colonists, and native populations with long tangents regarding what he views as misapprehensions on the part of other travel writers. On the subject of race and slavery, Howison's views were at once prey to the larger misapprehensions of the day, and at odds with the prevailing wisdom regarding the so-called natural inferiority of Africans. He seems to have been at some pains not simply to correct what he saw as the unjust labeling of blacks as naturally violent and depraved, but also to draw attention to the ills that slavery visited upon European colonists. For example, in his "West Africa" section he pauses to consider the conduct of Europeans toward Africans in influencing so-called bad behavior. He writes, "When we consider the general character and conduct of those Europeans who have hitherto been in the habit of frequenting the coast of Africa, we shall perceive that the Negroes must have found it necessary in their transaction with them to disregard integrity and justice, in order to avoid the chance of being maltreated, plundered and overreached."[46] At the same time, he describes the blacks of West Africa as "indolent" and "peaceable" thereby reproducing familiar stereotypes of lazy and childlike slaves. He is, however, clear in making the indolence less an inborn trait than a consequence of life in the tropics. For this reason, he takes a dim view of colonization in these areas. "A tropical climate has always been found to exert an unfavourable [*sic*] influence on the character of Europeans, even of a superior class, but it brutalizes and infuriates those of naturally low habits; and hence we may easily conceive what that society must have been, which consisted of an assemblage of foreign vagrants settled upon the fiery and fatal shores of West Africa."[47] Race, for Howison, seems more about climate theory than inborn qualities, though he does not seem so progressive when it comes to class. Phrasing like "naturally low habits" suggests that one's station and one's habits are unchangeable.

Despite this relatively elastic view on race and condition, Howison categorically rejects abolitionism. The subject is first brought up in his section on South Africa and elaborated on in his section on the West Indies. He praises South African colonists for practicing a more humane sort of slavery, noting the absence of either harsh labor or harsh punishment, and that slaves are often at liberty to hire themselves out when their masters have no work for them, keeping a portion of their earnings for themselves. He also points to the potential dangers posed by emancipation by citing an example of a homeless woman he spotted in Cape Town.

> I was never asked for charity in the streets of Cape Town but once. The applicant was an old woman, who, in answer to my inquiries respecting her condition, told me that she was formerly a slave, but that her mistress had recently died, leaving her "*nothing but her freedom.*" Let those hasty and intemperate emancipationists, who raise their voices so loud, consider the nature and consequences of the measure which they advocate—and let them scrupulously examine whether it will be for the benefit of those who are its objects, lest, in suddenly delivering them from bondage, the leave with, "*nothing but their freedom.*"[48]

Howison's views on colonialism in relationship to his views on slavery and emancipation reveal a kind of compassionate paternalism that is at once progressive and conservative. The repetition of the phrase "nothing but her/their freedom," obviously meant as a sarcastic jab at abolitionists who tout freedom over material cares, also implies that "freedom" is to blame for the ills of colonialism enumerated previously. Having plundered these colonies he argues, Europeans should cease their ventures and treat their slaves with as much compassion and temperance as possible.

> Let then the generous nations of Europe allow the Africans to enjoy their barbarism a few centuries longer. The continent of America has already been nearly depopulated of its aborigines by the introduction of the blessings of civilization. . . . It surely is time that the work of destruction

should cease; and since long and melancholy experience has proved us to be invariably unsuccessful in rendering happier, wiser, or better, the barbarians homes we have visited or conquered, we may now conscientiously let them alone and turn a correcting hand towards ourselves, and seek to repress those evils which the march of intellect has long been engendering, lest all vestiges of good should disappear from amongst us, and leave us without any qualities but our avarice, our selfishness, and our vices.[49]

This idea of abandoning colonial projects in favor for self-improvement not only appears to suggest magnanimously that Europeans have little business interfering with the lives of others given their own proclivities, but also implies—more than implies in fact—that the European character's worst qualities have been exacerbated by colonization and need of correction. In mourning the genocide of the Native Americans and fearing the same fate for the Africans, Howison's admonishment to let Africa "enjoy its barbarism" also reveals his own horror at the violence of the colonial process. He seems to be nostalgic for Britain's own barbaric past, for at least they were not complicit in the ruin of other peoples.

Where slavery fits in is more complicated. The Caribbean offers Howison the ideal example of how to run a colony and manage slavery successfully. It helps that he is able to point to the rapacious history of Columbus' conquest of St. Domingo as a useful foil for Britain's rule. The eradication of the indigenous peoples and accompanying atrocities allow him to condemn colonialism even as he praises its current incarnation in the character of the West Indian colonizer.[50]

> Buoyant in disposition, active in his habits, full of enterprise, jealous of his rights, devoted to business, and sensitive and spirited in all the relations of life, he is a totally different being from what we are accustomed to meet with anywhere else within the limits of the torrid zone. That monotony of ideas, languor of manner, and frigidity of expression, which are the general characteristics of European society in the tropical climates, are scarcely observable in the West Indies, where almost every one has an air of occupation and natural enjoyment, and where people appear to seek for sources of interest and excitement instead of idly waiting till these happen to present themselves.[51]

For this reason, West Indian emancipation is unnecessary. Howison's views on slavery veer to the disapproving only when the slaves are mistreated and the slave owners become greedy and indolent. While he approves ending the Atlantic Slave Trade, as indicated by his earlier remarks on West Africa, abolition is something else altogether. He condemns the British government for introducing slavery to the islands only to eradicate it without properly compensating the plantation owners.

Moreover, he views the abolition of the Atlantic trade as the beginning to the natural end of slavery. "When the root of a tree is destroyed, the shoots which it may have produced must quickly perish; and, in like manner, our present slave population will gradually disappear, and be absorbed in the mass of society, without the outrageous interference of the general emancipator, and the merciless and unjustifiable ruin of the West Indian agriculturalist."[52] Here, he anticipates abolitionist Thomas Clarkson's language in citing the end of the Atlantic Slave Trade as the tipping point to wholesale abolition.[53] This makes his anti-abolitionist rhetoric more pragmatic and humanist than conservative.

Given these viewpoints, it is little wonder that "The Florida Pirate" is such an interesting blend of pro and anti-slavery sentiments. Howison's lack of abolitionist sympathies is evident in his portrayal of the pirates as hardened criminals, even as his insistence on humanizing Manuel by giving him a harrowing backstory to explain his choices reveals a streak of anti-slavery sentiment. Nor, given his extensive travel experience, is it necessarily surprising that Howison should choose to set his story aboard a pirate ship. "The Florida Pirate" begins Howison's long career in writing sea tales, a few of which I will discuss later. What is curious is that Manuel's decisions to burn his master's plantation and then to turn pirate, taken together, produce a strain of that same revolutionary voice discussed in the Denmark Vesey case. Moreover, given the absence of reliable documentary evidence of Vesey's words, Manuel provides an accidental substitute for Vesey and all others like him. Likewise, the narrator, whose shadowy past indicates monetary recklessness, becomes the lens through which white readers can view their own role in creating insurrection.

The initial meeting aboard the pirate ship for a brief moment puts the narrator and Manuel on equal terms—both fugitives, both reluctantly consorting with criminals in order to escape certain death. The narrator writes:

> My anticipations respecting the life I was now to lead were gloomy and revolting. I scarcely dared to look forward to the termination of the enterprise on which I had embarked; but when I considered what would have been my fate had I remained on shore, I could not condemn my choice.—Contempt, abject poverty, and the horrors of want were the evils I fled from—tyranny, danger and an ignominious death, formed, those towards which I was perhaps hastening.[54]

The narrator's use of the term "revolting" captures the irony of his present dilemma even as it anticipates the larger theme of the story. Given his location in the Caribbean, his former life of leisure would have been due to the fruits of slavery. Likewise, his position aboard the pirate ship would not be possible but for the hardships that produce runaways. "Revolting" simultaneously evokes the magnetic pull of slavery's riches even as it raises the specter of insurrection. That the narrator's abhorrence of his situation does not prevent him from entering into a contract with pirates further complicates readers' possible reactions to his alleged disgust.

This contract, more than simply tying his fate to that of the fugitives, also forces him to engage with Manuel as an equal. Manuel tells the narrator that he hails from a plantation in South Carolina and was owned by a man named Mr. Sexton. Manuel's early experiences as a manservant put him in close proximity to whites, and he claims it was this experience that taught him to be dissatisfied with his lot in life, saying:

> Had I been forced to work in the fields, like the other negroes, I might not have repined at my condition because I would have known nothing better, and at the same time believed that my condition was irremediable, and consistent with the laws of nature. But being continually in the presence of Mr. Sexton and other white people, and daily hearing their conversation, I soon discovered that they were superior to us in nothing but knowledge; that they were mean, wicked, cruel, and unjust; and that they sometimes feared we would assert our rights, and overpower them by numbers.[55]

Rather than attribute Manuel's anger to his literacy, Howison points to constant contact with whites as the fuel behind the fire. Their loose talk combined with their hedonistic behavior, undermines their authority more than any furtively acquired political tract. The reference to their "rights" also reflects worries amongst slaveholders that political discussion surrounding the *Missouri Compromise* of 1820 would embolden the slaves to revolt.[56] While Howison's unwillingness to give Manuel full credit for arriving at insurrection on his own points to his paternal condescension regarding the ingenuity of slaves, it also leaves open the possibility for justification for insurrection.

As a result, Howison's narrator is unable to reconcile his fear of Manuel's crew with his burgeoning awareness of their plight. This becomes evident in the conversation the narrator overhears between two crewmembers regarding another pirate who was recently hanged, and how to avoid his fate.

> "We must keep a sharp look out. I guess our best plan would be to hinder any one from ever becoming a witness against us."—"How can we manage that?" demanded Mendez.—"Why, by *pinking* a hole in the bottom of our prizes, and making those on board of them drink our healths in salt water," said Mark. "Dead men tell no tales, you know." "Well I conclude it our only way," replied Mendez, "though I should feel a little

strange about sending a crew of white men to hell in a moment." "Why they must all go there at last you fool," returned Mark; "Think of the floggins you've got." "Ha your words sound my ear like the crack of a whip," cried Mendez. "But I wonder the Yankees don't know better than to hang us for being pirates. They can't suppose that we'll be so soft now as to let away the people who fall into our hands, and so give them a chance of informing against us. I'll bet you we'll kill five whites for every negro that is hanged." "Ay, and more too, if we choose," said Mark. "Oh, we've a weary time of it, for most people think that we blacks do not deserve to live, unless we are slaves and beasts of burden. Faith, I'm getting tir'd of sea-life. If I could but scrape together four thousand dollars, I would give up cruising, and go to St. Domingo."[57]

On the surface, this conversation reflects the greatest fears of slaveholders and abolitionists alike: two vengeful fugitives plot the murder of those who would bring them to justice and dream of one day settling in that ultimate insurrectionist utopia of San Domingo. Yet Howison also includes odd moments of justification citing the "crack of the whip" in Mark's words and the "slaves and beasts of burdens" allusion. The pirates' weariness of life at sea and longing for San Domingo also appears a justifiable yearning for a refuge from slavery and the precarious life of a fugitive in a haven that at least appears to provide respite from a life under the heel of a white hegemony. The old pirate maxim, "dead men tell no tales," seems both to speak to the narrator's fears as well as the pirates' sense of fatality. "Dead men" ostensibly refers to the crew of the prizes they seek, but also could refer to themselves: slaves turned pirates who choose to die as men rather than live as slaves. "Dead men tell no tales" also speaks to the silence that surrounds insurrection; the silencing of the conspirators by the authorities as well as the need to keep silent to succeed.

The narrator's uneasy friendship with Manuel reaches a tipping point when, upon sighting a ship in the distance, Manuel orders his crew to take it as a prize. Up until this point the narrator has been able to keep the reality of piracy at bay, merely remarking on the rough demeanor of the crew.

> The quiescent and monotonous life I had led since I came on board the schooner, had lulled me into a forgetfulness of my real situation, all the horrors of which now burst upon my mind, with appalling force. I had outlawed myself from society. I was surrounded with wretches, with whom I could have no community of feeling. I was soon to become, as it were an accomplice in the work of rapine and bloodshed.[58]

The narrator describes this moment not in terms of how this affects his friendship with Manuel but rather with how consorting with pirates implicates him in their actions. Howison implies that if proximity to slavery threatens to taint the colonist with evils of despotism, the only redemption is to stop insurrection when one can. Redemption is framed not in terms of rehabilitating an abused and wayward slave but rather rejoining civilization and putting the proper amount of distance between himself and piracy.

The opportunity for redemption is presented to the narrator in the form of two hostages, Mr. R and his daughter Elizabeth. The introduction of "innocent bystanders" turns this story into something less complex and more categorically cautionary. The narrator's sympathy with Manuel's crew now appears misplaced and it is only Manuel's lack of bloodlust that saves him in the eyes of potential readers. The new hero is the narrator who brings Manuel back to himself by reminding him of his humanity.[59] The attempted seizure of the ship, the fight with the American navy, and Manuel's loss of control over his crew all seem designed to undermine any sense of slave revolt as a real threat. Manuel's refusal to kill the captured whites enrages his crew, and it is only the arrival of the naval brig that diverts them from mutiny. During the ensuing scuffle, Manuel, rather than fight, attempts to sink the ship with gunpowder, crying out, "It is easy to see how this day will end, but I must hasten its termination."[60] This shift from Manuel as battle-ready to Manuel as ineffective and suicidal undermines the earlier sense that this story recognizes the impulse to revolt as something more than reactionary.

Yet Howison also includes some key details into the conclusion that complicate such an analysis. Upon their last meeting, in response to the narrator's declaration that Manuel does not deserve to die, he says, "Oh perhaps not . . . but law—law—law you know—However 'tis better I should. I've had a weary life of it. I was chased from the land, and took refuge on the sea; but notwithstanding that, I could not escape the bloodhounds of the Southern States of America."[61] Here Manuel's lack of contrition and his condemnation of the slave-holding south recall his earlier persona of the vengeful pirate. Likewise, the narrator's indignation on his behalf muddies our sense of him as standing in judgment over Manuel's more violent tendencies. That he "does not deserve to die," explicitly contradicts the later rhetoric of the Vesey court documents in which violent intent justifies the execution of the conspirators. This discrepancy between the defiant and contrite Manuel is never fully explored. Rather Howison returns his reader to the safe space of the "cautionary tale" by having Manuel leave the narrator all of his prize money, thereby solving the narrator's murky financial problems and enabling him to marry Elizabeth. In bequeathing his spoils to the narrator before he is executed, Manuel seems less a precursor for Denmark Vesey than for Uncle Tom and the trope of the martyred slave, his death making possible a future for a right-thinking sympathetic white ally. The question of the defensibility of insurrection seems settled.

When one considers Howison's politics surrounding slavery, the story's resolution, or lack thereof, makes a certain amount of sense. The narrator's inability to reconcile his unease with the ethics of slavery with his fear of slave insurrection is in keeping with Howison's noninterventionist position on both colonization and slavery. Returning to Great Britain offers the only ethical solution. But in making the narrator the heir to Manuel's ill-gotten gains, he also ensures that the narrator remains eternally complicit both in the insurrection and the practice of slavery. This also suggests that there is no ethical solution to the dilemma faced by the narrator, and that the practice of slavery traps all whites in an untenable and volatile limbo.

This limbo remains unresolved in Howison's later fiction. Rather, the ever-present menace of slave violence becomes the gothic element that torments his protagonists. This turn to gothic is noteworthy because it seems to be an attempt to continue to explore the literary possibilities of the story, while subsuming the revolutionary voice present in the "The Florida Pirate." As Gretchen Woertendyke has stated, "The Florida Pirate" does make use of the gothic to "relegate the threat of large-scale slave violence to the symbolic realm" even as it acknowledges its power "as both horrifying specter and utopia."[62] In Howison's later fiction, the gothic element is brought even more to the fore in what appears to be an attempt to explore white anxieties regarding slave violence and their own complicity without letting through the fugitive revolutionary voice.

Tales of the Colonies, published in two volumes in 1830, explores the fictional lives of colonists in Brazil and Mexico. In these later stories the slave presence shifts slightly away from white interaction with blacks as human and, to some extent, equal. Slaves in "The Colambolo" and "Sablegrove" appear in several ways: as servant figures to be treated well or poorly depending on the owner's predilections; as humans allegedly infused with supernatural powers or as ghosts of murdered slaves. In each instance, the slave is the vehicle through which the villains are punished appropriately and the protagonists are redeemed, usually monetarily. Howison seems to frame the redemption of the colonial project within the context of how well the protagonists manage both their slaves and their wealth. Bad plantation managers are also abusers of slaves and thereby subject to justice at the hands of either slaves or maroons.

Take for example "The Colambolo," which is a story of a couple, Emilia and Julian Labrodo from Rio, who find themselves penniless and relocate with a few slaves to one of their remaining estates. Their nearest neighbor, Don Ludlos, is something of a libertine with designs on Emilia. One day, the couple discovers gold dust in a nearby river and start collecting it to supplement their meager income. Fortuitously, a ship also appears in the harbor, and the husband trades the gold dust for goods they need. This must be kept secret, however, for "in Brazil the sale or exchange of gold-dust in any way whatever is totally prohibited by government," for tax reasons.[63] Don Ludlos discovers this and plots to use it as leverage for seducing the wife. Emilia, in the meantime, has discovered a creature called the Colambolo nearby, and gives it food. The Colambolo used to be a slave, but has run away from an evil master. His time in the forest has turned him into a monster. In return for Emilia's kind treatment, the Colambolo leads the couple and the blackmailing neighbor to the source of the gold dust, and during the journey kills the neighbor by pushing him down a waterfall. The Labrodos use the gold to restore their lost fortune. The Colambolo disappears back into the forest.

In "The Colambolo," we are told that the couple keep slaves but are good to them. This is in contrast to the neighbor who is wealthier but whose slaves are maltreated. Indeed, The Colambolo's instinctive antipathy towards him creates the sense that maltreatment of slaves is felt beyond the confines of the plantation. The Labrodos' skirting of the law by trading gold dust to the American trader in exchange for goods is thereby seen as a lesser sin than Don Ludlos's plan to use that knowledge to extort them and coerce Emilia into becoming his mistress. When the Colambolo disappears back into the forest, he seems less a flesh and blood being than a specter. Howison populates his other stories with dead slaves whose ghosts are believed to haunt abandoned plantations, as in "The Island."[64] Manuel, by contrast, is allowed his humanity despite his monstrous acts. His lack of a limb for the arson committed against his master could be used to conjure a figure more monstrous than human. Instead, Howison uses his narrator to parse the various shades of Manuel's motives. Nor does he allow a character to occupy the space of the "good" slave owner. The notion of the "good" slave owner seems to need this transformation of this slave figure from human into monster in order to facilitate the total redemption of the white protagonists.

The gothic here allows Howison to displace revolutionary violence entirely away from the question of what it means to *own* slaves and fixate it on how one should *treat* slaves. Focusing on poor treatment of slaves moves us away from thinking of insurrection as political and towards a more regressive mode of thinking of it as reflecting poorly on individual plantation owners. Moreover, having the protagonists find their way back to Europe further allows Howison to retreat from the scene of slavery and wash his hands of all political considerations of insurrection. Relegating slaves to specters or monsters at the beginning of the story allows him to fully disappear them by end.

Another story, "Sablegrove," is considerably more difficult to summarize. It is the story of a poor young man named Gerald, who travels to Brazil from Scotland after hearing he has inherited some property there. He is shipwrecked, confined to a plantation called Sablegrove where he saves an Obi woman, Unda, from drowning, falls in love with Miss Letitia, the young ward of his employer/captor, Mr. Marnledge, and attempts to escape with her only to have her die when they try to leave. Ultimately he is able to leave and dispose of his inheritance but only after a long and convoluted sojourn at Sablegrove involving Mrs. Dittersdorf, the jealous mistress of Marnledge, and her mulatto blackmailer, Mr. Palno.

The convoluted nature of the story seems to be due in part to the various threads of dysfunction Howison attempts to weave into this particular tale. The first thread, the antagonism between Gerald and Marnledge over the question of his inheritance is the easiest to parse. Gerald seeks out his inheritance not so much out of greed as out of a desire to escape poverty.[65] Described as a well-educated but underemployed man, Gerald seems to be positioned not as the greedy colonist or the slaveholder in need of reforming, but rather as a sort of tabula rasa figure whose impressions of slavery are readily shaped by his experiences. For this reason, Howison, by having him occupy this quasi slave position once he arrives at Sablegrove, allows the reader to engage with the question of slavery without ever really engaging sympathetically with the Negro slaves. The addition of Letitia, the young white beautiful damsel in distress, further displaces focus from the actual slaves populating the story and onto the doomed couple.

In this story, the place of the supernatural is also more complex. Unda, the Obi woman who comes to Gerald's aid, lives under a cage containing the corpse of a slave who allegedly murdered his master. Unda, in describing her choice to live there to Gerald, adopts a conspiratorial tone. "You white people laugh at the notion of *Obi*, and so do I; but I keep up the trick, because it enables me to live quiet and easy, and do what I please. No negro dare molest me, and Mr. Marnledge himself is fond to keep on good terms with me, because he knows I could frighten half the slaves off his estate if I choose to do so."[66] Unda in positioning herself as willing to engage in a certain amount of subterfuge to keep her position of limited privilege at Sablegrove, initially seems to undermine the notion that anything supernatural is afoot. Yet ghost sightings plague the plantation, causing slaves to run away. Mrs. Dittersdorf is increasingly agitated as though haunted. The death of Mr. Marnledge, which in a different kind of story might signal the end of strife and the restoration of the property to Gerald, only seems to deepen Gerald's dependence on those around him, further "enslaving" him to the plantation. Ultimately the ghostly sightings prove to be Mr. Palno, the mulatto who has been threatening Mrs. Dittersdorf with the revelation that she was guilty of murdering her first husband. The "haunting" therefore becomes a space for Howison to explore the sins of slavery and colonialism through the notion of crime in general.

It would seem then that the supernatural is merely a ploy by the slaves to discommode whites about their places of power in the Caribbean. Yet Howison leaves room for doubt in the final scene of the story. Having had the murder of her husband exposed by Mr. Palno, Mrs. Dittersdorf flees Sablegrove. Gerald, Unda, Mr. Palno and a party of slaves corner her at Unda's hut where, overcome by the hopelessness of her situation, she collapses in hysterics. Here, the presence of the supernatural reappears as Mrs. Dittersdorf realizes she is underneath the slave corpse.

> The light of every lantern was at once directed towards it, and at the same moment a human countenance appeared, and a loud shriek told that it was that of Mrs. Dittersdorf. Gerald and the mulatto advanced towards her, but she flung herself back exclaiming, "Shew your warrant! I was acquitted. No one can be put to trial twice for the same crime. Look above," continued she, pointing to the decayed body of the murder swinging from the tree. "Is this the mode of my punishment? What! are you now to place me beside him? Not alive, surely! Kill me first. Oh, do!"[67]

Gerald and his companions do not kill her. Instead, she contracts a fever and dies in that hut under Unda's care. Gerald sells off the property, now mostly depopulated of slaves who have run off into the forest, and returns to London "without further accident and adventure."[68] Unda in setting herself up as a kind of trickster character allows for the usual gothic trope to work itself out. There is no real supernatural danger. Rather the slave corpse works on pre-existing fears of Gerald and Mrs. Dittersdorf regarding their place within the community of Sablegrove. Yet the effectiveness of Unda's trick is far more sweeping than merely allowing her to live unmolested as she initially stated. The dissolution of the plantation and the death and exile of all masters and potential masters makes the haunting more literal. But, again, any notion of slavery as wrong for the slaves is lost. Rather, it is the corrupting influence of plantation life that Howison targets for critique. Gerald, who occupies a space of liminal freedom, and Letitia our tragic heroine, displace the proper slave figures as objects of sympathy. Unda, despite being given a privileged position as co-conspirator, never fully manifests as a character in the story. Mr. Palno, the mysterious mulatto, comes the closest to occupying a space of fully formed subjectivity. As the former slave of Mr. Dittersdorf and the unwitting administrator of the poison used to kill him, Palno's demands for justice seem less about the corrupt nature of slavers and more about his own thwarted ambition. In this way he could be seen as a doppelganger for Gerald. Yet Howison introduces him into the story too late to allow for the parallels to fully flesh out. Nor does he allow for Sablegrove to pass on to Mr. Palno, which might have injected into the end of the story, the possibility of transforming the plantation into a place free of slavery.

If, in these stories, slaves are agents of vengeance against the greedy and rapacious, they are also guardians of the wealth of the kind and moderate. Howison here deploys what becomes a familiar abolitionist strategy of pointing to slave violence as just desserts to slaveholders. What is lost here is a sense of the slave as an independent agent. Manuel, while portrayed as somewhat indecisive and inept, still retains that kernel of revolutionary possibility by being an assertive actor in his own fate. Likewise, his compatriots' unsavoriness is tempered by the wistful strain that accompanies the invocation of St. Domingo. The gothic, in Howison's hands, therefore begins as a way in which to expose revolutionary possibility inherent in slave insurrection and ends as a means to obscure and subsume that possibility as the flesh and blood slaves turn into specters who are silenced.

This fictional silencing of the violent slave figure mirrors the real response to the Vesey conspiracy. If the structure of "The Florida Pirate" foreshadowed key events from the Denmark Vesey conspiracy, the aftermath also mimicked Howison's subsequent output. Following the execution of the main actors, laws against slaves and free blacks gathering together proliferated across the South, the *Negro Seamen Acts* were passed, and the gag rule was instated in Congress.[69] These laws made the simple fact of being black into a crime, effectively turning free blacks in general, and black sailors in particular, into potential monsters. Howison, however, in his literary treatment of insurrection reveals to us both the unease of moderate anti-slavery whites and the futility of indefinite containment.

As to how these sentiments influenced anti-slavery factions in the 1820s, the example of the Pennsylvania Anti-Slavery Society is instructive. These abolitionists were rigidly opposed to anything violent, having come out against a plan to arm slaves in 1791, and having distributed copies of a British pamphlet titled *An Inquiry Into The Causes of the Insurrection of The Negroes in the Island of St. Domingo* (1792), which warned that abolition was the only way to stop a large scale black revolt.[70] Overall, anti-slavery factions shied away from the issue of violence and focused their energies on the Colonization question and westward expansion. Yet even Arnold Buffum, a friend to Garrison and an abolitionist who opposed violence, found himself considering the possibilities during a debate. In a letter to Garrison he writes that this opponent cried, "'Suppose slaves aboard a ship . . . that all slaves had a right to freedom,'—would not they 'murder the [white] officers and . . . drive the boat to the bottom of the sea?' I almost exclaimed," Buffum wrote, "then joy to the tempest that whelms them beneath and makes their destruction."[71]

At first glance, the Vesey conspiracy looked to be a boon to proslavery factions who sought both to isolate and scatter blacks physically and intellectually and to quell an increasingly vocal antislavery faction. But when one looks at the response not only for what it reveals about whites' reactions to slave conspiracy but also for how it revealed slave violence to be more organized, wider, and possibly more legitimate than anyone was willing to admit, the silencing seems less about political efficacy and more about stifling those fugitive whispers of revolutionary possibility. As has been posited by Levine, there is strong evidence to suggest that David Walker's *Appeal To The Coloured Citizens of the World* (1829–1830) came out of, in large part, Walker's acquaintance with Vesey and his reaction to the media frenzy surrounding the conspiracy.[72] Moreover, Walker's pamphlet, which was often confiscated from the bodies of black sailors in southern ports, was believed to have been part of what drove Nat Turner's Revolt in Southampton in 1831. The impossibility of fully containing those whispers would seem to indicate a direct failure on the part of southern legislatures. But what the appearance of "The Florida Pirate" before the conspiracy shows us is that revolutionary possibility was always already in the ether. And if Howison, a political moderate, could not help but be alive to it, the likelihood that slaves and free blacks would need it as "encouragement" to revolt seems remote.

Moreover despite the draconian nature of the *Negro Seamen Acts*, there is evidence that Haiti continued to loom large in the imaginations of antebellum African Americans. The conspiracy may have bolstered the entreaty on the part of Haitian President John Boyer who, in 1820 appealed to African Americans to emigrate to Haiti promising land and citizenship. "Black wounds would be 'healed by the balm of equality and their tears wiped away by the protecting hand of liberty.'"[73] Even in the years following the Vesey conspiracy[74] individual African Americans such as the Reverend Loring Dewey attempted to establish ties with Haiti and facilitate emigration. If the conspiracy was the invention of Charleston city officials, in presenting the fear of a coalition of Haitians and an army of local insurrectionists they would possibly be guilty of providing them with the best kind of fodder for that fantasy. Moreover, in the wake of the passage of the *Negro Seamen Acts*, black seaman would be further incentivized to desert or mutiny and make for St. Domingo.

At the end of *The Confessions of Nat Turner*, Thomas R. Gray asks Turner whether he knows of another revolt happening in North Carolina. When Turner denies any knowledge of this, and Gray looks at him skeptically, Turner's response is telling. "I see sir, you doubt my word; but can you not think the same ideas, and strange appearances about this time in the heavens might prompt others, as well as myself, to this undertaking."[75] Turner's reference to the "strange appearances" is in keeping with his claim that he was divinely inspired. Gray's skepticism on this point echoes the skepticism of the Charleston city officials who insisted that the conspiracy must be larger than witnesses initially claimed. Turner's denial here is not so much a rejection of the idea of a diasporic slave revolution as it is the rejection of the idea that slaves need guidance or organizing to rise up. As Eric J. Sundquist observes in *To Wake The Nations*, "revolt or rebellion need not be actualized in a state of intention or desire . . . or manifest itself as a threat."[76]

JOSEPH CINQUÉ, THE *AMISTAD* MUTINY,

AND REVOLUTIONARY WHITEWASHING

O N THE MORNING OF AUGUST 29, 1839, a "long low black schoo-
ner" was sighted and taken by the U.S. brig, the *Washington*, on suspicion of
piracy. Upon boarding the ship, called the *Amistad*, the navy men discovered the
ship to be manned by a band of fugitive slaves led by a Mendean called Joseph
Cinqué. Nearly two months earlier, Cinqué had picked the locks of his chains
with a nail, freed his companions, located a box of knives, and led a mutiny, killing
the captain and the cook in the process and keeping their "owners," José Ruiz and
Pedro Montes as their prisoners. The ship was confiscated, the slaves imprisoned,
and so began a lengthy process of determining the fate of the *Amistad* Africans.
The Africans' fate was complicated by two things. First, the mutiny and the ensuing
case exposed the problem of illegal slave trafficking that persisted despite the
Slave Trade Act of 1807 banning the Atlantic trade. The illegality of the acquisition of the Africans would categorically shift their status from chattel and force a
comparison between the Africans and black Americans, both slaves and free. Second, the *Amistad* affair opened the question of the applicability of natural rights
principles to slaves, the formerly enslaved, and free blacks by raising the question
of whether or not the killings of the ship's captain and cook were justified because
the Africans had been kidnapped rather than legally acquired. The Spanish Crown's
case rested on the assertion that the Mendeans had not been kidnapped in Africa
but had, instead, been born in slavery and were being transported from one port
to another. Should the case go against the Mendeans, they would be found guilty
of piracy.

The appellation of "pirate" in relation to the Mendeans, matters, not simply
because the term ironically designated the Africans as both the victims and the
alleged culprits of the same crime, but also because the initial framing of the Africans, and Joseph Cinqué specifically, as pirates is essential to understanding how

the abolitionist defense was able to undermine public perception of the *Amistad* Africans so effectively. While piracy was still considered a serious crime, by 1839 it was largely a matter of fiction. The popularity of maritime reading in the form of fictional stories and novels, sailor memoirs, and Barbary captivity narratives reached its height in the first half of the nineteenth century.[1] This was, in part, due to the massive role the maritime economy played in shaping the cultural life of the Early Republic, but not to a rise in the incidence of actual piracy. Rather, pirate stories, in particular, lent themselves to allegorical readings of the American Revolution by displacing anxieties regarding the justifiability of violent rebellion onto dubious figures, safely away from United States shores.

James Fenimore Cooper's *The Red Rover* helps us begin to understand how, in the case of the *Amistad,* the pirate label could be almost immediately unraveled and replaced by revolutionary heroism. In critiquing the role of violence in fomenting revolution—however justifiable—through fiction, Cooper is able to destabilize categories of criminal and hero by pointing to the necessity of an element of the former in creating the latter. Likewise, the abolitionists who got involved in the *Amistad* controversy by insisting on Africans' status as "kidnapped," forced observers to weigh the brutality of the Mendeans' actions against the necessity of gaining their freedom. In their hands, "pirate" re-signifies as revolutionary.

By the time the *Amistad* case went before the Supreme Court, the abolitionist press had effectively tied the actions of Cinqué and his comrades to the heroism of the American Revolution. The success of the case would potentially determine the way in which abolitionist rhetoric surrounding the role of slave violence would transform in the years to come. But although the ruling handed down by the Court was favorable to the Mendeans, its limitations also meant that, legally, the language of natural rights was not transferrable to American slaves. Additionally, the political efficacy of applying revolutionary rhetoric to American slaves would prove problematic even into the early years of the Civil War. The symbolic power of a figure like Joseph Cinqué remained powerful, but only in print.

Martin Robison Delany's *Blake or the Huts of America* and Frederick Douglass's short story, "The Heroic Slave," are the two imaginative works that most effectively use fiction to resituate the figure of the armed slave into the new revolutionary framework ostensibly made possible in the wake of the *Amistad* and *Creole* mutinies. But they also illustrate the difficulty of depicting slave violence as politically legitimate. Both texts sublimate violence beneath anxieties regarding a large-scale slave uprising. This sublimation of the idea of legitimate slave violence is a consequence, I argue, of the strategy of tying slave revolt to the American Revolution. While rhetorically effective and a much needed corrective to the unfinished project of creating a free republic, the act of reshaping the *Amistad* Africans into the heirs of the American Revolution unintentionally white-washed slave violence in such a way that made it impossible to view armed blacks as fully human. Delany and Douglass, in attempting to harness the symbolic power embodied by Joseph Cinqué and, later, Madison Washington, (whose revolt aboard the *Creole* in 1841 was the subject of Douglass's "The Heroic Slave") run up against the problem of representing the spectacle of violence.

In abolitionist literature, both fiction and nonfiction, scenes of violent slave abuse were often deployed as a means to move readers against slavery. As Saidiya V. Hartman writes in *Scenes of Subjection: Terror, Slavery, and Self-Making In Nineteenth-Century America* (1997), Douglass's description of his aunt's beating at the beginning of his 1845 *Narrative of the Life of Frederick Douglass* (1845) "establishes the centrality of violence in the making of the slave."[2] But even when these texts acknowledge that violence is integral to the master/slave relationship they often fail to recognize this violence as also virtually unavoidable for liberation. Instead, this strain of abolitionism tends to lament violence as a response to the excessive cruelty and inhumanity of slave owners. To mainstream abolitionists, violent slaves were victims of abusive behavior rather than political actors seeking their own liberation.

The radicalization of the abolitionist movement is a familiar story to antebellum scholars. Robert S. Levine's book, *Martin Delany, Frederick Douglass and the Politics of Representative Identity* (1997), explores how Harriet Beecher Stowe's radical conversion, following the publication of *Uncle Tom's Cabin*, was due to the influence of both Delany and Douglass.[3] In *Black Hearts of Men: Radical Abolitionists and the Transformation of Race* (2002), John Stauffer claims that the establishment of the Radical Abolitionist Party constituted a powerful, albeit brief, moment in which agreement on the necessity of an anti-slavery political party at last put both white and black abolitionists in perfect sympathy with each other.[4] Less familiar, though, is the way in which even that radicalization obscures the sanitization of black violence in abolitionist media.

Arguably, the abolitionists' focus on the slave as the victim of excessive violence can be traced to the *Zong* tragedy discussed in chapter 1. The crux of this case—the brutal treatment of slaves aboard ships—would come to frame the cause against slavery from the standpoint of the slave as victim of abuse within slavery, leaving aside the role of slaves as political actors capable of mounting organized resistance to their condition. The unintended consequence of this framing, which as we have seen was evident in the strategies of Thomas Clarkson, Olaudah Equiano, and the early British abolitionists, was the pitting of the abolitionist movement against the practice of slave insurrection. As a result, abolitionists tended to view the Middle Passage primarily as a space of slave victimization and rarely as the site of politicized violence against the loss of liberty, despite the fact that ship-board insurrection was a common occurrence throughout the whole of the Atlantic slave trade. While shipboard insurrection was common, particularly at the height of the Atlantic slave trade in the mid-eighteenth century, the *Amistad* mutiny stands out for the way in which American abolitionists seized upon it and made it into a cause célèbre. Within the context of abolitionist movement think-ing, the *Amistad* case represented a departure from previous reactions to slave violence. Whereas the *Zong* case had turned on the question of whether or not the property represented by enslaved Africans had been illegally destroyed, the *Amis-tad* case went to the heart of the question of who could and could not be defined as property. That definition turned on the killing of the ship's captain and cook, an act of violence which, had the Mendeans been legal slaves, would have subjected them to Spanish justice. Yet, because of the ban on the Atlantic slave trade, the Men-deans were deemed to be free Africans rather than slaves; having been kidnapped, they were able to justify the killing of the ship's captain and cook as self-defense instead of murder. Rather than dismissing the Mendeans as a band of savages, the abolitionists mounted a massive public relations campaign, celebrating them as heirs to the American Revolution.[5]

Despite this change, however, a closer look at the abolitionist debates before, during, and after the case reveals a persistent reluctance on the part of white aboli-tionists to grant slaves the full right to revolt. While the Mendeans' cause provided a useful moment to inject the rhetoric of natural rights into the argument against slavery, doing so was also the exception rather than the rule. Abolitionists remained divided over the place of violence well into the 1850s. The *Amistad* mutiny, and later the *Creole* mutiny, provided useful and compelling fodder for fiction, speeches, and political tracts, yet even those who embraced radical abolition harbored strong misgivings about the role of freemen and the formerly enslaved in the impending conflict. The *Amistad* case could not completely eradicate the fears borne out of the San Domingo uprising and the Nat Turner revolt.

The difference between the symbolic power of so-called black revolutionar-ies and literary depictions of these figures committing acts of violence is not simply a matter of sanitizing the legacies of complicated heroes. This difference goes to the heart of the way in which insurrection, or the fear of insurrection, is constantly deployed to specific political ends both in the eighteenth- and nineteenth-century abolitionist media. Black violence—first as evidence of the slave's essential savagery and later as byproduct of slavery's brutality—becomes in the aftermath of these mutinies, an opportunity to fold the history of insurrection into the grand legacy of American Revolutionary heroism. This process of mediation both sensationalizes black violence and erases details that might tarnish the image of heroism being projected. What is left in its place is a kind of chimera of a heroic black figure, at once menacing and eloquent that attaches itself to real-life figures.[6] The examples of Cinqué and Washington illustrate this process and the failure of even Delany and Douglass to see beyond this chimera.

Is it important that black figures be seen committing acts of violence in graphic manner? One might argue that a certain amount of omission is only natural given nineteenth-century representational norms for addressing genteel audiences. Even when abolitionists, for obvious reasons, felt compelled to describe graphic scenes of physical abuse meted out by slaveholders, they often did so with assurances that they had spared their readers the worst of these accounts. But omissions or distortions when it came to depicting black violence were not simply the result of the media taking into account audience sensibilities. Rather, the depiction of black violence against slaveholders tended to raise the question of whether this violence was a manifestation of the dehumanizing effects of enslavement (a claim most abolitionists were willing to credit) or whether it betokened an aggrieved population awaking to the idea that taking up arms for freedom and justice was the moral action called for (a more difficult possibility for many abolitionists to swallow). Indeed, coverage of black violence still resonates with these distortions. As such, depicting black violence calls into question the "dehumanizing" rhetoric that constantly accompanies abolitionist discourse of the consequences of slavery. The insistence that slave violence is always evidence of the inhuman robs the slave insurrectionist of political agency, something that is not simply a consequence of slavery but intentional on the part of the slaveholder.

Delany and Douglass both seem to embark on projects that would restore a sense of the "right to revolt" to the slave. They harness the imaginative energy of the *Amistad* and *Creole* insurrections in order to create characters who appear to thread the needle between eloquence and menace. More than merely providing fodder for the second half of Delany's *Blake* and Douglass's story, "The Heroic Slave," Cinqué and Washington's successes also infuse these stories with the powerful spectacle of slaves taking over a slave ship. This image unites the histories of those insurrections with that of the Middle Passage and turns the site of captivity and loss of agency into a site of victory. Douglass in particular, whose break with William Lloyd Garrison occurred in the immediate aftermath of these mutinies and whose relationship with those who would become the major figures behind the establishment of the Radical Abolitionist Party constitutes a pivotal moment within the history of antislavery politics, would most directly use the symbolic power of mutiny to demonstrate the revolutionary possibilities of slave violence.[7] Yet both abolitionist writers pause when the time comes to display their respective hero's organizational genius and show him in the heat of battle. The gaze of the imagined white reader dogs each text, forcing Delany and Douglass's narratives, in effect, to fade to black before the blood begins to run.

Although they took place at sea, where the political status of the actions of the mutineers could not be avoided, the *Amistad* and *Creole* mutinies nonetheless opened up the possibility that plantation rebellions, too, could be seen as collective acts of political liberation rather than reactions to physical mistreatment and abuse. However, in "The Heroic Slave" and *Blake*, the ocean, rather than providing a nationless maritime imaginary upon which to stage a successful revolt, becomes, instead, a safe space where a heavily mediated violence can occur away from the plantation zone. Thus the political promise of the revolts of Nat Turner, Gabriel Prosser, and Denmark Vesey is fulfilled, but only in part. On the one hand, the success of the *Amistad* and *Creole* reveal that the failures of these plantation insurrections prove to be the result of the structural issues rather than a lack of black gumption and intelligence. On the other hand, even the ocean proves a limited space upon which to imagine a successful black revolution. In what follows, I discuss this problem as being informed by both pro and anti-slavery forces in the years before the *Amistad* and *Creole* mutinies.

RADICAL ABOLITION FROM TURNER TO *AMISTAD*

Abolitionist accounts show that white northerners and southerners reacted similarly to black violence. Despite the fact that there were relatively few slave insurrections in the United States when compared to other sites in the Americas, the specter of insurrection loomed large. The abolitionist press reflects the changing views of black violence through its coverage of both the Turner revolt of 1831 and the *Amistad* mutiny. The (possibly) thwarted Vesey plot of 1822 and the Nat Turner rebellion nine years later, along with the continuing news of violence in Haiti, all served to create a sense of threat within the southern states.[8] In the north, the Turner revolt posed both a problem and an opportunity for abolitionists. Rumors circulated that the insurrectionists had been inspired to violence by reading both David Walker's *Appeal* (1829) and copies of Garrison's new periodical, the *Liberator*.[9] As a result, the *Liberator* confined itself to reporting on the capture of the ringleaders, the trial, and the execution.[10] By contrast, during the *Amistad* trials in 1839 and 1840, the *Liberator* rallied to the cause of captured slaves citing the slaves' natural right to revolt. The ways in which both cases circulated in the abolitionist press highlight an underlying narrative of black revolution within the history of abolition and insurrection that Delany and Douglass later use in their fiction.

While scholars of the history of abolition in the United States have typically understood opposition to slavery to be tied to Quaker pacifism, in Great Britain, as I have already discussed, those who opposed slavery on moral grounds found allies in plantation owners who saw the transatlantic slave trade as the culprit for continued slave insurrection.[11] Violence and abolition were therefore at odds from the beginning. The shift in tone from a more pacific separatist abolitionist rhetoric— one that favored gradual abolition and, in some cases, repatriation to Africa—to one that was more militantly in favor for ending slavery, has traditionally been attributed to the passing of the *Fugitive Slave Act* of 1850. John Brown's raid on Harper's Ferry constitutes, for many scholars of abolition and the Civil War, the first shot fired.[12] This characterization of the abolitionist movement, though, both fails to account for the earlier appearance of a more radical wing of abolitionists in the early 1840s and also presumes that the outrage caused by the *Fugitive Slave Act* alone produced a John Brown. Moreover, it portrays the abolitionist movement as a single entity rather than a fragmented, if growing, cohort that collectively shifted from a more pacific approach to calling for war.

In tracking the *Liberator's* response to slave violence before and after the *Amistad* case, one can see ostensibly a shift from a far more conservative approach with regards to the Turner revolt, to something both more secular and more revolutionary regarding Joseph Cinqué and his followers. In the wake of the *Amistad* decision, it became possible for the *Liberator* to speak of the "heroes" Toussaint L'Ouverture, Denmark Vesey, and even Nat Turner. Yet, while this case does appear to have precipitated the beginning of a more aggressive stance on abolition, Garrison and other abolitionists continued to harbor doubts about the desirability of an armed response and about armed slaves in particular. This lingering unease manifests even in the works of Delany and Douglass; the right to revolution for slaves and the formerly enslaved would remain, at best, rhetorical, merely providing the abolitionists with useful symbols in what would become the run-up to war. These limits on political imagination make themselves felt even on the plane of fiction.

In December of 1829, a white mariner delivered sixty copies of David Walker's *Appeal to the Coloured Citizens of the World* (1829) to a black minister in Savannah, Georgia. A four-part pamphlet meant to expose the atrocities unique to American slavery, the *Appeal* alarmed northern and southern whites alike with its call for slaves to "cast off their chains," as well as its predictions that God's vengeance would be visited upon the slaveholder.[13] This discovery led to the quarantining of all black sailors entering Georgia and new legislation against "seditious literature."[14] Despite these efforts, the pamphlet made its way up and down the coastal south, primarily through the hands of black sailors. On January 8, 1831, the *Liberator* published an editorial regarding the *Appeal*. In it, Garrison condemned the "spirit and tendency of this Appeal" and affirmed his own commitment to nonviolent solutions to slavery: "*We* do not preach rebellion—no but submission and peace. . . . We say, that the possibility of a bloody insurrection at [*sic*] the south fills us with dismay, and we avow, too, as plainly, that if any people were ever justified in throwing off the yoke of the tyrants, the slaves are that people."[15] Garrison's curious doublespeak simultaneously declares slave insurrection anathema even as it is granted justification. By putting himself at a remove from Walker, Garrison seems less interested in condemning violence outright than in removing the *Liberator* from the line of fire. Nor is he above pointing to the South's culpability for any violence in continuing to practice slaveholding: "It is not we, but our guilty countrymen, who put arguments into the mouths, and swords into the hands of the slaves." Displacing responsibility for insurrection onto the slaveholders allows Garrison to redeploy Walker's rhetoric for himself even as he dismisses the very premise of the *Appeal*. For Garrison, and quite possibly many of his allies, insurrection was less an autonomous act on the part of a thinking body of slaves than it was divine retribution for the sins of the South. Ignoring the obvious similarities between the *Appeal* and Thomas Paine's *Common Sense* (1776), Garrison describes the writing style as "natural and enthusiastic." His language highlights the volatile feeling behind the text rather than acknowledges the logic of Walker's arguments.[16]

Walker's clarion call to arms would appear to yield fruit that very year, as eight months later, Nat Turner led the bloodiest slave insurrection in North America. In response, Garrison would again redeploy this same strategy. On November 12, 1831, the *Liberator* reprinted a piece from the *Intelligencer* in Petersburg, Virginia, stating, "It is with much gratification we inform the public, that the sole contriver and leader of the late insurrection in Southampton, concerning whom such a hue and cry has been kept up for months, and so many false reports circulated—that Nat Turner, has at last been taken and safely lodged in prison."[17] That same year Garrison both disavowed the involvement of abolitionists in the Turner revolt and chastised the southerners for inviting this violence by insisting on keeping slaves. The final paragraph exhibits the *Liberator's* "official" position as one of pacifism:

> For ourselves, we are horror-struck at the late tidings. We have exerted our utmost efforts to avert the calamity. We have warned our countrymen of the danger of persisting in their unrighteous conduct. We have preached to the slaves the pacific precepts of Jesus Christ. We have

appealed to Christians, philanthropists, and patriots, for their assistance to accomplish the great work of national redemption through the agency of moral power—of public opinion—of individual duty. How have we been received? We have been threatened, proscribed, vilified, and imprisoned—a laughing-stock and a reproach. Do we falter, in view of these things? Let time answer. If we have been hitherto urgent, and bold, and denunciatory in our efforts,—hereafter we shall grow vehement and active with the increase of danger. We shall cry, in trumpet tones, night and day,—Woe to this guilty land, unless she speedily repent of her evil doings! The blood of millions of her sons cries aloud for redress! Immediate emancipation alone can save her from the vengeance of Heaven, and cancel the debt of ages![18]

Rather than address the potential validity of Turner's campaign, the *Liberator* takes refuge in the language of the early colonial jeremiad, casting abolitionists as proper Protestants in contrast to other nominal "Christians" who have failed to heed the abolitionists' warnings. This posture allows the *Liberator* to resituate its role in the Turner Rebellion; instead of being the instigator of violence, it is the ignored savior of the Union. The southern slaveholders cannot be the unwitting victims of the insurrection if they are also the instigators. The violence of Turner and his followers, while reprehensible, is only the natural consequence of the violence of slavery. Furthermore, this reaction suggests that the high-minded methods of the abolitionists do not register for slaveholders, implying that while violence may be abhorrent it seems to be the only language that pro-slavery factions understand. The slave owners, in having ignored "the precepts of Jesus Christ," have sinned against God, and the slave insurrectionists are the tools of His vengeance.

The *Liberator*, quick to distance itself from the revolt, was equally quick to point to black violence as a compelling reason for ending slavery. In September of 1831, this poem appeared in the paper:

> A shriek was heard by night!
> The startled eye but saw
> The gleaming axe, and the ear just caught
> The sable fiend's hurra!
> Out of the polished floor
> Ran the ensanguined flood;
> The babe slept on its mother's breast,
> And its bruised lips dashed with blood.
> Upon the cold hearth stone
> The unripened virgin lay,
> Crushed in her budding loveliness,
> And dawn of her opening day.[19]

In the very same issue, another piece declared: "*Wo* [*sic*] *to the innocent babe*—the guilty sire—*Mother and daughter*—friends of kindred tie! *Stranger and citizen alike shall die!* Red-handed Slaughter his revenge shall feed, And Havoc yell his ominous death-cry, And wild Despair in vain for mercy plead— While hell itself shall shrink and sicken at the deed! Read the account of the insurrection in Virginia, and say whether our prophecy be not fulfilled."[20] This rhetoric—despite the fact that it was intended to further the cause of abolition— essentially thrust Turner, his followers, and those who would emulate them, beyond the fringes of what was considered accepted action against slavery.[21] So long as plantation insurrection could be couched as unthinking violence perpe- trated by those driven to madness by slavery, slave insurrection would remain the realm of the "maladjusted" and "deviant" blacks. Turner's fanaticism while outwardly a problem for abolitionists reveals itself to be a boon to their cause.[22]

The *Liberator's* response to the Turner revolt reveals the underlying fear of black violence behind more pacifist approaches to abolition. The near-instinctive recoil from the Turner revolt goes beyond mere damage control. It speaks to an essential truth about the place of the formerly enslaved and free blacks within the abolitionist movement: that they were useful only as scarred examples of slavery's brutality or as proof that even though slaves could be as capable as whites, becom- ing educated and useful members of society, they could not become agents who could play an active role in securing their own freedom. This mode of presenting slaves as either victims and/or useful members of society is a legacy of British aboli- tion, in general, and Equiano, specifically, who presented slavery and the slave trade as inherently violent, and the ex-slave as ripe for civilizing. But because Turner's revolt—indeed, all slave revolts, including the Haitian Revolution—went against that prevailing narrative, these cases were presented as aberrations.

At the start of the *Amistad* case the question of violence became central to establishing both the validity of Spain's ownership of the slaves, and their right to prosecute them as pirates for the murder of the captain and cook. Indeed after Cinqué first appeared in court on August 29, the first case to be filed was against him and the other Africans for piracy and murder.[23] Piracy within the context of the *Amistad* case turned on the question of both the legality of the slave trade outside the United States and the criminality of the mutiny. Both the prosecution and the defense leveled the charge of piracy at each other—the prosecution for mutiny and murder, and the defense of the illegal slave smuggling. The definition ultimately depended on the question of the slaves' point of origin. Slave-trading via importation from Africa became defined as piracy in the United States in 1821, and in Spain in 1838. As such, should the abolitionists succeed in having Ruiz and Montes charged with piracy, they could redefine the Mendeans' violent actions as justifiable under natural law. "Pirate" within the legal framework becomes the operative term for re-designating slave violence as revolutionary. Moreover, in claiming the slaves as both property and criminals to be tried as pirates, the Spaniards risked undermining both cases in creating confusion as to whether the Africans were legally property or legally persons.

This fight over whether the Mendeans really deserved the designation of pirate in the case perhaps accounts for why Cinqué and his companions were characterized as "pirates" and "murderers." Cinqué, who early on distinguished himself as the leader, was singled out after reports of his speech to the Africans upon being captured circulated through the popular press. According to a story appearing August 31, 1839, Cinqué gave two speeches that were translated by a sailor-slave called Antonio. The first speech was as follows: "You had better be killed than live many moons in misery. I shall be hanged, I think, every day. But this does not pain me. I could die happy, if by dying I could save so many of my brothers from the bondage of the white man." In a second speech, Cinqué seems to rally and exhort his followers to rise up. "My brothers, I am once more among you, having deceived the enemy of my race by saying I had doubloons. I came to tell you that you have only one chance for death, and none for Liberty. I am sure you prefer death, as I do. You can by killing the white man now on board, and I will help you, make the people here kill you. It is better for you to do this, and then you will not only avert bondage yourselves, but prevent the entailment of unnumbered wrongs on your children. Come—come with me then."[24]

The *Sun* seized the opportunity and commissioned an engraving of Cinqué in which he is posed aboard a ship wearing a flannel shirt, white pants and sporting a machete. The image, by a J. Sketchley, is captioned, "Joseph Cinquez, Leader of the Piratical Gang of Negroes, who killed Captain Ramon Ferris and the Cook, on board the Spanish Schooner Amistad, taken by Lieut. Gedney, commanding the U.S. Brig Washington at Culloden Point, Long Island, 24th Augt. 1839."[25] Below was printed the text of the second speech.

Despite the framing text, the tension between the caption, the speech, and Sketchley's artistic rendering of Cinqué is obvious. The markers of criminality are absent. Even the blade lacks menace, appearing more like a gentleman's walking stick than a weapon. The desperate violent words don't match the noble bearing of the figure. Likewise, in depicting Cinque alone, Sketchley undermines the sense of menace implied by the phrase "piratical gang of negroes." Little is known about Sketchley, let alone his political leanings. What is known is that his image of Cinqué was immediately made into a colored lithograph and widely circulated. Aside from being in color, the lithograph was more or less the same as the engraving, save for the omission of the word "piratical." The alteration reveals what became a gradual shift away from the view of the *Amistad* Africans as a gang of pirates to something more heroic.[26]

When the southern press mentioned the case at all, they often referred to Africans as "pirates," "mutineers," and "murderers." Some also attempted to undermine the presentation of the Africans as civilized and nonviolent by reporting on their bad behavior while incarcerated.[27] This negative media may have put pressure on the abolitionist and northern press who, in turn, sought to emphasize the more civilized aspects of the Africans by making them available for public viewing to show off newly acquired reading skills and having Cinqué make speeches, first in his own language, and then later in broken English.[28] The abolitionist newspaper, the *Colored American*, published editorials in defense of the *Amistad* Africans as well as reprinted pieces from the mainstream press.[29] Turning the Africans into celebrities constituted both a massive media blitz, which included a traveling exhibition of wax likenesses made with hair from the captives and a concerted effort to quell incidents of violence in the jail between the Africans and the jailers, other prisoners, and each other. Moreover the language of violence became suffused with the rhetoric of natural rights. The *Liberator* took the lead in changing the conversation surrounding the *Amistad* insurrection.

Part of changing that conversation involved reframing the problem of piracy from the question of whether the Mendeans had committed mutiny to whether or not the Spaniards had captured them illegally. The *Amistad* case drew attention to the problem of illegal slave smuggling in the nineteenth century, thereby reframing piracy as stealing rather than mutiny. Despite the passage of the *Slave Trade Act* of 1807, the first major law passed by the United States to ban the African slave trade, according to W. E. B. Du Bois, enforcement of the law between 1807 and 1820 was erratic to non-existent.[30] In some cases American privateers, acting on behalf of the States against Britain in the War of 1812, engaged in illegal smuggling, at times openly flying American colors. It was not until 1819, when a large-scale slave smuggling operation on Amelia Island off the coast of Florida was discovered and shut down, that slave trading was officially termed to be piracy in the United States. Despite this, illegal trading would continue in the United States until the Civil War.[31] Additionally, slave smuggling proved lucrative in the years both preceding and following the Amistad case. The 1807 ban as well as the cotton boom drove the price of individual slaves up from $325 in 1820 to $500 in 1850, making the illegal trade highly lucrative.[32]

In the years before the *Amistad* case, the *Liberator* had often included notices from British newspapers about illegal smuggling activity.[33] In referring to the practice specifically as "piracy," the paper had already primed their readership to reject the argument that the Mendeans, having been kidnapped by pirates, could

JOSEPH CINQUEZ,

Leader of the gang of Negroes who killed Captain Ramon Ferrers and the Cook on board of the Spanish Schooner Amistad, Captured by Lieutenant Gedney, of the U.S. Brig Washington, off Gardiners Point, Long Island, August 26th, 1839.

Figure 2. James Sketchley. "Joseph Cinquez, Leader of the Piratical Gang of Negroes," for the *New York Sun* (1839), lithograph by John Childs. Stanley-Whitman House, Farmington, CT.

themselves be pirates.[34] In the weeks after the capture of the *Amistad*, the *Liberator* made its position known in no uncertain terms.

> These Africans are not guilty of piracy. By the laws of civilized nations, as well as by the laws of Nature, these Africans, by whomsoever thus seized, and wheresoever thus held in, had a right to assert their liberty, of which they had been deprived by force. They had a right to repel force by force, and to use all the force that was necessary to regain their liberty. They had precisely the same rights that an Englishman or an American would have, placed in a similar situation. They had a right to use all the force that was necessary to steer the schooner to the African coast, whence they were unlawfully taken. The killing of the captain and cook was on board a foreign vessel, beyond the jurisdiction of the U. States, and, *therefore,* if it ever amounted to murder, in the legal sense, the offenders cannot be tried under our laws.[35]

The language explicitly reframes the insurrection by moving it away from the term "piracy" and towards the rhetoric of natural rights. By calling the term "piracy" into question the *Liberator* directs the argument away from the murder of the captain and cook, and towards the legality of the act. This turn allows for other rhetorical moves. "African" becomes synonymous with "Englishman" and "American."

But even as this shift seems to signal a move towards acceptance of the place of armed insurrection in the abolitionist movement, it also frames that acceptance in a way that still categorizes violence in terms that are explicitly racialized. That "these Africans" have the same rights as Americans or Englishmen does not signify for other Africans or indeed African Americans. Instead Cinqué's heroism becomes a vehicle for white abolitionists who wanted to get away from gradualism.[36] The refrain of "Africanness" echoed the strategy of the defense, which depended on establishing that the Africans were in fact not born in the Spanish colonies but on the western coast of Africa. The evidence presented at the lower courts proved so persuasive that even the prosecution was forced to acknowledge that the Africans deserved to be returned to their homes. This ruling however also effectively nullified the defense's attempts to make a far-sweeping argument against the immorality of slavery wholesale.[37] Instead, the decision did not *free* them as such; rather it confined their freedom to their African citizenship. Judge Andrew T. Judson who presided over the district court trial was well known both as an avowed racist and a former member of the Colonial Society, and though opposed to slavery, he effectively blocked any attempts on the part of the defense to advance a natural rights argument.[38] Instead the Mendeans as Africans and therefore non-slaves were allowed the "right to revolt" within this limited definition of personhood. When the case was finally decided at the Supreme Court on March 9, 1841, this was the crux of the decision in favor for the Mendeans, not that slavery was *wrong* but that the Mendeans were *not slaves.*[39]

Despite the disappointment, brought on by the limited nature of the decision, the second opportunity presented by the *Creole* mutiny momentarily seemed to extend the energy for armed insurrection beyond the *Amistad* Africans to American slaves. The transformation of the Mendeans from pirates to heroes became, at least allegedly, the model for Madison Washington's own insurrection. According to the wealthy abolitionist, Robert Purvis, in the fall of 1841, Washington paid him a visit in Philadelphia as he was making his way back to Virginia. He arrived the same day as Nathaniel Jocelyn's portrait, "Sinque [*sic*], the Hero of the *Amistad*," was delivered and was "much taken" with the story of Cinqué and the other Africans.[40] Purvis, in telling the story, both imbues the *Creole* mutiny with the mythic power of the *Amistad* and retroactively amplifies the power of the story of the *Amistad* insurrection by showing a causal link between the two.[41] Gerrit Smith, in a speech at the New York State Abolition Convention in 1842, also suggested that the *Creole* would not have captured the attention of so many, had not the *Amistad* case paved the way.[42] Even if the court case limited the decision to illegally captured Africans, the story itself could extend beyond the boundaries of the law.

That the *Creole* was a domestic ship and its slaves were legally slaves who were made free only through Britain's deliberate refusal to recognize United States law underscored the imaginative power behind the insurrection. Here the question of freedom became infused with a romantic possibility due to the extralegal space of the ocean. In the *Amistad* case the ocean proved crucial to establishing jurisdiction. Not only did the position of the ship on the "high seas" allow for the case to be tried in district court, but the fact that the murder had taken place at sea, under the Spanish flag against Spanish law meant that the United States had no jurisdiction to try the Mendeans as pirates.[43] For this reason, pressing on the distinction between land and sea became a strategy by which abolitionists could use legal precedence to argue in favor for the *Creole* fugitives while also appealing to the imagination by invoking a more romantic notion of the freedom embodied by the high seas. "In the most notorious instance, Ohio Congressman Joshua Giddings introduced House resolutions arguing that the *Creole*, 'having left the territorial waters of Virginia, was no longer subject to its state laws but rather to the federal jurisdiction of the commerce of the high seas.'"[44] It is this difference between the law of the sea and the law of the land that Douglass seizes on in his retelling of the story of Madison Washington. Both Delany and Douglass take the arguments of Giddings and anti-slavery theorist William Jay, and use them to wed the revolutionary concept of natural rights to the cause of abolition. The sea acts as a leveler that proves the worth of any man who can demonstrate his prowess over nature. The relationship between freedom and the sea originated with Jay in a pamphlet called *The Creole Case And Mr. Webster's Dispatch* (1842). In it, he states, "the case is stronger for Liberty on the ocean than on the land—for the Earth may be, has been, subjugated by the iron hand of Power; but the free, the untamed sea disdains the puny grasp of the mightiest of earthly despots."[45] This contrast between the tyranny embodied by the land and the freedom embodied by the ocean highlights the artificiality of the rule of law in comparison to the realities of life at sea. The successful revolt, unfettered by the constraints of laws like the Fugitive Slave Act, reveals the true capabilities of Madison Washington and those like him.

The symbolic power of Washington's example, combined with Douglass's speeches on the subject, would reach beyond the confines of the abolitionist movement politics.[46] In his "Address on the Anniversary of the Emancipation of the Negroes in the British West Indies" delivered August 1, 1844, Ralph Waldo Emerson referred to "Toussaint and the Haytian heroes" as a way of praising the Barbados revolutionaries.[47] Emerson, who'd been largely silent if not outright skeptical regarding emancipation, used this address to signal his conversion to a robust and explicitly militant form of abolition.[48] Later, in his 1844 essay, "Character," he would muse:

> Is an iron handcuff so immutable a bond? Suppose a slaver on the coast of Guinea should on board a gang of negroes, which should contain persons of the stamp of Toussaint L'Ouverture: or let us fancy, under these swarthy masks he has a gang of Washingtons in chains. When they arrive at Cuba, will the relative order of the ship's company be the same? Is there nothing but rope and iron?[49]

This explicit reference to the *Creole* mutiny paired with the repeated mention of Toussaint L'Ouverture indicates that the mutiny captured Emerson's imagination to the point that he invokes it in an essay largely unrelated to the cause of abolition. Emerson's example seems to prove that the power of these mutinies fundamentally transformed the face of armed insurrection at least for a portion of the public already somewhat sympathetic to the cause of antislavery. And yet the manner in which he neatly folds the example of Washington into a larger discussion on the nature of character suggests that Emerson is willing to include these examples of slave resistance into his philosophical musings, but only to the extent to which they do not mar the American tapestry already in creation. That "under the swarthy masks" a gang of Washingtons exists indicates a special dispensation to Washington to revolt that does not extend beyond him.

The mainstreaming of armed insurrection would empty it of any real power to sanction slave rebellion. The co-opting of Cinqué and Washington as symbols of a new radical turn in abolitionist thinking would be effective in calling African Americans to arms in the Civil War but the long-term effects would be diminished as blacks bearing arms would fail to fully find acceptance.[50] In the next section I will look at how Delany's *Blake* and Douglass's "The Heroic Slave" attempt to negotiate the need to create a more militant vision of black emancipation with a menacing vision of armed slaves for a white readership.

SEA MUTINY AND THE PROBLEM OF VIOLENCE

If the *Amistad* and *Creole* mutinies made it possible to imagine a successful slave insurrection, one might expect fictional representations of slave mutiny to reflect this. However, both *Blake* (1861) and "The Heroic Slave" (1853) reveal a still-complicated relationship to slave violence. Delany forever delays the violent moment promised in his text. Similarly, while Douglass allows his hero, Madison Washington, to achieve a victory, he also mediates it so that the reader experiences the mutiny secondhand. In both texts, mutiny seems at first to stand as a different kind of violence from what usually appears in abolitionist texts, one that is made more legitimate by pitting the natural strength and ingenuity of the slaves against their white captors without the interference of the plantation community to give the advantage to the slaveholders. But violence also disappears in various ways from the reader's view, calling into question the full impact of these mutinies on the abolitionist movement. Though both writers were explicit about the efficacy of armed insurrection, the already fraught image of the armed slave inhibited their own revolutionary visions.

Douglass's early career is rife with this tension between the need for eloquence and the need for action. His work reflects a growing imperative to prove himself on the intellectual stage while simultaneously advocating for the right of blacks to bear arms in the early years of the Civil War. Because of these twin pressures, revolutionary rhetoric became useful in that it allowed him to place himself within a context of violence that was possibly more palatable than that of Turner's. More than that, in incorporating revolutionary discourse into his rhetoric, Douglass was able to define freedom for himself and not remain caught within the dichotomy of violent and non-violent ex-slave. His constant need to revise his autobiography is in part his attempt "to reach beyond resistance to slaveholding and beyond the attempt to redeem the flawed revolutionary ideals of the founding fathers to a further rebellion against the new bondage imposed upon him by white antislavery liberalism."[51] In the wake of the publication and popularity of Stowe's *Uncle Tom's Cabin*, Douglass—who publicly praised the novel—also seemed, both through his speeches and through the character of Madison Washington in "The Heroic Slave," to take pains to present himself as both a less childlike and more militant figure than Stowe's title character. By placing himself between Nat Turner and Uncle Tom, Douglass offers himself as an example of resistance who tempers violent impulse with revolutionary rhetoric.[52]

As Eric J. Sundquist, Levine, and others have noted, Douglass's preoccupation with his fight with the slave breaker, Covey, appears to reflect his evolving ideas of both the abolitionist movement and his place in it. In first framing it as a coming-of-age moment in *The Narrative of the Life of A Slave* (1845), and then, in *My Bondage and My Freedom,* revising it as a scene of collaborative resistance between himself and the other slaves present, Douglass appears to have brooded over the way violent resistance might be a means by which slaves could fully realize their capacities.[53] "The Heroic Slave," which appeared in *Autographs for Freedom* three years prior to the publication of *My Bondage and My Freedom* (1855), reveals that the *Creole* mutiny played a part in Douglass's thinking as he revised his autobiography. The speech titled "A Slave's Right to Revolt," delivered May 30, 1848, leaves little doubt to this. "Sir," he intones, "I want to alarm the slaveholders, and not to alarm them by mere declamation or by mere bold assertions, but to show them that there is really danger in persisting in the crime of continuing Slavery in this land. I want them to know that there are some Madison Washingtons in this country."[54] This would become even more pronounced after the publication of *My Bondage and My Freedom.* In the 1857 "West India Emancipation" speech, Douglass states outright that armed insurrection without the sanction of whites is the true path to emancipation. "I am aware that the insurrectionary movements of the slaves were held by many to be prejudicial to their cause. This is said now of such movements at the South. The answer is that abolition followed close on the heels of insurrection in the West Indies, and Virginia was never nearer emancipation than when General Turner kindled the fires of insurrection at Southampton."[55] He refers to Turner as "General Turner" as if to lend greater legitimacy to the idea of insurrection. As his aim was to rally northern blacks and later, to make a case for war against the south, it was in Douglass's interest to locate models that embodied active resistance. Madison Washington, the leader of the *Creole* mutiny, was the ideal picture of black resistance: "a black man, with wholly [*sic*] head, high cheekbones, protruding lip, distended nostril and retreating forehead, [who] had mastery of that ship."[56] Washington's name also ties this figure of slave resistance to two of the founding fathers and heroes of the American Revolution.

Douglass's decision to fictionalize the *Creole* case rather than the *Amistad* case appears calculated to capture the revolutionary spirit. Douglass, who, at least after 1851, viewed the Constitution as potentially a friend to abolition rather than the enemy that Garrison insisted it was, appears most concerned with arguing that Washington, Cinqué, and the other insurrectionists belong alongside the heroes of the American Revolution. For Douglass the politics of depicting slave violence necessitates engaging the white reader as a fellow heir of the American Revolution. He would later reinforce this point in his West Indian Emancipation speech when he would declare, "Madison Washington who struck down his oppressor on the deck of the *Creole*, is more worthy to be remembered than the colored man who shot Pitcairn at Bunker Hill."[57]

Delany's relationship to the American Revolution is more ambivalent. Blake is less an heir to the American Revolution than he is that of the Haitian Revolution. In a very public disagreement over Stowe's involvement with black improvement that played out in the pages of the *North Star*, Delany's hostility towards relying too heavily on the example of white abolitionists can be obliquely read as impatience with the white models of securing freedom. He wrote to Douglass, "In all due respect and deference to Mrs. Stowe, I beg leave to say, that she *knows nothing about us*, 'the Free Colored people of the United States,' neither does any other white person—and, consequently, can contrive no successful scheme for our elevation; it must be done by ourselves."[58] Delany's own career as a proto-black nationalist also comes through in *Blake* as he attempts to set the stage for the rise of a Caribbean black republic in the model of Haiti, not the United States. Delany toggled back and forth between outright hostility towards African emigration (the crux of his hostility towards Stowe) and arguing that the future of black Americans could be better realized outside of the United States. In his work *The Condition, Elevation, and Destiny of the Colored People of the United States* (1852), Delany proposes a model for African emigration that appears designed to both capture the revolutionary energy of the moment while distancing blacks from the white paternalism of current colonization projects. "Go or stay, of course each is free to do as he pleases, one thing is certain; our Elevation is the work of our own hands. And Mexico, Central America, the West Indies, and South America, all present now, opportunities for the individual enterprise of our young men, who prefer to remain in the United States, in preference to going where they can enjoy real freedom, and quality of rights, Freedom of Religion, as well as politics, being tolerated in all of these places."[59] Imbedded in this conviction that the future of black America lies in another region of the Americas, is a sense of that the feats of the American Revolution—escape, discovery, and the establishment of a new political order—need to be reenacted and transformed if black autonomy is to be realized.

This idea of reenactment might explain the way in which rehearsing conspiracy, rather than realizing its success, seems to be the structure around which the novel is built. Delany, who spends the first half of *Blake* exhaustively building up a slave insurrection only to have it never happen, simultaneously showcases the extent of slave revolutionary potential in the planning and scope of Blake's insurrection while also critiquing the emerging trope of tying slave insurrection to the American Revolution. During his journey through the south, Blake goes into the Great Dismal Swamp to meet with seven elders of the swamp maroon community known as the conjurers. Blake needs their blessing to pursue his own rebellion, and uses them to spread his message. But, despite the respect he shows them, he clearly views them as relics of the past rather than active participants in the present. This displays a certain amount of exasperation both with the tradition of *marronage* and the much-ballyhooed history of the blacks in the American Revolution.[60] That they are both confined by ancestral traditions and superstition and in thrall to the Founding Father myth suggests a problem with current modes of resistance. The seven conjurers still hold power within the swamp but spend little time doing much beyond recounting past glories. "In this fearful abode for years of some of Virginia and North Carolina's boldest black rebels, the names of Nat Turner, Denmark Veezie [*sic*], and General Gabriel were held by them in sacred reverence; that of Gabriel as a talisman. With delight they recounted the many exploits of whom they conceived to be the greatest men who ever lived, the pretended deeds of whom were fabulous, some of the narrators claiming to have been patriots in the American Revolution."[61] Here the exploits of Turner and Vesey represent the possible danger of stasis, of never moving beyond older models of rebellion, especially since those models have proven unsuccessful. Through Blake, Delany appears to recognize the need to break away from these older rebels. Even the fear represented by the swamp maroon has become a liability rather than an asset.

Delany's depiction of Blake's transition from plantation insurrection to sea mutiny can be read as an allegory of what he views as the history of insurrection before and after the *Amistad* and *Creole* incidents by depicting plantation insurrection as outdated and sea mutiny as both successful and an arena in which blacks can create their own revolutionary history. Reading this depiction of landed insurrection, or rather failed landed insurrections, as coming out of a post-*Amistad* context, allows Delany to suggest that the failure of landed insurrection might have less to do with structural issues of raising an army large enough to overturn the plantation system than with a preoccupation with past glories. The Great Dismal Swamp, an interstitial space between land and sea and a longstanding refuge for a sizeable maroon community, can be seen as a space for refuge and revolt.[62] But Delany also suggests that its durability is also a sign of its obsolescence. In fusing together the superstition of the conjurers with nostalgia for the American Revolution, Delany casts doubt on the lessons of the past as models for future victory. This fusion helps explain the rather abrupt shift from a land-based conspiracy to an ocean-based one. Failure is not failure but rather the only way to move forward.

Rather than seeing the revolt through to its end after transporting his family safely to Canada, Blake turns his attention to Cuba and to the job of securing a ship in order to spark a revolution on that island. He gets himself assigned to a position of leadership over the other black sailors and plots to take over the ship once the cargo of slaves has been acquired and he can add the captive slaves to his ranks of mutineers. The plan, relying as it does on both his superior knowledge of seafaring and the continued illegal slave trafficking, both highlights black ingenuity and strongly evokes the *Amistad* case in utilizing the captives.[63]

However, Blake's plans begin to unravel even before the ship sets sail, when a note signed by a co-conspirator, Placido, falls from Blake's pocket and is sighted by the first mate. The note is signed "Faithfully yours until the end of the war," alerting the crew to the possibility of an uprising, and causing them to take note of the words and actions of the black sailors serving aboard the ship.[64] A sea song, sung by the blacks, fixes their attention:

> Hurra, for the sea and its waves!
> Ye billows and surges, all hail!
> My brothers henceforth—for ye scorn to be SLAVES,
> As ye toss up your crests to the gale;
> Farewell to the land of the blood-hound and chain,
> My path is away o'er the fetterless main![65]

The song speaks to the promise of freedom engendered by the "fetterless main," and also heightens the sense of expectancy of violence to come—an expectancy made all the more potent by the thwarted insurrection discussed previously. The creation of a community of black sailors and their united purpose of freeing the future cargo also speaks of a desire not just to free future slaves, but to redress an old wrong. In returning to Africa for this purpose, they are also returning to the scene of the original crime of African enslavement. Yet the song also needlessly alerts the whites, putting Blake and his followers at risk. The whites, now aware of the possibility of the mutiny, spend the rest of the journey jumping at false alarms, until reaching Cuba. The only victory for Blake and his followers is that the slaves are rendered un-sellable due to the suspicion of mutiny.

During the voyage, in a moment that recalls the *Liberator*'s jeremiad in the aftermath of the Turner Rebellion, a vengeful God makes his appearance in the form of a storm that sends from the deep a creature "much larger than a grampus, and not so large as a whale" as "a sign of trouble"[66]:

> The black and frowning skies and raging hurricane above; the black and frowning slaves with raging passions below, rendered it dreadful without, fearful within, and terrible all around. Whilst the captain, mate, and crew were with might and main struggling against the fierce contending elements above, the master spirit of the captives seized the opportunity to release his fellow slaves from their fetters.[67]

This should be the moment at which Blake's plans come to fruition. The armed slaves are revealed in "a fearful flame of lightning" and the crew is too busy trying to subdue the ship to take notice. But when the white crewmembers take a second look, the freed slaves, rather than arming themselves, are raiding the stores for food. The storm, rather than aiding the slaves and sailor-slaves in their mutiny, merely amplifies the slavers' fears of an uprising.

This moment at sea, where Blake ostensibly has the advantage, haunts the story. Why does he not strike, given that the slaves outnumber the white crewmembers, not to mention the presence of the sympathetic British navy? Was the trip to and from Africa merely another interlude on the way to the true revolution in Cuba? Or was Delany, through Blake, unable, in the moment when all the slaves fall silent in the middle of the ocean, to break that silence with the necessary violence? For Delany to thwart his hero in this way calls into question the whole point of the novel: If one is going to create a black revolutionary hero, one must logically allow him his revolution. To answer these questions we must first acknowledge on a practical level that *Blake* suffers from bad timing. The *Weekly Anglo-African* began serializing it weekly in 1859. By the time the "complete" version appeared it was May of 1862. While the Civil War did not absolutely put the question of black emigration to rest (in 1862 "Lincoln was exploring the possibility of colonizing blacks to the tropics of Central and South America"), it definitely changed the focus of abolitionists.[68] In fact, upon hearing news of the secession of South Carolina while in Great Britain, Delany turned his efforts to the war.[69] Plans for a new black republic became sidelined in favor for joining forces with Douglass in making a case for the Civil War as a war of emancipation.

Another possible answer to the question of why *Blake* avoids graphic violence is that for Delany and his plans for a black republic, the depiction of a successful revolt is not the point. Instead, in repeatedly showing blacks in the act of conspiring, he is emphasizing the massive revolutionary potential of an enslaved population. For example, as we have seen, though the insurrection is thwarted, the rumors of an uprising "reduced the captives to a minimum price," allowing Blake and his comrades to purchase and free them.[70] In this way, the power of a collective resides not merely in the threat of violence, but in that collective's ability to capitalize on that threat without firing a shot. In neatly sidestepping the depiction of an insurrection, Delany avoids the problem of depicting a revolutionary figure in an act of violence. This avoidance raises the possibility that, his many objections to Stowe and *Uncle Tom's Cabin* notwithstanding, Delany, too, saw the advantages in keeping readers' eyes fixed on the evils of slavery rather than on the full character of the insurrectionists.

Delany's inability or unwillingness to portray a slave rebellion leaves Douglass's mutiny in "The Heroic Slave" as the sole literary representation by a black author of successful insurrection at sea. Douglass, whose only work of fiction is devoted to imagining the events leading up to the *Creole* mutiny, probably makes the most forceful case for the place of insurrection in abolition. For Douglass, the events aboard the *Amistad* and the *Creole* underline the concept of the right to revolution as a *natural right*, one that is embodied in revolt at sea, where the victor is not determined by statute but enacts his natural right to freedom by overcoming the oppressor and liberating himself. The example of the *Creole* in uniting the image of a slave insurrectionist with the American Revolution, and in occurring at sea, away from the power of the plantation, makes it a compelling narrative to which Douglass can attach his own philosophies regarding the possibilities of life for blacks in post-slavery America. However, despite the more positive approach, Douglass is careful to couch his endorsement of slave violence in the familiar revolutionary rhetoric employed by the Mendeans' more vocal white defenders. Our first sight of Madison Washington is through the eyes of his future friend and ally, Listwell, who, unseen by Washington, observes him praying. Moved by the sight, Listwell muses:

> Here is indeed a man . . . of rare endowments,—a child of God,—guilty of no crime but the color of his skin, hiding away from the face of humanity, and pouring out his thoughts and feelings, his hopes and resolutions to the lonely woods; to him those distant church bells have no grateful music. . . . Goaded almost to madness by the sense of the injustice done him, he resorts hither to give vent to his pent up feelings, and to debate with himself the feasibility of plans, plans of his own invention, for his own deliverance. From this hour I am an abolitionist. I have seen enough and heard enough, and I shall go to my home in Ohio resolved to atone for my past indifference to this ill-starred race, by making such exertions as I shall be able to do, for the speedy emancipation of every slave in the land.[71]

Listwell, as Washington's defender, mediates the readers' sympathies by drawing attention to Washington's humanity and decrying the Christians who have failed to abolish slavery. He then experiences his own epiphany and creates a short conversion narrative out of this moment. The reader, given the illusion of access to Washington's interiority as imagined by Listwell, ideally experiences a moment of conversion as well. Listwell is both the reader's conduit to Washington and the reader's screen from his true motives. The pun in the name Listwell affirms his reliability as a narrator, and commands the reader to follow the example he has set as a character.

Douglass highlights the impact of the depiction of a successful revolt by letting a white shipmate called Tom Grant tell the story after the fact. Grant, when confronted by a listener over the crew's incompetence in allowing the revolt to happen, retorts:

> It is one thing to manage a company of slaves on a Virginia plantation, and quite another thing to quell an insurrection on the lonely billows of the Atlantic, where every breeze speaks of courage and liberty. For the negro to act cowardly on shore, may be to act wisely; and I've some doubts whether *you*, Mr. Williams, would find it very convenient were you a slave in Algiers, to raise your hand against the bayonets of a whole government.[72]

Grant's reaction, and the communication of that reaction to his hearers, shows the act of revolution not simply as an end to itself but also as a performance for skeptical whites. It is almost as if Douglass has already responded to Garrison's complaint of the absence of emancipatory spirit on southern plantations. The sea brings out the true nature of the slave, whose apparent cowardliness on land is merely prudent and not an indication of his nature. His mention of Algiers is a reference to Barbary piracy through which the mate is claiming kinship with the slaves, realizing that in that earlier moment he might have been the victim of slavery as well.

Madison, having secured the ship, is now faced with guiding it through a violent storm. The focus of the battle is now transposed from man to the elements. Grant continues his story, noting that the first words Madison utters after the storm had slightly subsided are characteristic of the man. "Mr. Mate, you cannot write the bloody laws of slavery on those restless billows. The ocean, if not the land, is free."[73] In this moment, the story ceases to be one of insurrection and becomes a sea yarn that focuses on the dramatic depiction of a captain guiding his ship through a storm to safety. The mate grudgingly admits, "I confess, gentlemen, I felt myself in the presence of a superior man; one who, had he been a white man, I would have followed willingly and gladly in any honorable enterprise."[74] The sea as a space of freedom in this context is not just a grand metaphor for freedom but a challenging geography. Washington's mastery over the sea questions the legitimacy of anyone claiming to master him.

Most importantly, the secondhand narration also saves Douglass the trouble of depicting the actual insurrection. Reportage from the mouth of a former enemy, who was also knocked senseless early in the action and subsequently missed most of the battle, allows Washington's actions to be heroic without also being uncomfortably savage. Douglass neatly sidesteps having to address the account of a more savage vision of Washington as detailed in the "Protest" registered by the New Orleans-based crew of the *Creole*. According to testimony, Washington rallied his fellow slaves by saying, "Come up, every one of you, if you don't lend a hand, I will kill you all and throw you overboard!"[75] The killing of a white officer called Hewell is further described in graphic detail. "He [Hewell] advanced and they fell upon him with clubs, handspikes and knives. He was knocked down and stabbed in not less than twenty places, but he rose, got away from them and staggered back to the cabin exclaiming; 'I am dead—the negroes have killed me!'"[76] Douglass combats this by having Grant as the white witness. This tactic serves the same purpose within the text as the *Liberator* did during the *Amistad* case, namely, that of translating the mutiny to a white audience using the language of revolution. Readers, shielded from the graphic violence, only hear Washington's defense of his actions through Grant, "I have done no more to those dead men yonder than they would have done for me in like circumstances. We have struck for our freedom, and if a true man's heart be in you, you will honor us for the deed. We have done that which you applaud your fathers for doing, and if we are murderers, *so were they*."[77] The invocation of the American Revolution acts as almost a physical weapon against the accusation of murder. Indeed Grant describes himself as being "disarmed" by his words as though the blow were physical.

Yet in relying on secondhand narration and approval of white witnesses, "The Heroic Slave," makes slave violence palatable only by obscuring it. The secondhand narration creates the impression that the white sailors were subdued by their recognition of Madison Washington's manhood rather than the acts of violence perpetrated by the slaves themselves. The lack of a direct description of the mutiny and the disappearance of the mutineers into the hands of British justice also puts the spectacle at a physical remove. Moreover, in defending the mutiny by using the example of the American Revolution, Douglass does not so much expand the definition of revolution as he narrows the terms under which "right to revolt" is justifiable. Without access to the spectacle and only the tenuous word of the white sailors to go on, the *Creole* mutiny also vanishes both in the physical details and political impact. The loss of the violence through secondhand narration constitutes a vanishing of the slave voice.

In the end, it would be John Brown who would take up the cause for a slave revolution. Douglass, when asked, declined to join Brown in his raid on Harper's Ferry, and later, along with Delany, would throw himself into the war effort by insisting on commissioning black regiments into the Union army.[78] Despite the fact that the abolitionist movement eventually embraced war as the only solution, the role of blacks within the war remained a point of controversy. At Douglass's urging, President Lincoln would finally allow blacks to serve in the Union army in 1863, but not without objections from northern whites.[79] While the eventual inclusion of black soldiers in the war effort might be viewed as a victory for Douglass and Delany, one might view the Civil War as effectively ending the possibility of a slave revolution without having settled the question of whether or not it was justifiable for slaves to take up arms against their owners without the cover of state-sanctioned violence.

Once this limited rhetoric of violence became the language of the "mainstream" abolitionist movement, it became possible for moral suasionists such as Garrison and Harriet Beecher Stowe to adopt it and make it their own. In a speech on the event of John Brown's execution William Lloyd Garrison issued his most vocal defense of insurrection as a solution to slavery.

> A word upon the subject of Peace. I am a non-resistant—a believer in the inviolability of human life, under all circumstances; I, therefore, in the name of God, disarm John Brown, and every slave at the South. But I do not step there; if I did, I should be a monster. I also disarm, in the name of God, every slaveholder and tyrant in the world. (Loud applause.) For wherever that principle is adopted, all fetters must instantly melt, and there can be no oppressed, and no oppressor, in the nature of things. How many agree with me in regard to the doctrine of the inviolability of human life? How many non-resistants are there here to-night? (A single voice—"I.") There is *one*! (Laughter.) Well, then, you who are otherwise are not the men to point the finger at John Brown, and cry "traitor"—judging you by your own standard. (Applause.) Nevertheless, I am a non-resistant, and I not only desire, but have labored unremittingly to effect the peaceful abolition of slavery, by an appeal to the reason and conscience of the slaveholder; yet, as a peace man—an "ultra" peace man—I am prepared to say, "Success to every slave insurrection at the South, and in every slave country."[80]

Garrison's words suggest that it is Brown's example bolstered by the long history of insurrection that has proved the more compelling rather than the insurrection alone. Whiteness here provides the mantel of legitimacy over insurrection in a way that insurrection itself fails to do. Moreover, even as he wishes "success to every slave insurrection at the South" his words are qualified by his insistence on maintaining a position of non-resistance.

For Delany and Douglass it was, perhaps, more important to facilitate the adoption of a more radical approach to abolition than it was to think concretely about the possibilities of a Haitian-style revolution. But the lingering hesitance over literary depictions of slave violence signifies a disconnection between the rhetoric of violence and the practice of slave violence. Despite the application of revolutionary rhetoric to the actions of Cinqué and his followers, the *Amistad* case remains the exception rather than the rule within the history of landed insurrection and shipboard mutiny. Blake is suspended in Cuba on the verge of a coup that never occurs, and Madison Washington and his crew gain their freedom only due to the grace of the sympathetic British government. This failure by both authors is not merely the failure of imagination but also the failure of revolutionary rhetoric to exceed its limits. The invocation of the American Revolution for the cause of abolition succeeds only in reaffirming the American Revolution's legitimacy. Abolition, burdened by fear of slave insurrection, can only go so far in endorsing black violence on American soil. For a slave revolt to be truly revolutionary, one must face the possibility of slaves overthrowing the nation. Mutiny becomes a convenient way to remove the possibility of a successful slave insurrection from the mainland to the safe desolation of the ocean.

THE BLACK AND WHITE SAILOR

Melville's *Billy Budd, Sailor* and the

Case of Washington Goode

IN HERMAN MELVILLE'S FINAL PROSE work, *Billy Budd, Sailor,* the narrator introduces us to the title character by first recalling the sight of a black sailor who reminded him of the phenomenon of what Melville called, the "Handsome Sailor":

> In Liverpool now half a century ago, I saw under the shadow of the great dingy street-wall of Prince's Dock (an obstruction long since removed) a common sailor so intensely black that he must needs have been a native African of the unadulterated blood of Ham—a symmetric figure much above the average height. The two ends of a gay silk handkerchief thrown loose about the neck danced upon the displayed ebony of his chest, in his ears were big hoops of gold, and a Highland bonnet with a tartan band set off his shapely head. It was a hot noon in July; and his face, lustrous with perspiration, beamed with barbaric good humor. In jovial sallies right and left, his white teeth flashing into view, he rollicked along the center of a company of his shipmates. These were made up of such an assortment of tribes and complexions as would have well fitted to be marched by Anacharsis Cloots before the bar of the first French Assembly as Representatives of the Human Race.[1]

The chronological and spatial placement of the black sailor is crucial to our understanding of the significance of this reminiscence. Carolyn L. Karcher writes, "Melville introduces him in his own narrative voice, and the date and place correspond exactly with those of Melville's first voyage to Liverpool, in July 1839."[2] 1839 was also the year that the African, Cinqué, rallied his fellow slaves to mutiny against their captors aboard the ship *Amistad.* As for the significance of place, the town of Liverpool had been a leading slave port since 1750 and was one of the primary ports in Thomas Clarkson's research in the early part of the British abolitionist movement. It was there that he met his first informant on the horrors of the slave ship, a black sailor named John Dean who bore the marks of flogging on his back. Finally, by invoking Anacharsis Cloots, an ardent supporter of the French Revolution, who, on June 4, 1790, brought a delegation of nationalities before the French Assembly as representatives of the Human Race, Melville casts the ominous shadow of social upheaval over his picturesque scene. By 1790 the French Revolution was in its second year, and the Haitian Revolution was a year away. The image of the black sailor is striking but fleeting, as it vanishes almost immediately from the story to be replaced by Billy Budd whose beauty Melville's narrator describes as being almost completely the result of his "Anglo-Saxon" whiteness.

What is the import of the black sailor? Is he merely a picturesque means to introduce Billy Budd? Or was Melville, as scholar Gregory Jay has suggested, doing a sort of reverse minstrelsy in which Billy becomes an avatar for an antebellum slave archetype?[3] Or is he, as Karcher argues, a "reincarnation of Melville's long-dead faith in the essential nobility of man?"[4] Perhaps all of these ideas have some merit. There is, however, another possibility. In 1875, the Salem Register ran this brief item regarding a recent murder case:

> A hearing will be granted by the Governor's council on Tuesday of next week on the Pomeroy case. Several petitions have been presented, both for and against the commutation of the sentence, and the hearing will probably bring out numerous arguments on both sides.
>
> The murder of Mrs. Bingham may have much influence in deciding the fate of Pomeroy. Many are of the opinion that Webster would never have gone to the gallows, if Washington Goode, the poor colored sailor who while drunk had caused the death of a fellow being, had not so recently been hanged; so the murderer of Parkman could not consistently be pardoned, or have his sentence commuted. We hope something will be done in Pomeroy's case, to relieve the community of the feeling of insecurity his liberty would create.[5]

Jesse Pomeroy was believed to be a serial killer who at the age of fourteen was convicted of first-degree murder. The article in question refers to the surrounding debate regarding the issue of capital punishment. Pomeroy, a boy with a violent past, was believed to have killed both a ten-year-old girl and a four-year-old boy. The piece, in musing on the likelihood of commutation, makes reference to two of the most famous capital punishment cases in the antebellum period; the Parkman-Webster Case and the Washington Goode case, both tried in the year 1849.

The Parkman-Webster case is worth knowing given the pedigrees of both the parties involved.[6] But it is the Washington Goode case, which I argue, informs

Billy Budd, the story that constitutes Melville's final word on the subject of race and racism in the post-Civil War world. In 1849, a black sailor from the Boston area was tried and convicted of the murder of another African American. The presiding judge, as in the Parkman-Webster case, was Melville's father-in-law, Lemuel Shaw. The case ignited a massive anti-death penalty campaign due to the unprecedented nature of the sentencing and the highly circumstantial nature of the evidence used to convict Goode. His race, the poor reputation of sailors, and the fact that he was living in Boston's notorious Black Sea neighborhood, were all factors in this case.

Is Goode Melville's black sailor in *Billy Budd*? The differences at the outset might seem more striking rather than the similarities. *Billy Budd's* black sailor is exemplary: "jovial," a natural leader. Goode, by contrast, is "undisciplined in heart and mind" as well as "drunken" and "lust[ful]."[7] However, the circumstances that determine the murder convictions of both men are strikingly similar. Both are made examples of due to the fears on the part of Shaw and Vere that any sign of nuance or mercy might be interpreted as failing to take the threat of violence to the state seriously. That Goode is almost certainly innocent, and Billy is definitely guilty underscores that it is not the details of either case that determine the outcome but rather these larger social fears. I would like to propose that looking at the Goode case as yet one more piece of legal source material for *Billy Budd* adds a crucial piece to the puzzle of Melville's longer project regarding race and violence.[8]

Looking at the Goode case as source material for *Billy Budd* also demands that we examine the way in which race informs the critique of violence at play in the novella. To do that, I would like to propose that the black sailor at the beginning of the story invites us to revisit the scene of shipboard insurrection in *Benito Cereno* and the politics of race and punishment in *White-Jacket*. Washington Goode's case provides a concrete link between the characters of Billy Budd and *Benito Cereno's* Babo by simultaneously invoking the problematic justice surrounding violence and the politics of race. Both Babo and Budd present as figures whose "guilt" is at once undeniable and ambiguous, but for completely different reasons. Perceptions of Babo's guilt ultimately depend on the reader's view of the justness of slave insurrection and consequent willingness to accept the morally ambiguous manner in which Babo operates. Likewise, with the character of Budd, Melville sources insurrectionist impulse in an otherwise ideal citizen, thereby calling into question the very nature of revolutionary violence. In short, if Babo is a villain and Budd is a victim, to what extent does our acceptance of their actions depend, not only on their respective races, but the acts of violence themselves? While there's no textual evidence that *White-Jacket* was informed by Washington

Goode, the novel does provide an early example of Melville's engagement with abolitionist rhetoric as it applied to violence against sailors and slaves, as well as violence perpetrated by sailors and slaves. The fact that naval reformers not only were abolitionists but made direct comparisons between the culture aboard ships and the plantation system allows Melville to unpack the ways in which that comparison was both useful and limited. The treatment of flogging, specifically flogging as punishment for fighting, reveals Melville's anxieties about the relationship between authority and resistance to injustice.

The relationship between Melville and his father-in-law Shaw has been well covered by scholars.[9] Michael Paul Rogin has argued that Melville's depiction of Captain Vere is largely based on his sense that Shaw, despite holding more progressive sympathies, was all too enamored of the rule of law.[10] The Goode case would seem then simply just another example of this tendency and possibly a less significant one when compared with Shaw's high-profile defense of the Fugitive Slave Law.[11] Although Rogin and other scholars have not discussed the Goode case specifically, Melville's awareness of Shaw's rulings from the bench, the notoriety of the case itself, and Melville's own massive capacity for allusion make it probable that he was aware of it.

The ease with which Goode has been overlooked in Melville scholarship echoes the way that many readers forget about the black sailor at the beginning of the novella, whose intense blackness becomes obliterated by Billy's exceptional whiteness. Billy's fate, tied as it is to the specifics of navy life and the fear of insurrection in a time of war, has no obvious racial dynamic, particularly when one considers the explicit way in which Vere deliberately sets aside any sort of favorable prejudice. Indeed, it has been suggested that the fact that Billy's whiteness does not save him speaks to Melville's own latent racism, displayed earlier in *Battle-Pieces*.

Little is known about the specifics of Washington Goode's life. Barry Kritzberg and Louis P. Masur have written the most thorough accounts of the case.[12] Goode was perhaps born in Philadelphia, served under Zachary Taylor, during his Florida campaign in the Second Seminole War, and was, at the time of the murder, about twenty-nine years old and serving as a ship's cook.[13] He was a resident of the Boston neighborhood known as "The Black Sea"—a neighborhood the *Boston Post* describes as a place in which blacks and whites came together, "in dens and drunkenness [where] the passions are excited in all possible ways"— and was known to be courting a woman by the name of Mary Ann Williams. Williams, though, was married, and involved in a third relationship with another African American sailor, Thomas Harding.[14] On the night of the murder, June 28, 1848, Goode and Harding were seen to be arguing over a brightly colored handkerchief Harding had given to Williams. Harding was found dead later that same evening from both a blow to the head and a stab wound.[15]

District Attorney Samuel D. Parker tried the case in January of 1849. Despite the fact that, "no human eye saw the fatal blow given," Parker presented his case as though the verdict were a foregone conclusion.[16] The prosecution called sixteen witnesses, none of whom could swear absolutely to having seen Goode, though at least two claimed that Goode told them of his intention to kill Harding on the night in question. Goode's defense attorneys were William Aspinwall and Edward F. Hodges. Aspinwall, the lead chair, was distinguished but also young and had never tried a capital case. Aspinwall's defense rested both on the circumstantial nature of the evidence presented by the prosecution [one of the eye-witnesses was revealed to be near-sighted], as well as the inconsistency of the forensic evidence, as Harding's knife wound did not match the weapon Goode habitually carried.[17]

In spite of the apparent shakiness of the prosecution's evidence, Chief Justice Shaw's three-hour long charge to the jury cast the case in terms of lack of reasonable doubt rather than the presence of evidence of guilt.[18] Subsequently, the jury delivered a verdict of guilty after only thirty-five minutes of deliberation.[19] Before the reading of the sentence, Goode was asked if he wished to speak for the first time in the proceedings. In response to the question, "Have you anything to say why sentence of death should not be passed upon you?" he responded, "No I have nothing to say against it. . . . I know I am not innocent of the charge. I mean I am innocent of what charge has been made against me. I know if what the witnesses had sworn to was true, I would not have been here now. Every thing has been false that they have sworn to in the court. I have no more to say against passing the sentence upon me."[20] Shaw's words to Goode upon delivering his sentence are fairly indicative of the effect of Goode's statements.

> Washington Goode—you are guilty of the murder of a fellow being. To some of the circumstances attending the commission of the crime, we will briefly refer. The first is that you have been a visiter [sic]—a frequenter, an inmate, and a daily associate with parties, in a place that the resort of every thing [sic] in the shape of depravity and vice. It may be that there are similar places in other seaports, where similar scenes of intemperance, violence, and murder are of daily and nightly occurrence; but if so, it the more to be deplored, and to be provided against by the ruling authorities. Still more deplorable is it that these places have been so long allowed to exist as an allurement, especially to seamen—where vice holds out a premium to passions of the worst kind.[21]

Goode's conduct surrounding the murder—reports of drinking, the fact that he was in an adulterous relationship, and perhaps even the question of his being a sailor—appeared to have condemned him in the eyes of both judge and jury.

Massachusetts at the time did not have a long tradition of carrying out the capital punishment. Goode's conviction in some ways can be seen as Shaw's response to what he considered to be an upsetting trend of bad lawyering on behalf of the anti-capital punishment movement. For example, as Alan Rogers has already written, in an 1846 arson case that Parker also prosecuted before Shaw, the possibility that a guilty suspect had been acquitted case had galvanized activists. The lead defender was Rufus Choate who was by all accounts a clever if not altogether honest attorney who successfully argued that the crime was the result of somnambulism. The acquittal seemed typical. All told between 1835 and 1849 approximately twenty men were tried for murder. Of those twenty only four were sentenced to death, and of those four only one failed to have his sentence commuted. Goode's execution ended a long tradition of Massachusetts' resistance to the capital punishment.[22]

The outcry on Goode's behalf grew slowly and only gained momentum when the expected commutation of sentence failed to pass. Despite Goode's relative obscurity the case eventually attracted abolitionist attention because the abolition of capital punishment was a popular reform movement. Lydia Marie Child and Wendell Phillips were amongst those abolitionists agitating against capital punishment.[23] Henry David Thoreau, Ralph Waldo Emerson, and Frederick Douglass all spoke up for Goode. William Lloyd Garrison's the *Liberator* devoted considerable editorial attention to the case, as did the *North Star*. The *Liberator* opined, "A colored man too—one whom society most preeminently injures, doomed with such irreverent certainty to ignorance and vice, by cruel prejudice and wicked statutes in almost every part of the country—the child of an abused race. Let it not be said that the last man Massachusetts bore to hang was a colored man."[24] The *North Star*, in turn, praised the growing movement, declaring, "May the benevolent and philanthropic men who have taken up the case of this poor friendless victim of the debasing influence of Southern institutions, be successful in their efforts!"[25] Although the various defenses of Washington Goode did not mention or focus on his experiences aboard ships, navy or otherwise, the fact that Goode's defenders pointed to the known depravity of sailors, as was evidenced by the fact that Goode lived in the neighborhood called The Black Sea, indicates foreknowledge of flogging as one of the "hardening" aspects of sailor life.[26] We do know that William Garrison's brother's treatment at the hands of abusive captains led to his own participation in the naval reform movement. "James Garrison, elder brother of radical abolitionist William Lloyd Garrison and an unrestrained alcoholic since the age of fourteen, disappeared from his New England home for over two decades. In September of

1839, an unexpected summons from the Charleston Navy Yard reunited the editor of *The Liberator* with his long-lost brother, now a 'weather-beaten sailor'. . . . He had been whipped on several occasions for drunkenness and once placed in double irons for twenty-eight days."[27] Finally, Aspinwall's defense explicitly referenced Goode's race in such a manner as to make the link between anti-slavery and anti-death penalty rhetoric explicit. As he would later say in his address to the governor, "This man, for whose life I plead, is as ignorant of his duty towards God and toward man, as were those creatures your fathers stole. He came here darkened both in mind and soul—you did not take him by the hand and lead him to your schools and your altars, but you lured him into the haunts of infamy and crime."[28]

Defenses for Goode before and after sentencing only briefly dwell on the questionable nature of the conviction. What appears indisputable is that Goode's conduct was already relatively well known. His drunkenness, his relationship with a married woman, and his temper seem to have been matters of fact rather than speculation. As is evident above, speeches on his behalf, therefore, take on a curious hedging tone. He *might* be innocent of the crime, they acknowledge, but if he is guilty, which we are willing to believe given what we know of his character, it is our duty as enlightened Christians to preserve his life. Words like "hapless," "ignorant," and "friendless" abound in these editorials and speeches.[29]

As a sailor, Goode would have been vulnerable to stigma regardless of his race. Sailors had historically been seen as naturally depraved and "cut from the same cloth" as slaves, particular in the wake of the Boston anti-impressment riots in 1747.[30] Goode's bad behavior as such could be attributed to assumptions regarding both his race and his occupation. But given the climate of the 1840s and 1850s it is more likely that race played more into any bias against him than the stigma of being a sailor. While Marcus Rediker has often touted the multiracial makeup of ships as having revolutionary political potential, the impact of the Negro Seamens Acts created deep fissures between black and white sailors.[31] The 1840s and 1850s saw a sharp rise in sailors bringing abuse cases against bad captains and sharp decrease in instances of mutiny, but there were still instances of conflict when ships docked at southern ports. "In an 1853 case from New York, several black seamen were charged with revolt for refusing to accept the addition of an unscheduled port of call in the American South en route to their destination in South America. New York's Judge Betts agreed with the seamen that a stop not delineated in the articles—particularly one that could be seen as dangerous—could not be added without the crew's consent."[32] While instances like these showed the rule working at times in the favor of black sailors, the problem of southern ports would persist throughout the 1850s.

Goode was also a seaman in a moment that was beginning to see a precipitous decline in the participation of black men in the maritime industry. In New York alone, the percentage of African American sailors went from 14 percent in 1835 to 4.6 percent in 1866.[33] This was in large part due to a significant change in hiring practices. The tradition of captains choosing their own crew gave way to the introduction of middlemen known as "crimps" who would supply crews for ships for a fee, a practice that quickly lead to an informal "whites first" policy.[34] This change in securing crew members occurred just as maritime reformers, many of whom were also active in abolitionist circles, were introducing anti-slavery rhetoric into maritime reform with regards to flogging (as I will discuss in more detail in my section *White-Jacket*) and the shift from referring to ship's masters as *masters* to now more commonly accepted *captain*.[35] This paradox of the reform movement making progressive strides in rooting out abuse in the maritime industry as the maritime industry itself was becoming more and more segregated, speaks to the double bind in which Goode seemed to be caught. Add to his plight the history of murder acquittals in Massachusetts mentioned above and Shaw's rigid approach to the rule of law, and Goode becomes an avatar for the intersecting problems of both maritime life and race in the antebellum period.

The failure of activism on the part of abolitionists and reformers to save Goode speaks to the larger rhetorical problem of a movement, which borrowed freely from abolitionist rhetoric to empower sailors but failed to address the intrinsic problems of racism within maritime culture. This is where arguments about the egalitarian nature of the maritime industry break down and it matters that the key differences turn on issues of abuse and violence. While percentages of "revolt" cases against common seamen diminished and assault cases against officers increased, black seamen found themselves often unable to benefit from shift.[36] "In 1849 Captain Smiley of the *John E. Davidson* threatened his black steward, George Beckett, by warning that 'Becket[t] would never see New York again.' Whether the threat was murderous or implied that Beckett would be sold into slavery remained unclear, but it was Becket who ended up paying the price for his violent altercation with Captain Smiley. He was convicted of assault with a dangerous weapon and served three years in prison."[37]

In creating the white sailor Billy Budd, and using the memory of the anonymous black sailor to introduce him, Melville calls into question the sharp racial lines drawn between black and white sailors by first drawing them clearly, and then erasing them almost at once. This erasure ostensibly expunges the memory of black sailor as well, but if one considers that in criminalizing Billy Budd, Melville also racializes him, invoking this brief memory seems calculated to lull the readers into a tragic story about a good sailor with a minor yet significant flaw. The valorization of Billy's good points overshadows the kernel of violence that is contained within this flaw, and that valorization is underscored by Billy's pointedly racialized good looks. If Billy's aestheticized whiteness prevents us from understanding his violent potential, it also fails to save him in the end.

THE RACIALIZATION OF BILLY BUDD

At the end of *Battle-Pieces*, Melville includes a prose "Supplement" which appeals that his readers not forget the humanity of the South and expresses skepticism about integrating blacks into the polity. He writes:

> Those of us who always abhorred slavery as an atheistical iniquity, gladly we join in the exulting chorus of humanity over its downfall. But we should remember that emancipation was accomplished not by deliberate legislation; only through agonized violence could so mighty a result be effected. In our natural solicitude to confirm the benefit of liberty to the blacks, let us forebear from measures of dubious constitutional rightfulness toward our white countrymen—measures of a nature to provoke, among other of the last evils, exterminating hatred of race toward race. In imagination let us place ourselves in the unprecedented position of the Southerners—their position as regards the millions of ignorant manumitted slaves in their midst, for whom some of us now claim the suffrage.[38]

One could read Melville's critique of northern demonization of the South and the utopian visions of black elevation as late in life racism and encroaching conservatism rearing their ugly heads. But a more textured reading of the "Supplement" raises questions not simply regarding the role of whiteness and blackness in the post-Civil War era but the insistence on solving the race problem without first addressing the question of violence. In this way, Melville was allying himself against the Union victors but not necessarily with the southern losers. What seems to have outraged him was the manner in which northern triumphalism marched over the scores of dead bodies, bearing newly emancipated blacks on its shoulders as "cultural treasures" of the war.[39] At the center of his ambivalence is not the so-called "depraved" character of the slave but the method of emancipation. The fact that emancipation was effected only through "agonized violence" rather than "deliberate legislation" presents for Melville the primary obstacle to integrating the formerly enslaved into the newly defeated South. In asking his readers to imagine themselves as southerners extending suffrage to "millions of ignorant manumitted slaves," he echoes the racism of defeated Southerner but also chides the triumphant northerner for what he sees as their own romantic notions of emancipated blacks. In this way, he highlights the tension between the high-minded rhetoric of abolitionist and the brutal method through which emancipation was achieved.

To ask his readers to imagine the fear and loathing of the defeated southerners now forced to cohabit with their former slaves is also to revisit the fears of Thomas Clarkson's Parliamentary adversaries in the late eighteenth century who "foresaw nothing but insurrections of the slaves in our islands, and the massacre of their masters there" should the slave trade be abolished.[40] Also hovering over Melville was the shadow of the St. Domingo uprising in which emancipation was accompanied by mass brutality. In the years of writing *Battle-Pieces* and *Billy Budd*, Melville seems to have viewed the problems of Reconstruction as aftershocks not just of the Civil War and emancipation, but also of the longer history of insurrection, revolution, and abolition. So long as insurrection remained outside the context of the political, it burdened the abolitionist movement with evidence of black savagery.

Melville's later writings, particularly *Billy Budd*, however, suggest, instead, that the real issue was not how to extend the mantle of political legitimacy over slave insurrection, but whether or not *any* act of violence should be considered legitimate, regardless of the politics involved. This uncomfortable question demands that we set aside long-cherished concepts that "good" wars justify violence, and instead examine the nature of violence itself. In examining the nature of violence, Melville seems to indicate, through his deconstruction of Billy Budd's idealized persona, that in idealizing the kind of revolutionary spirit he represents, we risk excusing all of his violent acts. In endorsing an ethos of justifiable violence, we leave ourselves open to inventing a justification where none may exist. When violence becomes political we lose sight of what is problematic about violence.

In her discussion of *Billy Budd*, in *On Revolution*, Hannah Arendt reads Billy as embodying "goodness beyond virtue" who though good must die because, "goodness is strong, stronger perhaps even than wickedness, but that it shares with 'elemental evil' the elementary violence inherent in all strength and detrimental to all forms of political organization."[41] For Arendt then, the problem is that violence is only useful in clearing away the evil that is outside of the political. Conceptually, this reading is apt, but only if one assumes that Melville is primarily concerned with this question of absolute good and absolute evil. Placing the character of Claggart as the embodiment of "absolute evil" locates him as the threat, not only to Billy but also to the political integrity of the *Bellipotent*. But Melville, in locating in Billy all the external features of the heroic ideal only to have him commit murder at the first provocation, indicates that real threat is not Claggart but Billy whose very goodness obscures an unexamined propensity for violence. The loaded imagery that casts Billy in turns as Adam in the garden and "an angel of God," should warn experienced readers of Melville that to accept these metaphors and appellations at face value is probably missing something vital.[42] As with the whiteness of the whale in *Moby-Dick*, Billy's pure goodness is something his crewmates and higher ups read in him and do not necessarily point to that "absolute good" as the full expression of his nature.

One need only look at a moment early in the text for a flash of inscrutability. Upon being impressed into service aboard the *Bellipotent* from the merchant ship the *Rights-of-Man*, Billy who at first seemed to surrender cheerfully to his fate impulsively cries out as the boat departs, "And goodbye to you too, old *Rights-of-Man*."[43] The lieutenant who secures Billy for service on the *Bellipotent* is taken aback and reprimands him for this "terrible breach of naval decorum," but looks on this farewell not "as meant to convey a covert sally on the new recruit's [Billy Budd's] part, a sly slur at impressment in general."[44] The narrator at this point interjects, "for Billy, though happily endowed with the gaiety of health, youth and a free heart, was yet by no means of a satirical turn. . . . To deal in double meanings and insinuations of any sort was quite foreign to his nature."[45] In telling us to disregard any misgivings we might have regarding Billy's cheerful acquiescence to being impressed, Melville, through his narrator, again draws our attention not simply to Billy's nature but to the way in which inscrutability manifests.

Billy's inscrutability reveals itself in relationship to language. Here it is not clear whether or not he means anything. But it is made more explicit with the detail of his stutter, which only manifests in times of stress. This stress is usually in response to bullying. At the time of Billy's impressment, the captain of the *Rights-of-Man* recalls to the lieutenant an incident between Budd and another crewmember called Red-Whiskers. After a period of antagonism Whiskers, according to the captain, "gave him a dig under the ribs." Billy's response is swift. "Quick as lightening Billy let fly an arm. I dare say he never meant to do quite as much as he did, but anyhow he gave the burly fool a terrible drubbing."[46] This moment, spoken of in tones of admiration, is meant to set up Billy as an ideal seaman. He is only dangerous when pushed, and his strength is such that one cannot help but admire him. Red-Whiskers, rather than being outraged, becomes a devoted ally. Violence, at this early point of the novella, gets framed in a way that echoes the staged fight in Equiano's *Narrative*, namely as an initiation exercise. The assumption here is that the violence is not real violence because it does not proceed from motivation or intent but is merely a reaction.

This moment also brings us back to the detail of Billy's stutter as the obvious flaw in his character. Melville's narrator in bringing it up provides us with yet another Biblical metaphor in case we fail to note this as possible foreshadowing:

> Though in the hour of elemental uproar or peril he was everything a sailor should be, yet under sudden provocation of strong heart-feeling, his voice, otherwise singularly musical, as if expressive of the harmony within, was apt to develop an organic hesitancy, in fact, more or less of a stutter or even worse. In this particular Billy was a striking instance that the arch interferer, the envious marplot of Eden, still has more or less to do with every human consignment to this planet of Earth. In every case, one way or another he is sure to slip in his little card as much to remind us—I too have a hand here.[47]

The implication that the stutter represents a crack in Billy's otherwise pristine character operates as both heavy-handed foreshadowing and classic misdirection. For, as we find out later, it is, indeed, the stutter that leads to Billy's tragic fate, but only if one reads what happens in the most superficial way. His stutter stands as a physical sign of original sin only if one ignores the context of Billy's propensity towards violence. Aboard the *Rights-of-Man*, Billy's stutter and the subsequent drubbing of Red-Whiskers must be interpreted against the backdrop of the non-military status of the merchant ship. The stutter, which impedes and sometimes prevents speech, manifests within a context in which to act out violently against an individual of roughly equal rank does not challenge the political order. As a political allegory, Billy's loss of voice does not necessarily entail a loss of agency in defending himself.

The task of interpreting Billy's stutter is further complicated by the emphasis on his extraordinary good looks mentioned later in the text. Whereas the unnamed Handsome Sailor at the beginning of the text is spoken of in terms of his blackness, Billy's looks, likewise, seem to stem from his unmixed whiteness. "Cast in a mold peculiar to the finest physical examples of those Englishmen in whom the Saxon strain would seem not at all to partake of any Norman or other admixture, he showed in fact that humane look of reposeful good nature where the Greek sculptor in some instances gave his heroic strong man Hercules."[48] Billy here is presented as the negative doppelganger of the black handsome sailor of the "unadulterated blood of Ham" mentioned previously. But this emphasis on color, particularly coming after the story about Red-Whiskers, should alert the reader to the similarities of Billy to the black sailor rather than their more obvious differences. To be sure, the character of the black sailor remains a mystery. As mentioned at the beginning of this chapter we only have the allusion to the historical moment to give us some structure. But in creating a stark racial contrast, Melville asks us to look beyond the obvious markers of color.

Which, in turn, brings me back to Washington Goode, the black sailor, and the question of race. If we accept the narrator's Biblical interpretation of Billy's stutter we are also getting further away from the black sailor at the beginning of the chapter, and in doing so forgetting the specter of race that hangs over Billy's character description. In forgetting about the black sailor we are also accepting a non-racialized interpretation of both Billy's propensity towards violence and the implications behind his stutter. We are letting the fact of Billy's Anglo-Saxon purity overwhelm our sense of what is behind his actions.[49] To remember the black sailor is to be forced to reflect on what might be behind Billy's inscrutability and in turn what might be behind the black sailor's "barbaric good humor."[50] For as with Billy, what matters in the Goode case, particularly to his abolitionist defenders, is neither the truth of his innocence or guilt nor the motives behind the murder, an indifference that closes the distance between Goode's haplessness and abjectness and Billy's goodness.

Rather, if we do consider the "true" nature of Billy's motives we are also forced to confront the reality that Billy categorically does not have a revolutionary impulse in him. Melville makes this explicit by having him reject mutiny outright when approached by a fellow crewmate. Billy rebuffs him with, "D—d—damme, I don't know what are d—d—driving at, or what you mean, but you had better g—g—go where you belong! . . . If you d—don't start, I'll t—t—toss you over the r—rail!"[51] The manifestation of his stutter threatens to overwhelm him, but the crewmate retreats and the threat passes. Violence, or the threat of violence, is used here to avoid mutiny. His eagerness to serve diligently as well as his rebuff of the afterguardsman, point to a disposition still inclined to accommodate, rather than undermine authority. His goodness may include goodwill towards his fellow sailors, yet his compassion does not supersede his self-preservation. When witnessing the harsh justice administered aboard the *Bellipotent,* Billy's thoughts are only for himself. The narrator notes:

> This heightened alacrity had its cause, namely the impression made upon him by the first formal gangway-punishment he had ever witnessed. . . . When Billy saw the culprit's naked back under the scourge gridironed with red welts and worse. . . . Billy was horrified. He resolved never through remissness would he make himself liable to such visitation or do or omit aught that might merit even verbal reproof.[52]

As we shall see momentarily in my discussion of *White-Jacket*, Melville's reaction to flogging in the navy was explicitly political. Therefore to present Billy's reaction to flogging in terms so viscerally apolitical would seem to signify Billy's explicit lack of political awareness. Also, given how Billy's conviction plays out, the irony here should not be lost on anyone. However, there is also the manner in which Melville, by declaring Billy's antipathy towards mutiny specifically and disobedience in general, calls into question the relationship between intent and action. Billy's lack of intent and the spontaneity of his action are not revolutionary in the ideal sense of the word. But the fact that, despite this lack of intent, he still manages to commit an act that gets interpreted—or perhaps distorted—as revolutionary begs the question of exactly what constitutes revolutionary possibility. Is it, as has been the case in the previous chapters, the specific political intent behind acts violence perpetrated by slaves or free blacks? Or is it, as Melville seems to be suggesting here, the raw potential of violence to become revolutionary when unleashed in particular circumstances? If revolutionary possibility exists in raw form in ostensibly docile subjects like Billy, over-emphasizing the danger presented by someone like Washington Goode risks missing a closer more uncontrollable threat.

Just to be clear on what precisely happens in the story, the jealous master-of-arms, John Claggart, accuses Billy of mutiny and brings him before Captain Vere. When faced with Claggart's accusation, Billy cannot speak and strikes Claggart who dies instantly. Vere, while sympathetic to Billy, nevertheless convinces the drumhead court that the rule of law must be followed. Billy is, subsequently, convicted and executed for murder and conspiracy to commit mutiny. I will return to the conviction shortly, but I first want to focus on the details of the murder itself. Melville describes the moment that Billy kills Claggart as such: "Quick as a flame from a discharged cannon at night, his right arm shot out, and Claggart dropped to the deck." The act is oddly disconnected from Billy, as though his arm has the entire agency and he does not. Moreover, the reference to a "discharged cannon at night" evokes the poem "The Swamp Angel," which appeared in *Battle-Pieces and Aspects of the War*. The poem compares a maroon in the swamp to the infamous Union war cannon known as The Swamp Angel:

> There is a coal-black Angel
> With a thick Afric lip,
> And he dwells (like the hunted and harried)
> In a swamp where the green frogs dip.
> But his face is against a City
> Which is over a bay of the sea,

> And he breathes with a breath that is blastment,
> And dooms by a far decree.[53]

These two things, the passive language and the reference to the earlier poem, bring Billy's apparently involuntary and spontaneous act of violence into dialogue with the longer history of war, slavery, and slave insurrection. By naming the poem after the war cannon, Melville conflates the extralegal violence of slave insurrection with "legitimate" state violence of the Civil War. The Swamp Angel evokes all of the fears of violence, coalesced in a weapon of war that literally depicts the Union as weaponizing the violence of St. Domingo, Denmark Vesey, and Nat Turner. By allegorizing the target of the Swamp Angel as The City and not as a specific southern city or as the Confederacy, Melville calls into question whether the target of insurrectionist violence is the South or civilization at large. The description of the blow so distinctly echoes this moment that it suggests that, whether he knows it or not, something of this fugitive spirit exists within Billy. The taint of conspiracy is on him before the fateful meeting because a mutiny conspirator has already approached him, suggesting that every act of violence attaches the shadow of blackness to the culprit.

From this moment on, Billy's Anglo-Saxon good looks and personal purity not only fail to save him, but provide Vere the precise thing that the drumhead court is supposed to ignore. "They would think that we flinch, that we are afraid of them—afraid of practicing a lawful rigor singularly demanded at this juncture lest it should provoke new troubles."[54] Vere's words recall to us the case of Washington Goode, whose race Aspinwall invoked as a reason for the court to be lenient, only rather than whiteness as purity it is Goode's blackness and depravity the court should have taken into consideration. Contrast Aspinwall's use of "darkness" with the narrator's early description of Billy, whose alleged purity of blood obscures his propensity towards violence, even as we learn that when provoked, he stutters, and when he loses his voice he strikes. Vere's insistence on, as Gregg Crane has suggested, viewing the law as "a choice between opposed values" is literally viewing Billy's situation as black or white.[55]

In describing the murder, Melville seems to haven taken key details from the Goode case and inverted them in interesting ways. Authorities found Harding with both a knife wound to the abdomen and a blow to the head. Billy kills Claggart with a blow to the head. However, when the report of the crime appears in the naval chronicle *News of the Mediterranean*, as recounted in the text, Claggart is described as having been "vindictively stabbed to the heart by the suddenly drawn sheath knife of Budd."[56] By separating the blow from the stabbing in his telling of the story, Melville appears to be creating narrative confusion with regards to Claggart's murder—although the reader knows the blow is the true method, the stabbing transforms the spontaneous act of violence into an act more calculating.

The only difference between Goode and Billy is the assumed propensity toward violence attributed to the former and the known propensity toward violence in the latter. And as we recall Shaw's words to Goode at his sentencing, it was merely the *appearance* of his propensity toward violence that seems to have given judge and jury license to convict him. If our sensibilities are outraged at the treatment of Goode, it would seem that Melville is suggesting that our sympathy toward Billy may be misplaced. Yet Billy's "guilt" also sits uneasily with most readers. The shared fates of the real-life Goode and the fictional Billy Budd despite the differences in their guilt or innocence renders the condemned the same. What Melville shows is that the reason we cannot fully embrace violence by blacks is that we are not entirely certain we can embrace violence at all. But rather than confront this ambiguity, we render justice imperfectly and often in ways that insure more violence to come.

REVISITING RACE AND SHIPBOARD VIOLENCE IN *WHITE-JACKET*

If there is little direct evidence that the Goode case was on Melville's mind during the writing of *White-Jacket*, it is clear that he was already thinking about these specific intersections of race, violence, and the rule of law. In 1849, the year of the Goode case, Melville wrote *White-Jacket,* a fictionalized account of his years in the American Navy. Embedded in the satire is an impassioned three-chapter passage denouncing the practice of flogging. Although *White-Jacket* devotes the heart of its critique to flogging, as Elizabeth Barnes writes, "White-Jacket our narrator is also appalled by the number of offenses for which a sailor might be executed."[57] This section of the novel opens with a description of the flogging of several sailors for fighting amongst themselves.

> "You John, you Peter, you Mark, you Antone," said the Captain, "were yesterday found fighting on the gun-deck. Have you anything to say?"
> Mark and Antone, two steady, middle-aged men, whom I had often admired for their sobriety, replied that they did not strike the first blow; that they had submitted to much before they had yielded to their passions; but as they acknowledged that they had, at last, defended themselves, their excuse was overruled.

John—a brutal bully, who, it seems, was the real author of the disturbance—was about entering into a long extenuation, when he was cut short by being made to confess, irrespective of the circumstances, that he had been in the fray.[58]

Although the captain asks for their reasons, he quickly disregards motive in determining culpability and punishment. For our purposes, the fate of Peter, "a handsome lad about nineteen years old," who was "a great favorite in his part of the ship," is the primary focus of this analysis.[59]

That morning two of his young mess-mates had gone to his bag, taken out his best clothes, and, obtaining the permission of the marine sentry at the "brig" had handed them to him, to be put on against being summoned to the mast. This was done to propitiate the Captain, as most captains love to see a tidy sailor. But it would not do. To all his supplications the Captain turned a deaf ear. Peter declared that he had been struck twice before he had returned the blow. "No matter," said the Captain, "you struck at last, instead of reporting the case to an officer. I allow no man to fight on board here but myself. *I* do the fighting."[60]

The parallels to the character Billy Budd are fairly obvious: a handsome and popular youth defending himself is nevertheless condemned to suffer the consequences of his actions. Unlike Vere, however, Claret is clearly interested in the consolidation of power rather than the rule of law. The fact that he, and not his crewmembers, "does the fighting," undercuts his admonition that Peter should have respected the chain of command. Peter's attempt to mitigate his punishment by presenting himself to the captain as a tidy and civilized portrait also offers an interesting parallel to the notion in *Billy Budd* that a good and obedient sailor invariably looks the part. But the fact that White Jacket's captain is indifferent to Peter's appearance further underscores the irrelevance of individual character and behavior aboard navy ships. Peter takes his flogging harder than his shipmates, shouting, "*My God! Oh! my God!*" and writhing and leaping to escape the lash. Once it is over, he declares "I don't care what happens to me now. . . . I have been flogged once, and they may do it again if they will. Let them look out for me now!"[61] The implication here is that flogging has possibly placed Peter on the road to further insubordination and possibly insurrection. Subsequently, Melville uses this scene in the chapter "A Flogging," the ruining of a good sailor to launch his argument outlined in next three chapters titled "Some of the Evil Effects of Flogging," "Flogging Not Lawful," and "Flogging Not Necessary,"

No matter, then, what may by the consequences of its abolition; no matter if we have to dismantle our fleets, and our unprotected commerce should fall a prey to the spoiler, the awful admonitions of justice and humanity demand that abolition without procrastination; in a voice that is not to be mistaken, demand that abolition to-day. It is not a dollar-and-cent question of expediency; it is a matter of *right and wrong*. And if any man can lay his hand on his heart, and solemnly say that this scourging is right, let that man but once feel the lash on his own back, and in his agony you will hear the apostate call the seventh heavens to witness that it is wrong.[62]

His language echoes abolitionist calls for immediate emancipation of the nation's slaves regardless of the potential practical consequences. Melville's use of abolitionist rhetoric seems surprising given his well-documented ambivalence towards abolitionists. At this moment, however, Melville's commitment to the "essential dignity of man, which no legislator has a right to violate" supersedes any concern about order and control. Abolitionist rhetoric allows him to make this argument by providing the parallel of slave flogging in the South, which in highlighting the outrage done to the individual, also draws out the problem of treating large groups of individuals in such a way. As when Douglass describes the flogging of his aunt Hester in *The Narrative of the Life of a Slave*, and impresses on the reader the "terrible spectacle" of the "warm red blood . . . dripping to the floor," Melville's use of the example of Peter conjures a similar sense of outrage.[63] The charge for his readers to "feel the lash on [their backs]" in the same manner that Stowe repeatedly exhorts her readers to imagine the scenes she puts before them in *Uncle Tom's Cabin*, further emphasizes the links between the language of abolition and that of naval reform.

In a scene following the impassioned three-chapter diatribe against flogging, Melville describes an incident in which two black seamen are made to fight in a scene reminiscent of the mock fighting described in Equiano's *Interesting Narrative*, which I discussed in the first chapter. In *White-Jacket*, a man called May-Day, described as "a full-blooded *bull-negro*" and Rose-Water, described as a "slender and rather handsome mulatto," are compelled by Captain Claret to engage in head-bumping for his entertainment. "*Head-bumping* . . . consists in two negroes (whites will not answer) butting at each other like rams."[64] Whereas in *Interesting Narrative*, Equiano's adversary is a white sailor around his own age, which allows him to frame the fighting for sport in terms that suggest the ship as a space for the forging of bonds through fighting with and against each other, the dynamic here in *White-Jacket* is voyeuristic and compulsory.

That this is all about containment becomes apparent when, after the sport is over, May-Day, having won the "fight," doubles down on his victory by baiting Rose-Water in a deliberately incendiary fashion. The narrator reports:

Accordingly, after they had been bumping one evening to the Captain's content, May-Day confidentially told Rose-Water that he considered him a "*nigger*," which, among some blacks, is held a great term of reproach. Fired at the insult, Rose-Water gave May-Day to understand that he utterly erred, for his mother, a black slave, had been one of the mistresses of a Virginia planter belonging to one of the oldest families in that state. Another insulting remark followed this innocent disclosure; retort followed retort in a word, at last came together in mortal combat. . . . "Rig the gratings," said the Captain. "I'll teach you two men, though I now and then permit you to *play*, I will have no *fighting*. Do your duty, boatswain's mate!" And the negroes were flogged.[65]

First, it is worth noting that the nature of the argument turns on the deployment of "nigger" as a slur between two blacks. At issue here is the status May-Day has gained over Rose-Water in the eyes of Captain Claret. In having May-Day, a "full-blooded negro," calling Rose-Water, "a mulatto," "nigger" Melville seems to be suggesting that the pitting of black seamen against each other operates as a weapon of control in keeping this part of the crew at each other's throats. That this real fight, the result of a staged fight, also leads to a flogging further reinforces the larger theme of patriarchal control exercised in the navy.

But the key to the scene is Claret's words to the culprits: "I'll teach you two men, though I now and then permit you to *play*, I will have no *fighting*." This distinction between playing and fighting puts into stark relief the distinct manner in which racialized violence is categorized in terms of either useful spectacle or threat to order. Even a rather disheartening squabble over who is really a "nigger" seems to threaten to break into insurrectionist impulse. It is almost as if Claret recognizes, if May-Day and Rose-Water as yet do not, the political threat latent in the argument. At any moment the question of who really is a "nigger" threatens to become, who defines these terms and why do we accept them. The punishment of flogging, done to reinforce the distinction between blacks at *play* and blacks *fighting*, brings to the fore the strict categories in which blacks exist within the *Neversink*'s hierarchy. The use of the head-butting as a crucial mechanism of racial control reveals itself to be an imperfect method of releasing the specter of insurrection aboard the ship. Once it threatens to manifest concretely, flogging becomes the only way to exorcise it.

It is important to think about this scene in relationship to the impassioned diatribe against flogging mentioned above because, in showing the distinct conditions faced by blacks aboard the ship, Melville appears to introduce a possible wrinkle into the rhetoric of navy reformers that compared the treatment of sailors to the treatment of slaves. In most ways the treatment of May-Day and Rose-Water is not materially different from that of Peter and his companions. But the inciting factor, the head-butting command from Captain Claret, reveals how race, or rather the perception of racialized violence, alters the conditions under which violence both occurs and is dealt with. White sailors, Melville suggests, are not subject to being used in this kind of spectacle because white violence does not exist in the popular imagination in the same way that black violence does. While sailors of all ethnic stripes were stigmatized because of the supposed hardening effects of life at sea, black sailors whether or free or slave, carried with them the added menace of the threat of insurrection.[66] Yet, whether or not fighting aboard ships is mutinous, insurrectionist, or driven by personal grievances, the practice of flogging erases these distinctions. Claret's method of control is to keep the idea of black sailor violence distinct from that of white sailors. As White-Jacket himself observes following this scene as he contemplates Rose-water's fate:

> Poor mulatto! thought I, one of an oppressed race, they degrade you like a hound. Thank God! I am a white. Yet I had seen whites also scourged; for, black or white, all my shipmates were liable to that. Still there is something in us, somehow, that in the most degraded condition, we snatch at a chance to deceive ourselves into a fancied superiority to others, whom we suppose lower in the scale than ourselves.[67]

The effectiveness of Claret's use of racialized difference is shown by the fact that even White-Jacket, who has expressed an objection to flogging on the basis of its universal assault on the dignity of all men, is nevertheless prey to seeing his situation as a white sailor as fundamentally different from that of a black sailor. The apostrophic "Poor mulatto!" with its distinct overtones of romantic racialism acts as a distancing method even as he reluctantly admits the illusory nature of this comfort. While "whipping forces an identification between white and black men whose 'common bond' is powerlessness," its ties to racialized slavery also allow for race to create the perception of difference.[68]

   To return to the case of Washington Goode and Shaw's words at sentencing, the head-butting scene points to something disingenuous about ascribing Goode's supposed guilt to his having indulged in the worst aspects of sailor life. Shaw seems to be finding refuge from accusations of one kind of prejudice in another less incendiary one. If Goode's lack of moral fiber is one that is easily comparable to other white sailors, Shaw is only guilty of overzealous sentencing. But what this scene shows us is that the conditions under which black violence occurs are so circumscribed by fear of insurrection that justice that looks equal on the surface, is impossible so long as this fear persists. Shaw's failure, or refusal, to see this issue points to a fundamental problem with too-easy comparisons of sailor flogging with the poor treatment of slaves. Abolitionists who pointed to the poor treatment of sailors, as discussed in the first chapter, did so as a way of using that parallel to invite sympathy for the slave through the sailor. But what the Goode case demonstrates is the ways in which that comparison risks erasing fundamental differences in the way race bends our views of violent acts. Moreover, that comparison also misses the crucial fact that there is a very clear difference between the temporary deprivation of liberty that comes from enlisting or being impressed into service, and being somebody else's property.

The example of the Purser's slave Guinea drives this point home. Guinea is described as the very picture of a carefree seaman. "Faring sumptuously in the ward-room; sleek and round, his ebon face fairly polished with content; ever gay and hilarious; ever ready to laugh and joke, that African slave was actually envied by many of the seamen. There were times when I almost envied him myself. Lemsford once envied him outright. 'Ah Guinea!' he sighed, 'you have peaceful times; you never opened the book I read in.'"[69] White-Jacket here seems to fall into the kind of rhetoric which compares sailor and slave treatment in such a way that makes slavery seem more palatable. The depiction of Guinea is also resonant with the image of the handsome black sailor in *Billy Budd*, whose slave status is actually unknown. He further undercuts this image of the happy negro by describing the following scene:

> One morning, when all hands were called to witness punishment, the Purser's slave, as usual, was observed to be hurrying down the ladders toward the ward-room, his face wearing that peculiar, pinched blueness, which, in the negro, answers to the paleness caused by nervous agitation in the white. . . . "Where are you going, Guinea?" said this officer. . . . "*'Scuse* me, *massa*!" said the slave, with a low salutation; "I can't 'tand it; I can't, indeed, massa!" and, so saying, he disappeared beyond the hatchway. He was the only person on board, except the hospital-steward and the invalids of the sick-bay, who was exempted from being present at the administering of the scourge. Accustomed to light and easy duties from his birth, and so fortunate as to meet with none but gentle masters, Guinea, though a bondman, liable to be saddled with a mortgage, like a horse—Guinea, in India-rubber manacles, enjoyed the liberties of the world.[70]

White-Jacket here toggles between total earnestness and deep irony. The envy he feels at Guinea's exemption from the summons to witness a flogging, an ordeal he describes as the sound of "doom" to a sensitive seaman, is tempered by the clear sense that Guinea's position as a well-treated slave entails a kind of precariousness he cannot fathom.[71] This set of emotions, for Melville, presents a conundrum. The distinctions between slaves and freemen are such that comparisons between the flogging of sailors and the flogging of slaves become limited when one considers the permanence of slavery versus the temporariness of the sailor life. However, Billy's visceral fear of the lash in *Billy Budd* so exactly echoes Guinea's that it also raises the question of how much these distinctions should matter.[72]

Melville never solves the problem presented by May-Day, Rose-Water, and Guinea. Nor, as I mentioned at the outset, does this constitute evidence that Washington Goode lurks in some small way in these depictions. But it is worth looking at the interplay between flogging, mutiny, and race in *White-Jacket* for elements that he would explore in *Benito Cereno*. Here one might read the Goode case as providing further insight into the problems inherent in both using black violence as a rallying cry for emancipation and demonizing black violence as something separate and terrifying.

THE OTHER BLACK SAILOR

At the end of *Benito Cereno*, Melville's fictionalization of the shipboard mutiny aboard the *Tryal*, Amaso Delano and the traumatized Cereno reflect on the outcome of the shipboard insurrection. The discrepancy between Delano's contentment with the outcome and Cereno's continued unease could be attributed to the fact that Cereno suffered more at the hands of the slave. Initially, Cereno commends Delano for finally seeing through the charade: "So far may even the best man err, in judging the conduct of one with the recesses of whose condition he is not acquainted. But you were forced to it; and you were in time undeceived."[73] Cereno here appears to be implying a kinship with Delano forged over their shared experience and understanding. However, what follows is an exchange that reveals that a gulf still exists between what Cereno comprehends and Delano's vision:

> "You are saved," cried Captain Delano, more and more astonished and pained; "you are saved; what has cast such a shadow upon you?"
> "The negro."
> There was silence while the moody man sat, slowly and unconsciously, gathering his mantle about him, as if it were a pall.[74]

Delano's confusion at Cereno's fearful melancholy, even after the execution of his nemesis, Babo, reveals his faith in the rule of law after having tried and convicted the insurrectionists of the *San Dominick*. Despite the gaps in the deposition, Delano believes in the completeness of the narrative of the insurrection. In contrast, Cereno, who is the firsthand witness to the atrocities perpetrated by Babo and his followers, has more complete knowledge of the insurrection, knowledge that keeps him from celebrating their demise and silences him in the face of Delano's optimism.

The shadow of "the negro" cast over Cereno and the end of *Benito Cereno* would appear to reflect the fear of American southerners, as well as some in the North, that the plague of insurrection might spread, despite the best efforts at suppression. There is some ambiguity as to what—or who—it is that Cereno fears. Is "the negro" in question Babo, and does Cereno refrain from invoking his name for fear of conjuring him? Is it the body of slaves from the *San Dominick?* Or is it, in the end, all so-called "negroes"?

If *White-Jacket* contains within it a critique of importing abolitionist rhetoric to critique practices of flogging without fully understanding the fundamental differences in the way black and white violence is perceived,—*Benito Cereno*—expands on that critique by calling into question the heroic images that proliferated in the wake of the *Amistad* case. Melville's depiction of Babo as the deceptive ringleader of the mutiny forces us to consider the consequences of every act of insurrection through the same revolutionary lens. Babo, at once monstrous and opaque, appears as the very incarnation of racist fears of black violence. Yet, he also fails to fully materialize within the text, appearing either as the solicitous body servant of Cereno or the cold-blooded killer of the court deposition.

This failure to materialize could be read as failure of imagination on Melville's part. Indeed, the opacity of Babo and his fellow insurrectionists is so complete as to render them as merely shadows. But this reading only holds up if one insists on reading through Delano's lens as Melville's narrator somewhat ironically warns us not to do. His "singularly undistrustful good nature" is not framed as a positive but more as a possible sign of intellectual poverty. "Whether, in view of what humanity is capable, such a trait implies, along with a benevolent heart, more than ordinary quickness and accuracy of intellectual perception, may be left to the wise to determine."[75] The challenge issued to the reader here seems obvious: if one overvalues Delano's apparent goodness and misses his lack of intellect one cannot be numbered among "the wise."

Much has been made of Babo's cleverness in staging this elaborate charade. But what is striking about the novella, at least up to the point when all is revealed, is how close the charade is to failing at every moment in the text. The unfettered slaves, the open display of weapons, the odd moments of insolence and violence all alert the reader to the danger about to erupt. Babo's cleverness, therefore, has less to do with the quality of the deception he mounts than it does with how he understands his dupe. While Melville's narrator notes that Delano's failure to pierce the veil of the charade is, in large part, due to his "singularly undistrustful good nature," he is also careful to draw attention to every instance in which Delano perceives the danger around him and then fails to act on it.[76] Delano has been traditionally understood as standing in for white racist assumptions surrounding the character of blacks. At times aping the benign paternalism of the slaveholder or the romantic racialism of the white abolitionist, in the words of Eric J. Sundquist, "he constantly enacts the mechanics of oppression . . . in the sense that his refusal to understand the 'shadow' that has descended upon Benito Cereno is itself a psychological and politically repressive act that replicates the ideology of America's crisis over slavery."[77] But seeing Delano as both trusting and reflexively blind and racist does not quite get at the mechanics of the charade at play aboard the *San Dominick* during the bulk of the novella. Rather, the success of Babo's charade depends upon Delano deliberately ignoring the rather blatant cues that something is amiss.

These cues are not so much masked as they are offset by Babo's adoption of the devoted manservant role. While Delano notes the "noisy indocility of the blacks in general," it is Babo's "steady good conduct" that reassures him.[78] This suggests that insurrection is easily overlooked so long as there is at least one so-called happy slave to provide evidence of slavery as a benign institution. In Delano's case, Babo's act more than reassures him; it causes him to wax rhapsodic on the beauty of the master-slave relationship. "As master and man stood before him, the black upholding the white, Captain Delano could not but bethink him of the beauty of that relationship which could present such a spectacle of fidelity on the one hand and confidence on the other."[79]

Delano's failure to see beyond the tableau of happy slaves presented to him more than simply satirizing white myopia on race, explicitly calls out the failure of white anti-slavery activists to understand the specific politics of insurrection as not solely sourced in mistreatment but born out of resentment of the loss of liberty. But it is only effective because Babo read him correctly as being easily distracted by the "good slave act."

A closer look at the use of Atufal as decoy illustrates the layers of Melville's critique. Within the framework of the story, Atufal is meant to preempt Delano's suspicions that anything is amiss aboard the *San Dominick*.

> Captain Delano's attention was caught by the moving figure of a gigantic black, emerging from the general crowd below, and slowly advancing towards the elevated poop. An iron collar was about his neck, from which depended a chain, thrice wound round his body; the terminating links padlocked together at a broad band of iron, his girdle.
> "How like a mute Atufal moves," murmured the servant.

> The black mounted the steps of the poop, and like a brave prisoner, brought up to receive sentence, stood in unquailing muteness before Don Benito, now recovered from his attack.
>
> At the first glimpse of his approach, Don Benito had started, a resentful shadow swept over his face; and, as with the sudden memory of bootless rage, his white lips glued together.
>
> This is some mulish mutineer, thought Captain Delano, surveying not without a mixture of admiration, the colossal form of the negro.[80]

The use of Atufal as both a pantomime for Delano's benefit and a tool for Cereno's humiliation works in this scene because it allows Babo to play on both the romanticized idea of the black revolutionary and the more menacing image of the insurrectionist. Atufal's hulking chained presence makes a mockery of both images. Atufal is both the pro-slavery fantasy of containment as well as the anti-slavery fantasy of nobility barely contained. In making Atufal the very image of Douglass's "Herculean" yet "fettered" Madison Washington, Melville puts the performative aspects of slave revolution into sharp relief.[81] The tolling of the bell, the chains, the muteness, and the alleged repetition of the act over the course of sixty days reframes revolution as a set of scene directions, lines, and props. That Babo as orchestrator knows his audience so well points to the fundamental problem of white expectations of black revolution whether romanticized or sensationalized. Melville's question circles what we expect violence, particularly slave violence, to look like and how the reality of slave violence challenges white readers' views of both race and violence. As Jonathan Elmer notes, this scene "encodes a further political fantasy as well: Delano consumes a vision of domination and sovereign power uncontaminated by consent and capitulation. . . . Atufal's refusal is meant to suggest that freedom is not worth having under those conditions."[82] This tableau of the chained slave, so often used in abolitionist iconography, becomes in Melville's dark satire a pointed critique of abolitionist rhetoric that redeploys the ringing declaration—"Give me Liberty or give me death!"—in a manner that, nevertheless, insists on slave abjection even as it claims to abhor it. This satire becomes even more pointed once we realize that Babo's slavish devotion to Cereno obscures his true position aboard the *San Dominick*. That slave abjection has been the vehicle through which insurrection has succeeded, or temporarily succeeded, forces us to consider Delano's misrecognition of the true threat in light of our own racialized views of violence. If this masquerade is meant to argue that there is "no future . . . for the experiment of American democracy" so long as the issue of slavery remained unresolved, it also exposes the inability of whites to recognize insurrection less as a failure of imagination and more as a deliberate exercise in disavowal.[83] Delano's misrecognition of Atufal as the real threat further allegorizes the tendency of whites to see black violence in terms of either an aesthetic representation of an idealized hero or a brute safely contained. The danger of this binary is not simply the potential threat it poses to the new republic, but the threat it also poses to the idea of justice.

Cereno's unease at the end of the novella ostensibly speaks to the fear of future Babos. But, coming as it does in the wake of the trial and execution of Babo and the ringleaders, Cereno's fear of "the negro" implies not the dread of a mass uprising, but rather the opacity of "the negro" as a human subject. Neither Cereno's experience as a somewhat tolerant slave trader nor as the hostage of insurrectionists has been sufficient to reveal the true nature of Babo and his followers. Moreover, the deposition fails as a forensic exercise. Cereno's perception of the legal process gives him more reason to fear Babo than his ordeal aboard the San Dominick. We are only given "extracts" of the full deposition. We are also reminded that this is a translation from the Spanish, putting us as readers at a double remove from the text, triple if you consider that Spanish is, in all probability, not spoken by a number of the defendants. Finally, as Melville's narrator admits in his short preface, Cereno's own testimony was held in some doubt. "Some disclosures therein were, at the time, held dubious for both learned and natural reasons. The tribunal inclined to the opinion that the deponent, not undisturbed in mind by recent events, raved of some things which never could have happened. But subsequent depositions of the surviving sailors, bearing out the revelations of the strangest particulars, gave credence to the rest."[84] In an ironic twist of fate, Cereno finds himself in the position of Clarkson's slaves by needing the testimony of sailors to lend credence to his own experience of trauma aboard a slave ship. The administration of justice so heavily rests on the question of what could and could not happen in the eyes of the court alerts Cereno to the consequences of rendering slave insurrection "unthinkable." As a witness to insurrection, his own claims become subject to the same skepticism, thereby rendering his testimony "tainted." This taint, or shadow if you will, obscures the administration of justice to the point where knowledge of insurrection is always under threat of obfuscation or eradication.

Melville makes Cereno's unease our own by structuring the novella first in the style of a Gothic horror story, and then as merely the container for a legal case. This structuring destabilizes our sense of narrative by simultaneously giving us the sense that we know everything that happened and that we know nothing. The deposition gives the illusion of full disclosure but bars the reader from actually achieving complete understanding. The language itself has a distancing effect. On the one hand, the dryness of the long list of atrocities highlights the horror—the lack of embellishment adding starkness to the action described. "Babo commanded the Ashantee Martinqui and the Ashanti Leche to go and commit murder; that those two went down with hatchets to the berth of Don Alexandro; that, yet half alive and mangled, they dragged him on the deck; that they were going to throw him overboard."[85] And the strategic omissions create more questions even as they answer others. One such example describes the killing of the mate, Raneds, in the following fashion:

> [Various particulars of the prolonged and perplexed navigation ensuing here follow, with incidents of a calamitous calm, from which portion one passage is extracted, to wit:]
> —That on the fifth day of the calm, all on board suffering much from the heat, and want of water, and five having died in fits, and mad the negroes became irritable, and for a chance gesture, which they deemed suspicious—though it was harmless—made by the mate, Raneds, to the deponent, in the act of handing a quadrant, they killed him; but for this they afterwards were sorry the mate being the only remaining navigator on board except the deponent.[86]

The language here glosses over the actions of Raneds as harmless as stated by Cereno, the deponent in question, portraying the insurrectionists as both crazed by lack of food and water, and oblivious to long-term thinking concerning the killing of a navigator. However, when one considers the tool in question, the quadrant, the question of the harmlessness of the gesture becomes murky. While not ostensibly a weapon, one can imagine the quadrant being wielded as a weapon, in which case the gesture, be it merely a physical reflex or a genuine attempt at retaliation, becomes more difficult to interpret easily. As a legal text, the deposition nevertheless interprets the testimony in such a way that renders the insurrectionists actions as more chaotic than sensible.

Complicating all of this is the manner in which, despite Melville's critique of the justice system as it applies to race and violence, the text does in no way endorse slave insurrection as a viable solution to slavery. The same restrictive narrative construction that prevents us from confidently calling Babo and his followers evil also stands in the way of a reading that ascribes to them more noble motives than murder. If the slaveholder is blind to the character he seeks to control, the abolitionist is equally blind to that which he seeks to liberate. Moreover, the extreme brutality of their conduct combined with their unfortunate fate casts doubt on the morality of their actions. Melville's portrayal of Babo as a cunning mastermind directing his followers to kill Spanish sailors undermines any potential heroism. In setting the action of the novel aboard a slave ship and limiting Babo's capacity to control events, Melville makes it impossible for Babo to invert the master-slave relationship between Cereno and himself fully. Furthermore, although playing the part of the good slave solidifies his power, it also serves to undermine his control. In silencing Cereno by forcing him to "play" the role of master, Babo also silences himself. His words throughout the text are those of the slave, and if he speaks to assert his control, his words must be those of a slave.

This failure of insurrection to upend the slave system and become truly revolutionary is emblematized by Babo's persistent silence throughout the text. This silence, characterized first by the false voice of the happy slave and then by the secondhand voice of the deposition, is at the heart of Melville's critique of both the slaveholding south and northern abolitionists. The insistence on perceiving insurrection either through the lens of brute savagery or revolutionary heroism ignores the absence of a legal framework that allows for black subjects to speak for themselves. The consequences of perceiving black violence as either wholly outside of the political realm or operating within the confines of abolitionist rhetoric are, firstly, that black subjects who commit violent acts must either be above reproach, as was the case with Joseph Cinqué, or pitied as abject brutes, as was the case with Washington Goode. This means that legal cases involving black defendants never escape getting trapped in one of these two narratives.

Secondly, the perception that black violence is wholly different from the kind of violence committed by whites threatens not only to cement imbalances in the application of justice but allows for atrocities to be perceived as more or less justified depending on the race of the alleged culprit. If we take the example of Jesse Pomeroy mentioned at the beginning of the chapter, the commutation of the death sentence for a convicted serial killer, versus that of Washington Goode, the execution of a man convicted under highly dubious circumstances, we see that violence loses meaning in relationship to race. If we expand on this example to take the comparative justness of the American Civil War with the savageness of the Haitian revolution into account, one sees not only how wars get narrated as "good" or "bad" but how this narration is not possible without the complicity of ostensibly progressive political movements. In lionizing the Cinqués and demonizing the Babos and the Veseys, we force a morality upon human subjects while at the same time treating their very humanness as still up for debate. In doing the same with large-scale conflagrations, we also elide atrocity done in the name of the good. For this reason, the question of Babo's heroism or villainy is irrelevant. Whether he is guilty or innocent, justice should look at his actions with disinterest. In a world in which his actions are never his own to explain but rather open to interpretation under this false binary, passing as a hero is no guarantee that he will be viewed as fully human but rather as a kind of avatar of the savagery of the Haitian revolution.

Babo, perceiving the impossible situation he is in, decides that his only recourse is becoming silent voluntarily. "Seeing all was over, he uttered no sound, and could not be forced to. His aspect seemed to say, since I cannot do deeds I will not speak words."[87] The lesson he appears to have learned is that a fully realized revolution is unavailable to him outside of the abolitionist narrative of revolution. Silence becomes both a defense mechanism against having his story coopted and the acknowledgment of defeat in the face of opposing forces, pro and anti-slavery, that insist on narrow constructions of revolutionary violence. The treatment of his body following his execution completes the process of rendering him voiceless. "The body was burned to ashes; but for many days the head, that hive of subtlety, fixed on a pole in the Plaza, met, unabashed, the gaze of the whites."[88] The figurative death of the slave persona and the literal death of the insurrectionist empty Babo of any identity save that of "the negro."

The absence of a fully realized subject calls to mind the court documents of the Denmark Vesey trial and silenced defendants and the anonymous shipboard insurrectionists from Thomas Clarkson's collected testimonies. His silence both seems to confirm his monstrousness but also calls into question the very nature of insurrection itself. By stripping away that idealist revolutionary framework Melville essentially forces defenders of insurrection to confront their own racist assumptions about what constitutes justifiable violence. And while this text has the most tenuous relationship to the Washington Goode case of the three discussed in this chapter, in challenging readers' to see beyond the framework of race in assessing the guilt or innocence of a particular black subject, *Benito Cereno*—obliquely critiques the outcome of that case. If we have fewer questions regarding Babo's guilt than we do regarding Goode's, we also have possibly as many questions regarding his "true character."

CONCLUSION

Melville's abhorrence of violence appears not only to be a reaction to the brutality of the Civil War but also to the rhetoric of justified force taken up by the Union. These misgivings manifest themselves in earlier texts such as *White-Jacket, Moby-Dick, Benito Cereno,* and in *Battle-Pieces.* In taking up slavery, the Union inoculated itself against moral quandary. While almost all of his readers agree that the violence of the war dismayed Melville, discussion of his Civil War poems tends to revolve around his sympathy for the South and the failure of Reconstruction.[89] Rather than viewing his disillusionment as "a shift in his sympathies away from the slaves his antebellum fiction champions, and towards their defeated masters," it is perhaps more accurate to view it instead as his frustration with the unstable and vulnerable position of blacks in the Reconstruction-era South.[90] For Melville, the abolitionists' eventual embrace of violence constitutes a naïve and overly positive approach to the slavery problem.

If, as Maurice S. Lee writes, the Melville who wrote *Benito Cereno* was "compel[led] to imagine a future discussion in which, hopefully, speech is more profitably practiced and some truths are not beyond words," the Melville at the time of *Billy Budd*'s conception despaired altogether of discourse as a revelatory tool. In *Billy Budd,* lack of eloquence is tied to violent acts, and the return of eloquence does not reveal any truths or provide any comfort. Instead, discourse becomes a means of obfuscation and rationalization. Billy's blow becomes criminalized for the good of the *Bellipotent* and the British Navy. Captain Vere becomes the avatar for the role of discourse in manufacturing political narratives of violence in service to a larger political narrative regarding violence and mutiny. Lost in this narrative is the sense of Billy's humanity.

Billy Budd, Sailor ends with a sailor's song called "Billy In The Darbies," darbies being nautical slang for "irons or handcuffs."

> So I'll shake a friendly hand ere I sink.
> But—no! It's dead then I'll be, come to think.
> I remember Taff the Welshman when he sank.
> And his cheek it was like the budding pink.
> But me they'll lash in hammock, drop me deep.
> Fathoms down, fathoms down, how I'll dream fast asleep.
> I feel it stealing now, Sentry, are you there?
> Just ease these derbies at the wrist,
> And roll me over fair!
> I am sleepy, and the oozy weeds about me twist.[91]

This song acts as a counter-narrative to the news piece that appeared regarding Billy's crime in *News of the Mediterranean*. Lost is any sense of Billy as the perpetrator of a crime, and what remains is merely the lament of the dead sailor. Written in the style of a "corpse poem," "Billy In The Darbies," instead focuses on the tragedy of loss while also burying the crime.[92] The poem sits uneasily with the reader, performing a different kind of erasure than that of the libelous news item. It also carries the promise, or threat, if you will, of possible future mutinies as this song escapes the confines of the *Bellipotent* and makes its way to other ships and other sailors. The drowned corpse conjures images of drowned slaves from the *Zong* atrocity, recalling us once again to the Black Sailor at the beginning of the text doubling the sense of loss and mystery. Billy's fate becomes tied to that of the *Zong* slaves as well as Denmark Vesey, Washington Goode, and his fictional counterpart Babo.

WHILE ONE MUST ALWAYS BE cautious in drawing direct lessons from the past when confronting the problems of the present, it is difficult not to see some possible resonances between the story I have told over the previous four chapters and several issues that concern us at present. As we have seen in that story, while the rooting of abolitionist arguments against the slave trade in objections to the treatment of enslaved Africans was successful in eliciting public outrage against mistreatment and abuse, this strategy limited the capacity of abolitionists to see and depict slave insurrection as deriving from rational claims by the enslaved that they deserved full consideration as political equals with the whites who were oppressing them. Even the most radical foes of slavery like Frederick Douglass found it difficult to escape the reticence of abolitionist discourse around insurrection. And as Melville correctly showed, the "hive of subtlety" that was the mind of Babo remained opaque if not invisible to the Captain Delanos of the north who continued to imagine that blacks just might be suited for subordinate roles, provided they were treated well by their masters. Equal protection and liberty under the law remained unimaginable. The violence of *Benito Cereno* starkly illustrated the outcome of such blindness. In Babo, Melville created a character who escapes the white gaze. The reader knows that their view of him is woefully blinkered but cannot see beyond that awareness to the real person beyond. This suggests that while Melville could see the necessity of insurrection in creating "a more perfect union," he could not fathom a future in which this fact was recognized by whites.

When Billy Budd unwittingly bids farewell to the *Rights of Man* and is left mute in the face of injustice, his violent response seems almost required. His obliviousness to the loss of freedom resulting from impressment reflects the way in which whiteness obscures underlying inequalities and in doing so creates within whites a potentially dangerous blindness. Billy's inability to articulate the helplessness he feels reminds us of the dangers of failing to allow the marginalized a political voice. It is only through the actions of Captain Vere before the drumhead court that we are able to identify Billy with someone like Washington Goode. It is also a stark warning to those who see whiteness as providing wholesale protection against injustice. For it is not simply that Billy's whiteness fails to protect him but that it also fails to allow others to note his propensity towards violence as a potentially fatal flaw. If the danger presented by Babo is in the failure to recognize the political import of the violence he commits, the danger presented by Billy is in the failure to see the potential for violence in an idealized white body.

In the years since starting this project, first as a dissertation and then as a book, the issue of racialized violence has exploded onto the public imagination in the wake of the murders of Trayvon Martin, Mike Brown, and Freddie Gray to name a few. Over the last few years, as evidenced by such phenomena as the rise of #BlackLivesMatter and the emergence of Ta-Nehisi Coates as a prominent commentator on racial inequality, reckoning with the consequences of lethal violence has appeared to energize new forms of political protest. These voices of protest have been eloquent in drawing attention to the lifeless and brutalized bodies of unarmed black citizens who have become victims of police violence. In drawing attention to the traumatic image of the black body either in pain or in death, both Coates and #BLM took the proliferation of videos and images from police shootings and beatings and deployed them for their political power. For example, on the "Resources" page of the *Black Lives Matter* website the first three items are toolkits related to commemorating the death of Trayvon Martin, one for black people and non-black People of Color (POC) organizers, a Spanish-Language tool-kit, and another toolkit for white people.[1] The toolkits are primarily built around utilizing discussions of commemoration as a reminder to continue the struggle. The language of the header for the Trayvon Taught Me Toolkit: For Black and Non-Black POC Organizers states:

> The #TrayvonTaughtMe digital campaign highlights the beginnings of the Black Lives Matter movement, and how Trayvon's extrajudicial murder and his family's commitment to ending gun violence and strengthening communities catalyzed a generation of organizers and activists to take action for Black lives. Five years later, the same conditions that led to Trayvon's death have been exacerbated under the Trump administration. Anti-Blackness is pervasive and implicit, and Black children and adults continue to be put on trial for our own murders. The perceptions of Black people and Blackness in America, and globally, have resulted in the refusal to acknowledge the unique cultural contributions of Black people.[2]

By situating the movement around the murder of Trayvon Martin, #BLM shows the articulation of the movement's energy with the image of imperiled black bodies. The focus on the black body in peril is also the motif of Coates's 2015 book *Between the World and Me.* The book, presented as a letter to his teenaged son, frames the problem of race as the fragility of black bodies. Coates writes,

> And you know now, if you did not before, that the police departments of your country have been endowed with the authority to destroy your body. It does not matter if the destruction is the result of an unfortunate over-reaction. It does not matter if it originates in a misunderstanding. It does not matter if the destruction springs from a foolish policy. Sell cigarettes without proper authority and your body can be destroyed. Resent the people trying to entrap your body and it can be destroyed. Turn to the dark stairwell and your body can be destroyed.[3]

Coates's repeated warning of the way in which the black body can be destroyed distills the problem of racism to this one stark fact. But, as indicated by the difficulty that #BLM had in articulating a positive vision for the nation and Coates's pessimism, we may be seeing the rhetorical and imaginative limits of this strategy, which looks troublingly like the strategies of early crusaders against the slave trade.[4] Specifically, as #BLM remains primarily a protectionist movement it risks remaining on the outer rims of political organizing in a way that calls to mind the early Garrisonians and Colonization Society. While pointing out the discrepancy between the relative safety white people feel around law enforcement and the sense of feeling unsafe reported by black people can open up discussions, the calls to retreat or boycott events where high police presence is a factor are likely to do little more than foster a widespread sense of outrage against the police. For real change to occur what needs to happen is something more comprehensive, something that calls attention to the ways in which "safe spaces" for whites in the form of gated communities and highly segregated neighborhoods exacerbate this discrepancy between feeling safe and un-safe around law enforcement. If there is something to be learned from the radical turn to abolition, it is that the move towards declaring the right to revolt provided a much-needed turn from the defensive to the offensive. The right to be "safe" from police is a retreating move, an appeal to the negative freedom from oppression rather than a demand for the positive freedom of rights. And if there is a further lesson to be learned from the failures or limits of radical abolition, it is that the privileging of the "black body as victim as the best tool to end the oppression" may perpetuate the problem of seeing black Americans as perfect victims, as objects of pity rather than as fellow citizens with whom other Americans must work to achieve a better society.

There may also be darker lessons to be learned from the histories of insurrection and revolution. When people in power dismiss the needs of the many, catastrophic violence is often the consequence. In this respect, one lesson of the history of abolition that this book only touches on but is worth emphasizing here is that part of abolitionists' failures, particularly in the eighteenth century, centered on their unwillingness to attack the sugar trade wholesale, which in turn forced them into a devil's bargain with the proslavery faction who favored "natural increase." The abolitionists' failure to successfully tie the sins of capitalism to the sins of slavery reflects an ongoing problem in liberal reform. The decoupling of antiracism from anticapitalism has some roots in the desire of abolitionists to make their case by highlighting the "usefulness" of people like Equiano, Cinqué, and Douglass, and the concomitant necessity to downplay or disavow those such as Turner, Prosser, and Vesey. In this way while showcasing the piety, literacy, and other so-called "civilized" aspects of the enslaved and formerly enslaved was invaluable in proving the capacity of these people for learning and working, it also perhaps unwittingly divides African-Americans into categories of useful and useless. This is why it is essential to restore to histories of violence some accounting of the political nature behind such acts. It is all very well to restore concepts like "natural rights" and "right to revolt" to those deprived of them. But the true threat of insurrectionist and revolutionary violence is to the economic power centers, and the suppression of such movements has as much to do with the preservation of that power as it does to the preservation of human life. And such categories do not merely divide a society racially. Individuals deemed useless have little reason to see our social and political institutions as worthy of respect and preservation—and when our institutions seem for so many to be disconnected from what contributes to living a good life, it is hard to see how they can command such respect.

This book would not have been possible without grants from the Colgate University Research Council, which subsidized my research trips to the American Antiquarian Society and the Huntington Library. I am grateful to Paul Erickson, formerly of the American Antiquarian Society, for accepting me as a scholar in residence during the summer of 2014. The time there proved invaluable in helping me find the shape of my book.

I am grateful to my friends at Colgate University, my professional home of the last five years. The wilds of Central New York would be a cold and lonely place were it not for my friend, neighbor, and partner-in-crime Meg Worley whose insistence on carving out a space for research and cheerful resilience in the face of professional setbacks have proven both reassuring and inspiring. I am also grateful for my friends in the English and Theater Departments, Ben Child, John Connor, Christian DuComb, Amelia Klein, and Nimanthi Rajisingham who read chapter drafts of this book. Your feedback and encouragement were integral in pushing this project forward. I am also deeply indebted to Phil Richards, Kezia Page, Constance Harsh, Jennifer Brice, Alan Cooper, and Margaret Maurer for their mentorship and encouragement during my time here.

This book began with a seminar paper in Nancy Ruttenburg's class, at New York University (NYU) and I am extraordinarily grateful to her for telling me I was "onto something with Melville." I am also grateful to my dissertation committee members Bryan Waterman, Cyrus Patel, and Elizabeth McHenry. Over the years my work has benefited from the guidance of my colleagues in the field. I have been extraordinarily fortunate to have the support of Hester Blum, Hoang Phan, and Hélène Quanquin for being sounding boards and mentors.

To my Central New York crew, Kim Germain, Susan Wooley, Tiffany Tai, Jen and Tristan Tomlinson, Wenhua Shu, Karla Loveall, David Gray, Brooks Sommerville, Jacob Mundy, Susan Thomson, Lora Woodford, Spring Knapp, and Anna Rios, I am so happy to have discovered such dear friends at a time in my life when the prospects for new friendships are often few and far between. Thank you for the trivia nights, barbeques, crawfish boils, and many other social events big and small that add flavor and joy to life in between classes, meetings, conferences, and sabbaticals.

Thank you for letting me into your homes, and letting me play with your pets and children.

A very special thank you to my own New York University crew, Meghan Hammond and Yohei Igarashi. If I had to identify two grad school war buddies you would be it. I would also like to thank Seth Rudy for providing humor, encouragement, and swift kicks in the rear as needed. And for also understanding the darker turns of mood this profession often triggers.

To my oldest dearest friends, Mary Hollingsworth, Sanjay Hukku, and Mikka Tokuda-Hall there is little I can say to express how much I have needed you. Mary, my partner in crime, you are still my rock and the person who still shows me my best self. Mikka, you are in some ways an extension of the most whimsical part of my brain. Sanjay, I owe you a special note of thanks for helping getting me unstuck at a crucial point in this writing process, and for being the friend who more than anyone else has taught me the value of going the against the grain.

My family has seen the best and the worst of this process. My sister Mercedes, my brothers Marcus and Gregory, you remind me every day to take myself less seriously. I am lucky to have a sister-in-law, Yajaira Giuiàn, who is generous and patient and the mother of the best baby on the planet. I have no words to thank my long-suffering parents Kenneth and Maria whose support, love, patience, and willingness to proofread have at times kept me from giving up.

And last, to my partner Robert Scott: you have been the best most unexpected gift, and you have shown me how little I know about love and life in the best possible way.

INTRODUCTION

1. J. M. W. Turner, "Fallacies of Hope" (1812), quoted in Jerrold Ziff, "John Langhorne and Turner's 'Fallacies of Hope,'" *Journal of Warburg and Courtauld Institutes* 27 (1964), 341.
2. Douglass H. Maynard, "The World's Anti-Slavery Convention of 1840," *Mississippi Valley Historical Review* 47, no. 3 (1960): 452–53.
3. Marcus Rediker, *The Slave Ship: A Human History* (New York: Viking, 2007), 240–41.
4. Ian Baucom, *Specters of the Atlantic: Finance Capital, Slavery, and the Philosophy of History* (Durham, NC: Duke University Press, 2005), 212.
5. Robin Blackburn, *The Overthrow of Colonial Slavery: 1776–1846*, (London: Verso, 2011), 468.
6. Paul Gilroy, *The Black Atlantic: Modernity and Double Consciousness* (Cambridge, MA: Harvard University Press, 1993), 16.
7. Hester Blum, "The Prospect of Oceanic Studies," *PMLA* 125, no. 3 (2010): 3.
8. Edgar Allan Poe, "The Philosophy of Composition," in *Edgar Allan Poe: Poetry, Tales and Selected Essays* (New York: Library of America, 1996), 1379. The precise quote is "the death, then of a beautiful woman is, unquestionably, the most poetical topic in the world."
9. Frederick Douglass, *My Bondage and My Freedom* (1855), ed. John David Smith (New York: Penguin, 2003), 265–66.
10. John Stauffer, *The Black Hearts of Men: Radical Abolitionists and the Transformation of Race* (Cambridge, MA: Harvard University Press, 2002).
11. Manisha Sinha, *A Slave's Cause: A History of Abolition* (New Haven, CT: Yale University Press, 2016), 210–13.
12. David Brion Davis, *The Problem of Slavery in the Age of Revolution*, 1770–1823 (Ithaca, NY: Cornell University Press, 1975).
13. Peter Linebaugh and Marcus Rediker, *The Many-Headed Hydra: Sailors, Slaves, Commoners, and the Hidden History of the Revolutionary Atlantic* (Boston: Beacon Press, 2000), 4.
14. See Saidiya V. Hartman, *Scenes of Subjection: Terror, Slavery, and Self-Making in Nineteenth-Century America* (New York: Oxford University Press, 1997).
15. Ibid., 52.
16. See Olaudah Equiano and Werner Sollors, *The Interesting Narrative of the Life of Olaudah Equiano, Or Gustavus Vassa, the African, Written by Himself* (New York: Norton, 2001).
17. Frederick Douglass, "The Heroic Slave," Edited by Julia Griffiths, and the Rochester Ladies' Anti-slavery Society. *Autographs for Freedom*. Boston: J. P. Jewett, 1853–1854.
18. Vincent Carretta, *Equiano, the African: Biography of a Self-made Man*. Athens: University of Georgia Press, 2005. Cathy N. Davidson, "Olaudah Equiano, Written by Himself," *NOVEL: A Forum on Fiction* 40, nos. 1–2 (2006): 18–51.
19. Walter Johnson, "Possible Pasts: Some Speculations on Time, Temporality, and the History of Atlantic Slavery," *Amerikastudien / American Studies* 45, no. 4 (2000): 489.
20. Michel-Rolph Trouillot, *Silencing the Past: Power and the Production of History*. Boston: Beacon Press, 1995.

CHAPTER 1 — WITNESS TO THE ATROCITIES: OLAUDAH EQUIANO, THOMAS CLARKSON, AND THE ABOLITION OF THE SLAVE TRADE

1. Olaudah Equiano, *The Interesting Narrative and Other Writings* (New York: Penguin, 2003), 70.
2. Vincent Carretta, *Equiano, the African: Biography of a Self-made Man* (Athens: University of Georgia Press, 2005), 349, 361–62.
3. See Baucom's *Specters of the Atlantic.* See also Rediker's *The Slave Ship.*
4. Eric Robert Taylor, *If We Must Die: Shipboard Insurrections in the Era of the Atlantic Slave Trade* (Baton Rouge: Louisiana State University Press, 2006); and David Richardson, "Shipboard Revolts, African Authority, and the Atlantic Slave Trade," *William and Mary Quarterly: New Perspectives on the Transatlantic Slave* 58, no. 1 (2001): 69–92.
5. Robin Blackburn, *The Overthrow of Colonial Slavery, 1776–1848* (New York: Verso, 2011), 20, and *The Making of New World Slavery: From the Baroque to the Modern, 1492–1800* (New York: Verso, 1997), 324.
6. Taylor, *If We Must Die,* 1.
7. Richardson, "Shipboard Revolts," 75.
8. Stephen D. Behrendt et al., "The Costs of Coercion: African Agency in the Pre-Modern Atlantic World," *Economic History Review* 54, no. 3 (2001): 467, fig. 2.
9. John Locke, *Two Treatises of Government,* ed. Peter Laslett, 2nd ed. (Cambridge: Cambridge University Press, 1988), 284–85.
10. Ibid., 284. "This is the perfect condition of slavery, which is nothing else, but the state of war continued, between a lawful conqueror and a captive: for, if once compact enter between them, and make an agreement for a limited power on the one side, and obedience on the other, the state of war and slavery ceases, as long as the compact endures: for, as has been said, no man can, by agreement, pass over to another that which he hath not in himself, a power over his own life."
11. See Thomas Clarkson, *The Abstract of the Evidence Delivered Before a Select Committee of the House of Commons, in the Years 1790 and 1791 On the part of the Petitioners For the Abolition of the Slave Trade* (Cincinnati, OH: American Reform Tract and Book Society, 1855), 18–19.
12. See Carretta, *Equiano,* 3–9. For a rebuttal see Cathy N. Davidson, "Olaudah Equiano, Written by Himself," *NOVEL: A Forum on Fiction* 40, nos. 1–2 (2006): 18–51. Also see Paul E. Lovejoy's "Olaudah Equiano or Gustavus Vassa—What's in a Name?" *Atlantic Studies* 9, no. 2 (2012): 165–84; and "Autobiography and Memory: Gustavus Vassa, Alias Olaudah Equiano, the African," *Slavery and Abolition* 27, no. 3 (2006): 317–47.
13. W. Jeffrey Bolster, *Black Jacks African Americans in the Age of Sail* (Cambridge, MA: Harvard University Press, 1998), 19. Numbers of enslaved sailors varied colony by colony sometimes amounting to only 3 or 4 percent of the maritime population and at other times rising to almost 15 percent.
14. David Brion Davis, *Inhuman Bondage: The Rise and Fall of Slavery in the New World* (New York: Oxford University Press, 2006); and Davis, *The Problem of Slavery in the Age of Revolution, 1770–1823* (Ithaca, NY: Cornell University Press, 1975). See also Seymour Drescher, *Abolition: A History of Slavery and Antislavery* (Cambridge: Cambridge University Press, 2009); and Claudius K. Fergus, "'Dread of Insurrection': Abolitionism, Security, and Labor in Britain's West Indian Colonies, 1760–1823," *William and Mary Quarterly* 66, no. 4 (2009): 757–80.
15. Taylor, *If We Must Die,* 41–42.
16. Ibid., 197.
17. Blackburn, *Overthrow of Colonial Slavery,* 57–58.

18. Michel-Rolph Trouillot, *Silencing the Past: Power and the Production of History* (Boston: Beacon Press, 1995), 83.
19. Fergus, "Dread of Insurrection," 758. See also Edward Long, *The History of Jamaica; Or, General Survey of the Antient and Modern State of That Island* (London: T. Lowndes, 1774), in 3 vols. Blackburn suggests that "natural increase" led to the rise in free people of color in Jamaica, particularly those who were "inured to local disease, environment, and spared the rigours of forced labor," which in turn lead to the abolition of slavery in the British colonies. (Blackburn, *Overthrow of Colonial Slavery*, 424)
20. Thomas Clarkson, *Three Letters (One of Which Has Appeared Before) To The Planters and Slave-Merchants Principally On the Subject of Compensation. By Thomas Clarkson, M.A. Author of Several Essays On the Subject of the Slave-Trade* (London: Phillips and Fardon, 1807), "To the Planters and Merchants Concerned In The African Slave-Trade," Letter 1, London, January 28, 1807. "In another part of your Petition, you seem to urge the proximity of St. Domingo to be the most important of the British Islands in the West Indies as an Argument against the Abolition of the Slave Trade. But surely You seem to have overlooked how imperiously this proximity calls on You for its Abolition. In case of any sudden rupture between St. Domingo and You, or between St. Domingo and Great Britain, where would be your safety, inclosed [*sic*] by a multitude of newly imported Slaves?"
21. Long, *History*, vol. 2, 445.
22. Ibid., vol. 2, 444; emphasis in the original.
23. Ibid., vol. 2, 472; emphasis in the original.
24. Ibid., vol. 2, 502; emphasis mine.
25. Claudius K. Fergus, *Revolutionary Emancipation: Slavery and Abolitionism in the British West Indies* (Baton Rouge: Louisiana State University Press, 2013), 41. "Beginning with James Ramsay, abolitionists consistently made Long their principal authority for creolization as the antidote for internal security, often quoting extensively from his *History of Jamaica* or simply extracting from it data that had become axiomatic by the 1790s."
26. Clarkson, *An Essay on the Impolicy of the African Slave Trade: In Two Parts* (London: Francis Bailey, 1788), 85–86, 93.
27. Thomas Clarkson to Auguste Jean Baptiste Bouvet de Cressé, December 1789, Thomas Clarkson Papers, Huntington Library, San Marino, California.
28. Letter from Thomas Clarkson to Honoré-Gabriel Riqueti, Comte de Mirabeau, November 13, 1789 , Thomas Clarkson Papers, 1787–1847 (ibid.).
29. Letter from Thomas Clarkson to Honoré-Gabriel Riqueti, Comte de Mirabeau, December 9, 1789, (ibid.).
30. Clarkson, *Essay on the Impolicy*, 93.
31. Blackburn, *Overthrow of Colonial Slavery*, 138–39. I will also be going into this in further detail with my discussion on Clarkson's work.
32. Clarkson, *Essay on the Impolicy*, 6–20.
33. Clarkson's brother John was charged with escorting a number of escaped slaves from Nova Scotia to Sierra Leone and was the first governor of the colony. See Thomas Clarkson, *The History of the Rise, Progress, and Accomplishment of the Abolition of the African Slave-Trade by the British Parliament* (New York: J. S. Taylor, 1836), vol. 2, 272–73.
34. Ibid., vol. 1, 182.
35. Equiano, *Interesting Narrative*, 55.
36. Ibid., 61.
37. Thomas Clarkson, *The Substance of the Evidence of Sundry Persons on the Slave-Trade* (London: James Phillips, 1789).
38. Ian Baucom, *Specters of the Atlantic: Finance Capital, Slavery, and the Philosophy of History* (Durham, NC: Duke University Press, 2005), 214.

39. Blackburn, *Overthrow of Colonial Slavery*, 57. Insurrections in the colonies were fairly sporadic through the latter half of the eighteenth century. As Blackburn notes: "From the mid-1760s slave rebellions became far rarer in Jamaica as the colony embarked on rapid growth. Colonies that were growing and prosperous attracted settlers and could afford the upkeep of patrols, militia units and garrisons." For this reason, including the high incidence of shipboard insurrection provides a more complete picture of the status of slave revolt in this period.

40. Clarkson, *History*, vol. 2, 156.

41. Ibid., vol. 1, 217.

42. Ibid., vol. 1, 219.

43. Clarkson, *Evidence*, iv.

44. Ibid., iv.

45. Clarkson, *History*, vol. 1, 225.

46. Ibid., vol. 1, 56–57. One of Clarkson's aims was to show that English slave traders were not just buying slaves from African slavers but kidnapping free Africans either by going inland themselves or luring them aboard the ships under some pretense. It was commonly believed that the Africans were just as avid participants in the trade as were the British and other Europeans. In gathering accounts of kidnapping, Clarkson was also trying to prove that British rapaciousness was more of a key feature than previously known.

47. Ibid., vol. 2, 198–99.

48. Ibid.

49. Clarkson, *Evidence*, 19–20.

50. Ibid., 19.

51. Ibid., 21.

52. Ibid., 9.

53. Ibid., 105n01.

54. Clarkson, *History*, vol. 2, 28–29.

55. Equiano, *Interesting Narrative*, 139.

56. Taylor, *If We Must Die*, 194–96.

57. Ibid., 273–74.

58. C. L. R. James, *The Black Jacobins: Toussaint L'Ouverture and the San Domingo Revolution* (New York: Dial Press, 1938), 68.

59. Thomas Clarkson to Auguste Jean Baptiste Bouvet de Cressé, December, 1, 1789, Thomas Clarkson Papers, 1787–1847. Thomas Clarkson Papers, Huntington Library, San Marino, California.

60. Clarkson, *History*, vol. 2, 180.

61. Ibid.

62. Marcus Rediker, *The Slave Ship: A Human History* (New York: Viking, 2007), 310–11; Clarkson, *History*, vol. 3, 200. This broadside featured the diagram for the plan of the slave ship the *Brooks*, graphically illustrating how slaves were stowed. Clarkson said that this image "made up the deficiency of language" regarding the horrors of the Middle Passage.

63. Clarkson, *History*, vol. 2, 267–68.

64. This incident occurred in 1774. Annis's master who'd freed him in 1774 later tried to kidnap him. According to Equiano, Annis sought Sharp's help and was hopeful, but was later deceived by the attorney he'd engaged. Annis was sent back to St. Kitt's where he died. (Equiano, *Interesting Narrative*, 179–181, 288n505.)

65. Charles R. Foy, "Uncovering Hidden Lives: Developing A Database of Mariners In the Black Atlantic," *Common-Place* 9, no. 2 (2009): http://www.common-place.org/vol-09/no-02/tales/.

66. Equiano, *Interesting Narrative*, 56.

67. Ibid., 57.
68. Ibid., 65–66.
69. Ibid., 69, 73, 84.
70. Ibid., 124–25.
71. Ibid., 104, 123.
72. Ibid., 104.
73. Ibid., 105.
74. Ibid., 107.
75. Clarkson, *Evidence*, 77–78.
76. Equiano, *Interesting Narrative*, xxv.
77. Ibid., 112.
78. Ibid., 147.
79. Ibid., 148.
80. Ibid., 63. In chap. 3, he refers to a brief period when his master called him Jacob, and then Michael after the archangel before settling on the name Gustavus Vassa.
81. Ibid.
82. Ibid., 149.
83. Ibid., 55.
84. Ibid., 149–50.
85. Ibid., 151.
86. Ibid., 234.
87. Bolster, *Black Jacks*, 268.
88. Ibid., 33.
89. David Brion Davis, *The Problem of Slavery in the Age of Emancipation* (New York: Alfred A. Knopf, 2014), 170.

CHAPTER 2 — DENMARK VESEY, JOHN HOWISON, AND REVOLUTIONARY POSSIBILITY

1. One wonders if the sighting of a suspicious ship was inspiration for James Fenimore Cooper who used a similar device in *The Red Rover*, written in 1827. Ostensibly a historical novel about piracy during the Revolutionary war, Cooper's tale also uses the trope of piracy to raise difficult and interesting questions about slave violence. Cooper's pirate ship itself is initially mistaken for a slave ship. And in the story, Scipio, the faithful black companion to the hero, Wilder, sacrifices his life in a bloody scene that portrays him as simultaneously heroic and savage. Here, too, revolutionary possibility is framed as a thing of the past, and the single black figure is killed. Cooper, *Sea Tales: The Pilot, The Red Rover* (New York: Library of America, 1991).
2. John Howison, *The Florida Pirate, Or, An Account of a Cruise of the Schooner Esperanza, with A Sketch of the Life of Her Commander* (New York: W. Borradaile, 1823), 3.
3. James Hamilton Jr. and City of Charleston, South Carolina, *An Account of the Late Intended Insurrection Among A Portion of the Blacks of This City, Published by the Authority of the Corporation of Charleston*, 2nd ed. (Charleston, SC: A. E. Miller, 1822), 4–5.
4. Eric J. Sundquist, *Empire and Slavery in American Literature, 1820–1865* (Jackson: University Press of Mississippi, 2006), 144.
5. W. Jeffrey Bolster, *Black Jacks: African Americans in the Age of Sail* (Cambridge, MA: Harvard University Press, 1998), 230.
6. Donald J. Ratcliffe, "The Decline of Antislavery Politics, 1815–1840," in *Contesting Slavery: The Politics of Bondage and Freedom in the New American Nation*, ed. John Craig Hammond and Matthew Mason (Charlottesville: University of Virginia Press, 2011), 269–71.

7. See Douglas R. Egerton, *Gabriel's Rebellion: The Virginia Slave Conspiracies of 1800 and 1802* (Chapel Hill: University of North Carolina Press, 2000).

8. Daniel Rasmussen, *American Uprising: The Untold Story of America's Largest Slave Revolt* (New York: Harper Collins, 2011), 1–2.

9. Bolster, *Black Jacks*, 146.

10. John Howison, "The Florida Pirate," *Blackwoods Edinburgh Magazine*, August 1, 1821, 516–31.

11. Howison, *Florida Pirate, An Account* (1823).

12. Howison, *Florida Pirate, An Account* (Pittsburgh: Cook and Schoyer, 1834).

13. Bonnie Shannon McMullen, Review of "The Florida Pirate," by John Howison, *Washington Gazette*, November 20, 1821. Howison's other work appears to have been widely read, but "The Florida Pirate" was initially published anonymously in *Blackwood's*.

14. See Carrie Hyde, "Novelistic Evidence: The Denmark Vesey Conspiracy and Possibilistic History," *American Literary History* 27, no. 1 (2015): 26–55.

15. Robert S. Levine, *Dislocating Race and Nation: Episodes in Nineteenth-Century Literary Nationalism* (Chapel Hill: University of North Carolina Press, 2008), loc. 1167, Kindle.

16. Hamilton, *An Account* (1822), 17.

17. Lionel Henry Kennedy and Thomas Parker, *An Official Report of the Trials of Sundry Negroes Charged with an Attempt to Raise An Insurrection in the State of South Carolina: Preceded by an Introduction and Narrative* (Charleston, SC: James R, Schenck, 1822), 30.

18. Hamilton, *An Account* (1822), 17n. The footnote describes Vesey as being "always looked up to with awe and respect" and also "ungovernable and savage."

19. Michael P. Johnson, "Denmark Vesey and His Co-Conspirators." *William And Mary Quarterly* 58, no. 4 (2001): 940. While criticism of Johnson's piece is well-founded, I still find certain details regarding who does and does not speak useful for reasons I will elaborate on both here and in subsequent chapters.

20. Hyde, "Novelistic Evidence," 32–35.

21. Andy Doolen, "Reading and Writing Terror: The New York Conspiracy Trials of 1741," *American Literary History* 16, no. 3 (2004): 377.

22. See Jill Lepore, *New York Burning: Liberty, Slavery, and Conspiracy in Eighteenth-Century Manhattan* (New York: Vintage Books, 2006).

23. Ibid.

24. Edlie L. Wong, *Neither Fugitive nor Free: Atlantic Slavery, Freedom Suits and the Legal Culture of Travel* (New York: New York University Press, 2009), 194; emphasis in the original. Wong is quoting Governor Aiken in "Massachusetts and South Carolina," *The New Englander*, (1846), 195.

25. Douglas R. Egerton, *He Shall Go Free: The Lives of Denmark Vesey*, rev. ed. (Lanham, MD: Rowman & Littlefield, 2004), 180.

26. Ibid., 176.

27. M. P. Johnson, "Denmark Vesey," 952. Johnson's argument here is based on what he views as Charleston city authorities' main goal, namely the dissolution of the African Methodist Episcopal Church. Douglas Egerton, in his rejoinder to Johnson, points out that the church "was routinely in violation of two state laws, which is why city authorities consistently closed it down." Douglas R. Egerton, "Forgetting Denmark Vesey; Or, Oliver Stone Meets Richard Wade," *William and Mary Quarterly* 59, no. 1 (2002): 150.

28. Egerton, "Forgetting Denmark Vesey," 152.

29. Levine, *Dislocating Race and Nation*, 81. See also, James O'Neil Spady, "Power and Confession: On the Credibility of the Earliest Reports of the Denmark Vesey Slave Conspiracy," *William and Mary Quarterly* 68, no. 2 (2011): 287–304.

30. Ibid., 87–96.

31. Hyde, "Novelistic Evidence," 34.

32. Hamilton, *An Account*, 17.

33. Kennedy and Parker, *An Official Report*, 28.

34. Ibid., 41–42; emphasis in the original.

35. Ibid., 62, 111; emphasis in the original.

36. Ratcliffe, "Decline," 272–82.

37. This contrast is most starkly felt when one compares these documents to the press coverage surrounding the Nat Turner case, which I will discuss in chap. 3.

38. Marcus Rediker, *Villains of All Nations: Atlantic Pirates in the Golden Age* (Boston: Beacon Press, 2004), 139.

39. Ibid., 60–82.

40. Bolster, *Black Jacks*, 15.

41. See Sarah E. Johnson, *The Fear of French Negroes: Transcolonial Collaboration in the Revolutionary Americas* (Berkeley: University of California Press, 2012), for a discussion on the role of black pirates in slave smuggling and the problem of locating hard numbers for black pirates in the early nineteenth century.

42. Rediker, *Villains*, 54.

43. Claudius K. Fergus, *Revolutionary Emancipation: Slavery and Abolitionism in the British West Indies* (Baton Rouge: Louisiana State University Press, 2013), 187.

44. Howison, *Florida Pirate, An Account* (1823), 6–7.

45. Ibid., 4, 6, 14.

46. John Howison, *European Colonies, in Various Parts of the World: Viewed in Their Social, Moral, and Physical Condition, by John Howison, of the Honourable East India Company's Bombay Service, And Author of, "Sketches of Upper Canada," "Foreign Scenes and Traveling Recreations"* (London: Richard Bentley, 1834), vol. 1, 58.

47. Ibid., vol. 1, 148.

48. Ibid., vol. 1, 375–76; emphasis in the original.

49. Ibid., vol. 1, 99–100.

50. Ibid., vol. 1, 287–91. With regards to Columbus, Howison absolves him of total responsibility by pointing to King Ferdinand's greed as having forced Columbus to press the natives more than was prudent.

51. Ibid., vol. 1, 326–27.

52. Howison, *European Colonies*, vol. 2, 337.

53. Howison anticipates language almost exactly in that Clarkson's words were "For, by aiming at the abolition of the Slave Trade, they [the committee] were laying the axe at the very root." Clarkson, *History*, vol. 2, 214.

54. Howison, *Florida Pirate, An Account* (1823), 4.

55. Ibid., 6–7.

56. The trial records indicate that the conspirators used newspaper reports of the debate to recruit followers. Kennedy and Parker, *An Official Report*, 42, 128. See also Levine, *Dislocating Race and Nation*, 84.

57. Howison, *Florida Pirate, An Account* (1823), 13.

58. Ibid., 14.

59. Ibid., 13.

60. Ibid., 22.

61. Ibid., 24.

62. Gretchen Woertendyke, "John Howison's New Gothic Nationalism and Transatlantic Exchange," *Early American Literature* 43, no. 2 (2008): 324.

63. John Howison, *Tales from the Colonies in Two Volumes* (London: Henry Colburn and Richard Bentley, 1830), vol. 2, 328.

64. Howison, *Tales from the Colonies*, vol. 1, 3.
65. Ibid., vol. 1, 221–22.
66. Ibid., vol. 1, 294.
67. Howison, *Tales from the Colonies*, vol. 2, 77.
68. Ibid., vol. 2, 79.
69. Ratcliffe, "Decline," 281.
70. Richard S. Newman, *The Transformation of American Abolitionism: Fighting Slavery in the Early Republic* (Chapel Hill: University of North Carolina Press, 2002), 26–27.
71. Ibid., 128.
72. Levine, *Dislocating Race and Nation*. 67–118.
73. Manisha Sinha, *A Slave's Cause: A History of Abolition* (New Haven, CT: Yale University Press, 2016), 168–69.
74. Ibid., 169.
75. Nat Turner and Thomas R. Gray, *The Confessions of Nat Turner, the Leader of the Late Insurrection in Southampton, Va.: As Fully and Voluntarily made to Thomas R. Gray, in the Prison Where He was Confined, and Acknowledged by Him to be such when Read before the Court of Southampton: With the Certificate, Under Seal of the Court Convened at Jerusalem, Nov. 5, 1831, for His Trial: Also, an Authentic Account of the Whole Insurrection, with Lists of the Whites Who were Murdered, and of the Negroes Brought before the Court of Southampton, and there Sentenced, &c.* (Baltimore: Lucas & Deaver Print, 1831), 18.
76. Eric Sundquist, *To Wake the Nations: Race in the Making of American Literature* (Cambridge, MA: Belknap Press of Harvard University Press, 1993), 43. Sundquist's reading of *The Confessions of Nat Turner* is illustrative of my larger point regarding of how slave voices compromise the legal framework of texts. Gray, like Hamilton, Kennedy, and Parker before him attempts to use Turner's own voice to condemn him but is successful only to a point.

CHAPTER 3 — JOSEPH CINQUÉ, THE *AMISTAD* MUTINY, AND REVOLUTIONARY WHITEWASHING

1. *White Slaves, African Masters: An Anthology of Barbary Captivity Narratives*, ed. Paul Baepler (Chicago: University of Chicago Press, 1999), 24.
2. Saidiya V. Hartman, *Scenes of Subjection: Terror, Slavery, and Self-Making in Nineteenth-Century America* (New York: Oxford University Press, 1997), 3.
3. Robert S. Levine, *Martin Delany, Frederick Douglass, and the Politics of Representative Identity* (Chapel Hill: University of North Carolina Press, 1997), 148–49.
4. John Stauffer, *The Black Hearts of Men: Radical Abolitionists and the Transformation of Race* (Cambridge, MA: Harvard University Press, 2002), 40.
5. See Howard Jones, *Mutiny on the Amistad: The Saga of a Slave Revolt and Its Impact on American Abolition, Law, and Diplomacy*, rev. ed. (New York: Oxford University Press, 1987); Marcus Rediker, *The Slave Ship: A Human History* (New York: Viking, 2007); and Ian Baucom, *Specters of the Atlantic: Finance Capital, Slavery, and the Philosophy of History* (Durham, NC: Duke University Press, 2005).
6. Eric Sundquist, in particular, points to the *Amistad* case as having been over-celebrated by the abolitionists who "lost sight of the fact that Story's decision had done nothing to dislodge the notion that 'legal' slaves were property and they had no rights under American law." Sundquist (1997, 178). Maggie Montesinos Sale has discussed the *Amistad* case as it relates to both racialist discourse and the construction of black masculine identity in *The Slumbering Volcano: American Slave Ship Revolts and the Production of Rebellious Masculinity* (Durham, NC: Duke University Press, 1997). Iyunolu Osagie has productively, if somewhat inaccurately, argued that the "Amistad case also produced a major paradigm shift in the approach of the U.S. North to the problem of slavery" in *The Amistad Revolt: Memory,*

Slavery and the Politics of Identity in the United States and Sierra Leone (Athens: University of Georgia Press, 2000), xi.

7. Stauffer, *Black Hearts of Men*, 109–94. Stauffer gives a good account of Douglass's turn towards militancy and the enthusiasm with which the Radical Abolitionists courted President John Quincy Adams; however he makes no mention of Adams's role in the *Amistad* case nor does he cite the *Amistad* case as a meaningful moment within abolitionist discourse at all. See also Robert S. Levine, *The Lives of Frederick Douglass* (Cambridge, MA: Harvard University Press, 2016). Levine's book deals primarily with the role of the *Creole* mutiny in his analysis of Douglass's turn to militancy.

8. Vesey, a sailor from Haiti, more directly brought with him the fear of widespread black violence so effectively that, to this day, it is a matter of some debate as to how real the plans were for revolt, as was discussed in chap. 2. The Nat Turner revolt resulted in the deaths of as many as sixty men, women, and children. In retaliation southerners killed around 200 supposed conspirators and passed a series of draconian laws against black literacy and congregation. The publication and circulation of Thomas R. Gray's *The Confessions of Nat Turner* also served to create the aura of a region under threat. See Turner and Gray, *The Confessions of Nat Turner, the Leader of the Late Insurrection in Southampton, Va.: As Fully and Voluntarily made to Thomas R. Gray, in the Prison Where He was Confined, and Acknowledged by Him to be such when Read before the Court of Southampton* (Baltimore: Lucas & Deaver Print, 1831).

9. Patrick T. J. Browne, "'To Defend Mr. Garrison': William Cooper Nell and the Personal Politics of Antislavery," *New England Quarterly* 70, no. 3 (1997): 415–42. One of the more vocal accusers was the Governor of Virginia who demanded that the mayor of Boston arrest Garrison. The accusations never went beyond rumor.

10. Citations from the *Liberator* are from Accessible Archives, Columbia University (New York: New York, 2018), http://library.columbia.edu/locations/dhc/usaetexts.html. See the *Liberator* issues: September 10, 1831; October 29, 1831; November 5, 1831; November 12, 1831; November 19, 1831; November 26, 1831; December 3, 1831, for a sampling.

11. See Christopher Leslie Brown, *Moral Capital: Foundations of British Abolitionism* (Chapel Hill: University of North Carolina Press, 2006), for a deep dive in the role of the Society of Friends in both British and American Abolitionist movements.

12. See David S. Reynolds, *John Brown, Abolitionist: The Man Who Killed Slavery, Sparked the Civil War, and Seeded Civil Rights* (New York: Knopf Doubleday, 2006). See also Hannah N Geffert, "John Brown And His Black Allies: An Ignored Alliance," *Pennsylvania Magazine of History and Biography* 126, no. 4 (2002): 591–610.

13. David Walker, *David Walker's Appeal to the Colored Citizens of the World* (1829), ed. Peter Hinks (University Park: Penn State University Press, 2003), 8.

14. Ibid., xxxix.

15. *Liberator*, January 8, 1831; emphasis in the original.

16. Ibid.

17. *Liberator*, November 12, 1831.

18. *Liberator*, September 3, 1831.

19. *Liberator*, September 3, 1831; and March 10, 1832.

20. Ibid.; emphasis in the original.

21. *Liberator*, March 2, 1833. In a piece entitled "Food for Thought" reprinted from the *Village Record*, Turner and his followers were referred to thusly:

> In the trifling insurrection at Southampton of "Nat Turner, and his deluded handful of followers," was not the first thing thought of, and prayed for— the assistance of the troops of the United States? Was not the application of the Committee of the citizens of Southampton immediately to the President

for men and arms? And was not this from the inhabitants of the 'old domin-
ion,' which they are disposed to consider, and perhaps with propriety—as the
most chivalrous state in the Union? And is it persons in this situation, exposed
daily and nightly to the knife and torch of the assassin and incendiary, whose
vindictive nature is roused to vengeance by a keen sense of long suffered
wrongs—a foe within their houses and on their own hearths—is it persons
in this situation who talk of nullifying the laws and withdrawing themselves
from the protection of the free states of the Union?

22. Manisha Sinha argues that Garrison, in defiance of his white coadjutors admired Turner
and may have anonymously penned an admiring review of Walker's *Appeal* as well as writing sympathetically about the Haitian Revolution. Yet it is not clear that this personal view
of Garrison's was influential on the overall direction of the *Liberator* (Sinha, *A Slave's Cause:
A History of Abolition* [New Haven, CT: Yale University Press, 2016], 218–19).

23. Bruce A. Ragsdale, "Incited by the Love of Liberty: The *Amistad* Captives and the Federal
Courts," *Prologue* 35, no. 1 (2003): 3–5. This question of criminal and property meant that
the Africans were eventually arrested under two warrants; a warrant of seizure which allowed
the government to hold all goods, and the criminal warrant for piracy.

24. Marcus Rediker, *The Amistad Rebellion: An Atlantic Odyssey of Slavery and Freedom* (New
York: Penguin Books, 2012), 99–100.

25. Ibid.

26. Ibid., 114–21, 138–42, 160–68.

27. "Lynch Law Amongst the Africans," *New Hampshire Gazette*, October 12, 1939, 2. The
Southern press became particularly active after the Africans were transported back to Africa
in reporting the missionaries' disappointment with Cinqué's conduct. During the trial, much
was made of the allegation that Cinqué himself was a slave trader. For more on this, see Joseph
Yannielli, "Cinqué the Slave Trader: Some New Evidence on an Old Controversy," *Common-
Place* 10, no. 1 (October 2009), http://www.common-place-archives.org/vol-10/no-01
/yannielli/.

28. Rediker, *Amistad Rebellion*, 141, 153–59. The education of the Africans began after a series
of damaging articles appeared about fighting and weapons in the jail. A traveling exhibition was put on shortly after they won the court case to raise funds for transport back to
Africa. See also Jones, *Mutiny on the Amistad*.

29. For example: "Keep Cool," *Colored American*, November 2, 1839; "The Africans of the *Amistad*," *Colored American*, June 6, 1840; and "An Appeal to Abolitionists," *Colored American*,
October 10, 1840.

30. W. E. B. Du Bois, *The Suppression of the African Slave-Trade to the United States of America,
1638–1870* (New York: Longmans, 1896), 112–15.

31. Ibid., 1.

32. Ibid., 162.

33. See the following selections from the *Liberator* for a sampling: "Capture of a Slaver—A
Letter from Havana," January 4, 1834; "Smuggling of Slaves—Lt. Bagot of the British
schooner," June 14, 1834; "The Slave Trade," February 4, 1837; and "Slavery in Brazil,"
June 28, 1837.

34. See for example, "NATIONAL ANTI-SLAVERY SOCIETY," the *Liberator*, October 5,
1833. "The laws of this country make it a capital crime for her citizens to engage in the
foreign slave trade, yet a traffic in slaves is still tolerated and pursued under the eye of the
federal government, equally atrocious in character and cruel in practice, with that on
the African coast. Husbands and wives are separated from each other—children are
torn from their parents and sold to those who trade in the flesh and blood of human
beings. Thus while the foreign slave trade is denounced as piracy, the domestic trade, no

less shocking to humanity, and equally revolting to the feelings is openly and shame-lessly prosecuted."

35. *Liberator*, September 13, 1839; emphasis in the original.

36. *Liberator*, December 16, 1859.

37. Ragsdale, "Incited by the Love of Liberty," 29–30.

38. Jones, *Mutiny*, location 1838.

39. Rediker, *Amistad Rebellion*, 190. See also THE UNITED STATES, APPELLANTS, v. THE LIBELLANTS AND CLAIMANTS OF THE SCHOONER AMISTAD, HER TACKLE, APPAREL, AND FURNITURE, TOGETHER WITH HER CARGO, AND THE AFRICANS MENTIONED AND DESCRIBED IN THE SEVERAL LIBELS AND CLAIMS, APPELLEES. SUPREME COURT OF THE UNITED STATES 40 U.S. 518; 10 L. Ed. 826 JANUARY, 1841 Term. It, then, these negroes are not slaves, but are kidnapped Africans, who, by the laws of Spain itself, are entitled to their freedom, and were kidnapped and illegally carried to Cuba, and illegally detained and restrained on board of the *Amistad*; there is no pretence [*sic*] to say, that they are pirates or robbers.

40. Rediker, *Amistad Rebellion*, 224–25.

41. Without written corroboration from Washington, we cannot rule out the possibility that the story is apocryphal. We only have Purvis's account of this. "A Priceless Picture," *Philadelphia Inquirer*, December 26, 1889. See also Richard J. Powell, "Cinqué: Antislavery Portraiture and Patronage in Jacksonian America," *American Art* 11, no. 3 (1997): 68. Levine also points to another essay that corroborates Purvis's account in the *National Anti-Slavery Standard*, April 28, 1842 (Levine, *Lives of Frederick Douglass*, 329n14).

42. Gerrit Smith, *Gerrit Smith and the Vigilant Association of the City of New-York* (New York: John A. Gray 1860), 20–21.

43. Jones, *Mutiny*. See also *United States v. Bevans* 16 U.S. 336 (1818): Congress has power to provide for the, punishment of offenses committed by terms serving on board a ship of war of the United States, wherever that ship may lie. But Congress has not exercised that power in the case of a ship lying in the waters of the United States; the words 'within any fort, arsenal, dockyard, magazine, or in any other place or district of country under the sole and exclusive jurisdiction of the United States,' in the third section of the Act of 1790, ch. 9, not extending to a ship of war, but only to objects in their nature fixed and territorial.

44. Eric J. Sundquist, *To Wake The Nations: Race in the Making of American Literature* (Cambridge, MA: Belknap Press of Harvard University Press, 1993), 116–17. Joshua R. Giddings, *Speeches in Congress (1841–1852).* (Boston: J. P. Jewett, 1853), 23.

45. William Jay, *The Creole Case And Mr. Webster's Dispatch; With Comments of the N.Y. American* (New York: New York American, 1842), 117.

46. Len Gougeon, "Militant Abolitionism: Douglass, Emerson, and the Rise of the Anti-Slave," *New England Quarterly* 85, no. 4 (2012): 631–632. In February of 1844, Douglass gave two lectures in Concord, one of which was reported in the *Herald of Freedom* by Nathaniel P. Rogers, who wrote: "He reminded me of Toussaint among the plantations of Haiti.— There was great oratory in his speech—but more of dignity and earnestness than what we call eloquence. He was not up as a speaker—performing. He was an insurgent slave taking hold on the right of speech, and charging on his tyrants the bondage of his race." (*The Frederick Douglass Papers*. Vol. 4, *Series One: Speeches, Debates, and Interviews, 1864–80*, ed. John W. Blassingame and John R. McKivigan [New Haven, CT: Yale University Press, 1979], 23–24). As Gougeon has already noted, there is reason to believe that Emerson may have taken his cues from this report if not the lecture itself for his own address.

47. Ralph Waldo Emerson, "Address," in *Essays and Lectures* (1844) (New York: Library of America, 1983), 32.

48. Gougeon, "Militant Abolitionism," 623.

49. Emerson, "Character," in *Essays and Lectures* (1844), 498.
50. L. Diane Barnes, "Insurrection as Righteous Rebellion in *The Heroic Slave* and Beyond," *Journal of African American History* 102, no. 1 (2017): 32–33. Rediscovering and reassessing Frederick Douglass's novella, the "Heroic Slave," Barnes takes a far less pessimistic view of the influence of the language of "natural right" to revolt than I. As I will show through a close reading of both texts, Douglass and Delany are hampered by needing to define "natural right" to revolt within the parameters of the American Revolution.
51. Sundquist, *To Wake The Nations*, 87.
52. Levine, *Lives of Frederick Douglass*, 146, "For good reason, the novella sometimes has the feel of a play starring Frederick Douglass."
53. Ibid., 135. According to Levine, this transformation is evident even earlier. Just days before the publication of his *Narrative*, Douglass was moving toward an even more radical position on black violence. He proclaimed in a speech delivered in New York City in May 1845: "You say to us, if you dare to carry out the principles of our fathers, we'll shoot you down. Others may tamely submit; not I. You may put the chains upon me and fetter me, but I am not a slave, for my master who puts the chains upon me, shall stand in much dread of me as I do of him."
54. Ibid., 140. See also *Frederick Douglass Papers*, vol. 2, 131.
55. *Frederick Douglass, Selected Speeches and Writings*, ed. Philip S. Foner and Yuval Taylor (Chicago: Chicago Review Press, 2000), 368.
56. *North Star*, May 11, 1849.
57. Douglass, *Selected Speeches and Writings*, 367.
58. *North Star*, April 1, 1853; emphasis in the original.
59. Martin Robison Delany, *The Condition, Elevation, Emigration, and Destiny of the Colored People of the United States* (Philadelphia: M. R. Delany, 1852); *Martin R. Delany: A Documentary Reader*, ed. Robert S. Levine (Chapel Hill: University of North Carolina Press, 2003), 210. Delany's position on emigration can at best be described as mercurial. In the 1850s, most of his energy went into raising funds in support of his own emigration projects, namely the establishment of a free black nation in South or Central America (Martin Robison Delany, *Blake; Or, the Huts of America, a Novel* [Boston: Beacon Press, 1970], xiv). An autonomous black nation, he claimed, "would, by its economic and political potency, contribute to the downfall of American slavery" (Ibid.). Later he would devote his energy to the Civil War. For more see Levine, *Martin Delany, Frederick Douglass*, 184, and Levine, *Lives of Frederick Douglass*, 218–23.
60. Marronage refers to the practice of fugitive slaves or "maroons" creating "independent groups and communities on the outskirts of slave societies." Marjoline Kars. "Maroons and Marronage," http://www.oxfordbibliographies.com/view/document/obo-9780199730414/obo-9780199730414-0229.xml. See also, Monique Allewaert, "Swamp Sublime: Ecologies of Resistance in the American Plantation Zone." *PMLA: Publications of the Modern Language Association of America* 123, no. 2 (2008): 340–357. William Cooper Nell, *The Colored Patriots of the American Revolution, with Sketches of several Distinguished Colored Persons: To which is Added a Brief Survey of the Condition and Prospects of Colored Americans . . . with an Introduction by Harriet Beecher Stowe* (Boston: Robert F. Wallcut, 1855). Nell's book was published during the time that Delany was at work on *Blake*. Stowe wrote the introduction.
61. Delany, *Blake*, 115.
62. Herbert Aptheker, "Maroons within the Present Limits of the United States," *Journal of Negro History* 24, no. 2 (1939): 168. The most noted of such communities was that located in the Dismal Swamp between Virginia and North Carolina. It seems likely that about two thousand Negroes, fugitives, or the descendants of fugitives, lived in this area. They

carried on a regular, if illegal, trade with white people living on the borders of the swamp. Such settlements may have been more numerous than available evidence would indicate, for their occupants aroused less excitement and less resentment than the guerrilla outlaws.

63. This could also be an oblique tribute to Denmark Vesey who was also a former sailor.
64. Delany, *Blake*, 202.
65. Ibid., 207.
66. Ibid., 231.
67. Ibid., 234.
68. Levine, *Martin Delany, Frederick Douglass*, 217.
69. Ibid., 220.
70. Delany, *Blake*, 238.
71. Ibid., 181–82.
72. Frederick Douglass, "The Heroic Slave," in *Autographs for Freedom*, Edited by Julia Griffiths and Rochester Ladies' Anti-slavery Society. Boston: J. P. Jewett, 1853-1854228; emphasis in the original.
73. Ibid.
74. Ibid.
75. "Protest of the Officers of the *Creole*," *Niles National Register*, January 22, 1842, 323.
76. Ibid., 324.
77. Douglass, "Heroic Slave," 235; emphasis in the original.
78. Geffert, "John Brown," 599. Geffert argues that from his first meeting with Douglass in 1847, Brown believed that the key to a successful slave revolt was the involvement of powerful black leaders. "Although Douglass agreed with Brown's objective and rationale, he could never quite believe that John Brown's tremendous plan was humanly possible. Douglass and other black leaders also knew that if the project failed, black men would pay the cost." Brown also approached Delany, who refused as well.
79. Levine, *Lives*, 219.
80. Harriet Beecher Stowe, "Getting Ready For A Gale," *Independent*, April 15, 1861, 1; emphasis in the original. "Our sons and brothers whom we are sending take their lives in their hands and may never return," she wrote, "but this is a cause to die for—and, thanks be to God, our young men embrace it as a bride, and are ready to die" ("No Union With Slaveholders," *Liberator*, December 16, 1859).

CHAPTER 4 — THE BLACK AND WHITE SAILOR: MELVILLE'S *BILLY BUDD, SAILOR* AND THE CASE OF WASHINGTON GOODE

1. Herman Melville, "Billy Budd, Sailor," in *Melville's Short Novels: Authoritative Texts, Contexts, Criticism*, ed. Dan McCall (New York: Norton, 2002), 103–72, at 104.
2. Caroline L. Karcher, *Shadow Over the Promised Land: Slavery, Race, and Violence in Melville's America*, PhD diss., University of Maryland, 1980 (Baton Rouge: Louisiana State University Press, 1980), 354.
3. Gregory Jay, "Douglass, Melville, and the Lynching of Billy Budd," in *Frederick Douglass & Herman Melville: Essays in Relation*, ed. Robert S. Levine and Samuel Otter (Chapel Hill: University of North Carolina Press, 2008), 388.
4. Caroline L. Karcher, "Melville and Revolution," in *Melville's Short Novels: Authoritative Texts, Contexts, Criticism*, ed. Dan McCall (New York: Norton, 2002), 354.
5. *Salem Register*, April 5, 1875.
6. Brook Thomas, "The Legal Fictions of Herman Melville and Lemuel Shaw," *Critical Inquiry* 11, no. 1 (1984): 40–41. Dr. George Parkman was allegedly murdered by chemistry

professor James Webster. The case was made famous both because of the gruesome details of the crime (the body was partially dismembered and cremated) and the controversial conduct of Chief Justice Lemuel Shaw. According to Shaw's critics, Shaw was overly permissive with the prosecution instructing the jury that direct evidence was not essential to their decision.

7. "Washington Goode," *New Bedford Mercury*, May 4, 1849.
8. While Franklin, H. Bruce discusses "Billy Budd" in relationship to the argument of capital punishment, Washington Goode does not figure in his argument. "Billy Budd and Capital Punishment: A Tale of Three Centuries." *American Literature* 69, no. 2 (1997): 337–59
9. See Thomas, "Legal Fictions"; Michael Paul Rogin, *Subversive Genealogy: The Politics and Art of Herman Melville* (New York: Alfred A. Knopf, 1983); Robert K. Wallace, "Fugitive Justice: Douglass, Melville Shaw," in *Frederick Douglass & Herman Melville: Essays in Relation*, ed. Robert S. Levine and Samuel Otter (Chapel Hill: University of North Carolina Press, 2008), 39–68; and Hershel Parker, *Herman Melville: A Biography, Volume 1, 1819–1851* (Baltimore: Johns Hopkins University Press, 2005).
10. Rogin, *Subversive Genealogy,* 281.
11. Wallace, "Fugitive Justice," 60–61. This would be his ruling that the slave Thomas Sims should be returned to Georgia in 1851.
12. Barry Kritzberg, "A Pre-Civil War Struggle Against Capital Punishment: Charles Spear, Concord, and the Case of Washington Goode," *Concord Saunterer* 2, no. 1 (1994): 102–16; Louis P. Masur, *Rites of Execution: Capital Punishment and the Transformation of American Culture, 1776–1865* (Oxford: Oxford University Press, 1989).
13. Alan Rogers, "Under Sentence of Death: The Movement to Abolish Capital Punishment in Massachusetts, 1835–1849," *New England Quarterly* 66, no. 1 (1993): 42.
14. *Boston Post,* January 2, 1849. See also Kritzberg, "Pre-Civil War Struggle," 104.
15. *Salem Observer,* July 1, 1848.
16. Kritsberg, "Pre-Civil War Struggle," 105.
17. Rogers, "Under Sentence of Death," 43–44.
18. Kritzberg, "Pre-Civil War Struggle," 106.
19. Masur, *Rites of Execution*, 12.
20. *Boston Courier,* January 26, 1849.
21. Ibid.
22. Rogers, "Under Sentence of Death," 39–40.
23. Ibid., 40–41.
24. *Liberator*, March 30, 1849; *Boston Courier*, April 9, 1849; and *New-Bedford Mercury*, May 4, 1849.
25. *North Star,* April 20, 1849.
26. Myra C. Glenn, "The Naval Reform Campaign Against Flogging: A Case Study in Changing Attitudes Toward Corporal Punishment, 1830–1850," *American Quarterly* 35, no. 4 (1983): 419–420:

> [John Parker] Hale was a staunch and controversial antislavery advocate. After being read out of the of the Democratic party in 1845 because of his refusal to vote for the annexation of Texas, Hale became a Free Soiler and later a well-known Radical Republican. . . . Besides Hale, the leading congressional critics of the lash included Hannibal Hamlin, the Democratic senator from Maine who later served as Lincoln's Vice President during the Civil War, Salmon P. Chase, a Free Soiler from Ohio and, later, a leader of the Radical Republicans; and John M. Niles, Democratic senator from Connecticut who joined the Republicans in the early 1850s.

These senators denounced naval flogging in much the same way that they condemned slavery. . . . Like the institution of slavery, naval flogging was a "reproach" to civilization and Christianity, a "stumbling block" to the progress of an "enlightened humanity."

27. Leon Fink, *Sweatshops At Sea: Merchant Seamen in the World's First Globalized Industry, from 1812 to the Present* (Chapel Hill: University of North Carolina Press, 2011), 47–48.

28. *Prisoner's Friend: A Monthly Magazine Devoted to Criminal Reform, Philosophy, Science, Literature, and Art.*, ed. John Murray Spear and Charles S. Spear (Boston, 1849), 399.

29. See *Liberator*, April 13, 1849.

30. W. Jeffrey Bolster, *Black Jacks: African American Seamen in the Age of Sail* (Cambridge, MA: Harvard University Press, 1998), 27.

31. Peter Linebaugh and Marcus Rediker, *The Many-Headed Hydra: Sailors, Slaves, Commoners, and the Hidden History of the Revolutionary Atlantic* (Boston: Beacon Press, 2000).

32. Matthew Taylor Rafferty, *The Republic Afloat: Law, Honor, and Citizenship in Maritime America* (Chicago: University of Chicago Press, 2013), 192.

33. Bolster, *Black Jacks*, 221–22.

34. Ibid., 226–28.

35. Rafferty, *Republic Afloat*, 47, 63.

36. Ibid., 115–16.

37. Ibid., 191.

38. Herman Melville, *Battle-Pieces and Aspects of the War: Civil War Poems* (Amherst, NY: Prometheus, 2001), 243–44.

39. Ibid., 391.

40. Thomas Clarkson, *The History of the Rise, Progress, and Accomplishment of the Abolition of the African Slave-Trade by the British Parliament* (New York: J. S. Taylor, 1836) vol. 2, 141.

41. Hannah Arendt, *On Revolution* (London: Penguin Books, 1990), 83, 87.

42. Melville, "Billy Budd, Sailor," in *Melville's Short Novels*, 110, 146.

43. Ibid., 108.

44. Ibid.

45. Ibid.

46. Ibid., 106.

47. Ibid., 111.

48. Ibid., 109.

49. Herman Melville Papers, 1761–1964. "Billy Budd. A.Ms.; [n.p., n.d.]," MS Am 188 (363). Houghton Library, Cambridge, MA, Harvard University. In the edited manuscript, cross-outs on pages 2, 4, and 5 indicate that Melville took some pains to make the racial significance of both the unnamed black sailor and Billy Budd clear.

50. Melville, "Billy Budd, Sailor," in *Melville's Short Novels*, 104.

51. Ibid., 133.

52. Ibid., 122–23.

53. Melville, *Battle-Pieces*, 52–53.

54. Melville, "Billy Budd, Sailor," in *Melville's Short Novels*, 155.

55. Gregg Crane, "Judgment in *Billy Budd*," in *The New Cambridge Companion to Herman Melville*, ed. Robert S. Levine (Cambridge: Cambridge University Press, 2014), 145.

56. Melville, "Billy Budd, Sailor," in *Melville's Short Novels*, 168.

57. Elizabeth Barnes, "Fraternal Melancholies: Manhood and the Limits of Sympathy in Douglass and Melville," in *Frederick Douglass & Herman Melville: Essays in Relation*, ed. Robert S. Levine and Samuel Otter (Chapel Hill: University of North Carolina Press, 2008), 252.

58. Herman Melville, *Redburn, His First Voyage; White-Jacket, Or, the World in a Man-of-War; Moby-Dick, Or, the Whale*, notes by G. Thomas Tanselle (New York: Literary Classics, 1983), 490.
59. Ibid.
60. Ibid.; emphasis in the original.
61. Ibid., 492; emphasis in the original.
62. Ibid., 500–501; emphasis in the original.
63. Frederick Douglass, *Autobiographies: Narrative of the Life of Frederick Douglass, An American Slave, My Bondage and My Freedom* (New York: Library of America, Penguin, 1994), 19.
64. Melville, *Redburn, His First Voyage; White-Jacket*, 639; emphasis in the original.
65. Ibid., 639–40; emphasis in the original.
66. Glenn, "Naval Reform Campaign," 411. "During the antebellum period Jack Tar symbolized a life of transiency, vice, and crime. The flogging of seamen, therefore, posed a crucial challenge to antebellum reformers. The latter believed that there were more enlightened ways to discipline deviant behavior on land as well as at sea. The achievement of effective naval discipline without the lash would vindicate this belief."
67. Melville, *Redburn, His First Voyage; White-Jacket*, 641.
68. Barnes, "Fraternal Melancholies," 251.
69. Melville, *Redburn, His First Voyage; White-Jacket*, 747.
70. Ibid.; emphasis in the original.
71. Ibid., 488.
72. "For the slave Guinea to stand and watch a sailor being flogged would be to render the sailor not "like" a slave but beneath a slave. Before such an audience, the defining hierarchical space between the two terms would collapse." Samuel Otter, *Melville's Anatomies*, (Berkeley: University of California Press, 1999), 83.
73. Melville, "Benito Cereno," in *Melville's Short Novels*, 101.
74. Ibid.
75. Ibid., 35
76. Melville, "Benito Cereno," in *Melville's Short Novels*, 35.
77. Eric J. Sundquist, *To Wake the Nations: Race in the Making of American Literature* (Cambridge, MA: Belknap Press of Harvard University Press, 1993), 149.
78. Melville, "Benito Cereno," in *Melville's Short Novels*, 40–41.
79. Ibid., 45.
80. Ibid., 49–50.
81. Frederick Douglass, "The Heroic Slave," *Autographs for Freedom*. Edited by Julia Griffiths, and Rochester Ladies' Anti-slavery Society. Boston: J. P. Jewett, 1853–1854, 176–78.
82. Jonathan Elmer, *On Lingering and Being Last: Race and Sovereignty in the New World* (New York: Fordham University Press, 2008), 95.
83. See Sybille Fischer, *Modernity Disavowed: Haiti and the Cultures of Slavery in the Age of Revolution* (Durham, NC: Duke University Press, 2004).
84. Melville, "Benito Cereno," in *Melville's Short Novels*, 89.
85. Ibid., 92.
86. Ibid., 94.
87. Ibid., 102.
88. Ibid.
89. See Carolyn L. Karcher, "White Fratricide, Black Liberation: Melville, Douglass, and Civil War Memory," in *Frederick Douglass & Herman Melville: Essays in Relation.*, ed. Robert S. Levine and Samuel Otter (Chapel Hill: University of North Carolina Press, 2008), 349–68; and Maurice S. Lee, "Melville, Douglass, the Civil War, Pragmatism," in *Frederick Douglass*

& *Herman Melville: Essays in Relation*, ed. Robert S. Levine and Samuel Otter (Chapel Hill: University of North Carolina Press, 2008), 396–415.

90. Karcher, "White Fratricide," 351.
91. Melville, "Billy Budd, Sailor," in *Melville's Short Novels*, 170.
92. See Diana Fuss, "Corpse Poem," *Critical Inquiry* 30, no. 1 (2003): 1–30.

CODA

1. "Resources" *Black Lives Matter*, https://blacklivesmatter.com/resources/.
2. "Trayvon Taught Me Toolkit: For Black and Non-Black POC Organizers," *Black Lives Matter,* https://blacklivesmatter.com/resource/trayvon-taught-me-toolkit-for-black-and-non -black-poc-organizers/.
3. Ta-Nehesi Coates, *Between the World and Me* (New York: Random House, 2015), 9.
4. Darren Sands, "What Happened to Black Lives Matter," *Buzzfeed*, June 21, 2017, https://www.buzzfeed.com/darrensands/what-happened-to-black-lives-matter?utm_term= .jrqGKnZ7AP#.xoB9JE6BVX); see also R. L. Stephens, "Between the Black Body and Me," *Jacobin Magazine*, May 31, 2017, https://www.jacobinmag.com/2017/05/ta-nehisi-coates -racism-afro-pessimism-reparations-class-struggle.

Accessible Archives. Columbia University. New York: New York, 2018. http://library
.columbia.edu/locations/dhc/usaetexts.html.

Allewaert, Monique. "Swamp Sublime: Ecologies of Resistance in the American Plantation
Zone." *PMLA: Publications of the Modern Language Association of America* 123, no. 2 (2008):
340–357.

Aptheker, Herbert. "Maroons within the Present Limits of the United States." *Journal of Negro
History* 24, no. 2 (1939): 167–84.

Arendt, Hannah. *On Revolution*. London: Penguin Books, 1990.

———, ed. *White Slaves, African Masters: An Anthology of American Barbary Captivity Narratives*. Chicago: University of Chicago Press, 1999.

Barnes, Elizabeth. "Fraternal Melancholies: Manhood and the Limits of Sympathy in Douglass
and Melville." In *Frederick Douglass & Herman Melville: Essays in Relation*, edited by Robert S.
Levine and Samuel Otter, 233–56. Chapel Hill: University of North Carolina Press, 2008.

Barnes, L. Diane "Insurrection as Righteous Rebellion in *The Heroic Slave* and Beyond." *Journal of African American History* 102, no. 1 (2017): 21–34.

Baucom, Ian. *Specters of the Atlantic: Finance Capital, Slavery, and the Philosophy of History*.
Durham, NC: Duke University Press, 2005.

Behrendt, Stephen D., David Eltis, and David Richardson. "The Costs of Coercion: African
Agency in the Pre-Modern Atlantic World." *Economic History Review* 54, no. 3 (2001):
454–76.

Blackburn, Robin. *The Making of New World Slavery: From the Baroque to the Modern, 1492–
1800*. London and New York: Verso, 1997.

———. *The Overthrow of Colonial Slavery, 1776–1848*. New York: Verso, 2011.

Black Lives Matter. "Resources" *Black Lives Matter*, https://blacklivesmatter.com/resources.

———. "Trayvon Taught Me Toolkit: For Black and Non-Black POC Organizers," *Black
Lives Matter,* https://blacklivesmatter.com/resource/trayvon-taught-me-toolkit-for-black
-and-non-black-poc-organizers/

Blum, Hester. "The Prospect of Oceanic Studies." *PMLA* 125, no. 3 (2010): 670–77. Reprint as
pdf. 1–14.

Bolster, W. Jeffrey. *Black Jacks: African American Seamen in the Age of Sail*. Cambridge, MA:
Harvard University Press, 1998.

Brown, Christopher Leslie. *Moral Capital: Foundations of British Abolitionism*. Chapel Hill: University of North Carolina Press, 2006.

Browne, Patrick T. J. "'To Defend Mr. Garrison': William Cooper Nell and the Personal Politics of Antislavery." *New England Quarterly* 70, no. 3 (1997): 415–42.

Carretta, Vincent. *Equiano, the African: Biography of a Self-made Man*. Athens: University of
Georgia Press, 2005.

Clarkson, Thomas. *The Abstract of the Evidence Delivered Before a Select Committee of the House
of Commons, in the Years 1790 and 1791 On the part of the Petitioners For the Abolition of the
Slave Trade*. Cincinnati, OH: American Reform Tract and Book Society, 1855.

———. *An Essay on the Impolicy of the African Slave Trade: In Two Parts*. London: Francis Bailey, 1788.

———. *The History of the Rise, Progress, and Accomplishment of the Abolition of the African Slave-Trade by the British Parliament*. 3 vols. New York: J. S. Taylor, 1836.

———. *The Substance of the Evidence of Sundry Persons on the Slave-Trade*. London: James Phillips, 1789.

———. Thomas Clarkson Papers, Huntington Library, San Marino, California.

———. *Three Letters (One of which has Appeared before) to the Planters and Slave-Merchants, Principally on the Subject of Compensation. By Thomas Clarkson, M.A. Author of Several Essays On the Subject of the Slave-Trade* London: Phillips and Fardon, 1807.

Coates, Ta-Nehesi. *Between the World and Me*. New York: Random House, 2015.

Cooper, James Fenimore. *Sea Tales: The Pilot, The Red Rover*. New York: Library of America, 1991.

Crane, Gregg [D.] "Judgment in *Billy Budd*." In *The New Cambridge Companion to Herman Melville*, edited by Robert S. Levine, 142–54. Cambridge: Cambridge University Press, 2014.

Davidson, Cathy N. "Olaudah Equiano, Written by Himself." *NOVEL: A Forum on Fiction* 40, nos. 1–2 (2006): 18–51.

Davis, David Brion. *Inhuman Bondage: The Rise and Fall of Slavery in the New World*. New York: Oxford University Press, 2006.

———. *The Problem of Slavery in the Age of Emancipation*. New York: Alfred A. Knopf, 2014.

———. *The Problem of Slavery in the Age of Revolution, 1770–1823*. Ithaca, NY: Cornell University Press, 1975.

Delany, Martin Robison. *Blake; Or, the Huts of America, a Novel*. Edited by Floyd J. Miller. Boston: Beacon Press, 1970. Reprint. 2000. First published 1861–1862.

———. *The Condition, Elevation, Emigration, and Destiny of the Colored People of the United States*. Philadelphia: M. R. Delany, 1852.

———. *Martin R. Delany: A Documentary Reader*, edited by Robert S. Levine. Chapel Hill: University of North Carolina, 2003.

Doolen, Andy. "Reading and Writing Terror: The New York Conspiracy Trials of 1741." *American Literary History* 16, no. 3 (2004): 377–406.

Douglass, Frederick. *Autobiographies: Narrative of the Life of Frederick Douglass, An American Slave, My Bondage and My Freedom*. New York: Library of America, Penguin, 1994.

———. *The Frederick Douglass Papers*. Vol. 4, *Series One: Speeches, Debates, and Interviews, 1864–80*. Edited by John W. Blassingame and John R. McKivigan, New Haven, CT: Yale University Press, 1979.

———. *Frederick Douglass: Selected Speeches and Writings*. Edited by Philip S. Foner and Yuval Taylor. Chicago: Chicago Review Press, 2000.

———. *My Bondage and My Freedom* (1855). Edited by John David Smith. New York: Penguin, 2003.

Drescher, Seymour. *Abolition: A History of Slavery and Antislavery*. Cambridge: Cambridge University Press, 2009.

Du Bois, W. E. B. *The Suppression of the African Slave-Trade to the United States of America, 1638–1870*. New York: Longmans, 1896.

Egerton, Douglas R. "Forgetting Denmark Vesey; Or, Oliver Stone Meets Richard Wade." *William and Mary Quarterly* 59, no. 1 (2002): 143–52.

———. *Gabriel's Rebellion: The Virginia Slave Conspiracies of 1800 and 1802*. Chapel Hill: University of North Carolina Press, 2000.

———. *He Shall Go Out Free: The Lives of Denmark Vesey*. Rev. ed. Lanham, MD: Rowman & Littlefield, 2004.

Elmer, Jonathan. *On Lingering and Being Last: Race and Sovereignty in the New World*. New York: Fordham University Press, 2008.

Emerson, Ralph Waldo. *Essays and Lectures* (1844). New York: Library of America, 1983.

Equiano, Olaudah. *The Interesting Narrative and Other Writings*. New York: Penguin, 2003.

Equiano, Olaudah, and Werner Sollors. *The Interesting Narrative of the Life of Olaudah Equiano, Or Gustavus Vassa, the African, Written by Himself*. New York: Norton, 2001.

Fergus, Claudius K. "'Dread of Insurrection': Abolitionism, Security, and Labor in Britain's West Indian Colonies, 1760–1823." *William and Mary Quarterly* 66, no. 4 (2009): 757–80.

———. *Revolutionary Emancipation: Slavery and Abolitionism in the British West Indies*. Baton Rouge: Louisiana State University Press, 2013.

Fink, Leon. *Sweatshops at Sea: Merchant Seamen in the World's First Globalized Industry, from 1812 to the Present*. Chapel Hill: University of North Carolina Press, 2011.

Fischer, Sibylle. *Modernity Disavowed: Haiti and the Cultures of Slavery in the Age of Revolution*. Durham, NC: Duke University Press, 2004.

Foy, Charles R. "Uncovering Hidden Lives: Developing a Database of Mariners in the Black Atlantic." *Common-Place* 9, no. 2 (2009). http://www.common-place.org/vol-09/no-02/tales/.

Franklin, H. Bruce. "Billy Budd and Capital Punishment: A Tale of Three Centuries." *American Literature* 69, no. 2 (1997): 337–59.

Fuss, Diana. "Corpse Poem." *Critical Inquiry* 30, no. 1 (2003): 1–30.

Garrison, Wendell Phillips, and Francis Jackson Garrison. *William Lloyd Garrison, 1805–1879: The Story of His Life Told by His Children*. New York: Century, 1886.

Geffert, Hannah N. "John Brown and His Black Allies: An Ignored Alliance." *Pennsylvania Magazine of History and Biography* 126, no. 4 (2002): 591–610.

Giddings, Joshua R. *Speeches in Congress (1841–1852)*. Boston: J. P. Jewett, 1853.

Gilroy, Paul. *The Black Atlantic: Modernity and Double Consciousness*. Cambridge, MA: Harvard University Press, 1993.

Glenn, Myra C. "The Naval Reform Campaign Against Flogging: A Case Study in Changing Attitudes Toward Corporal Punishment, 1830–1850." *American Quarterly* 35, no. 4 (1983): 408–25.

Gougeon, Len. "Militant Abolitionism: Douglass, Emerson, and the Rise of the Anti-Slave." *New England Quarterly* 85, no. 4 (2012): 622–57.

Grainger, James. *The Sugar-Cane: A Poem, in Four Books, with Notes*. London: R. and J. Dodsley, 1764.

Griffiths, Julia, and Rochester Ladies' Anti-slavery Society. *Autographs for Freedom*. Boston: J. P. Jewett, 1853–1854.

Hamilton, James, Jr., and City of Charleston, South Carolina. *Negro Plot: An Account of the Late Intended Insurrection among a Portion of the Blacks of This City. Published by the Authority of the Corporation of Charleston*. 2nd ed. Charleston, SC: A. E. Miller, 1822.

Hammond, John Craig, and Matthew Mason, eds. *Contesting Slavery: The Politics of Bondage and Freedom in the New American Nation*. Charlottesville: University Of Virginia Press, 2011.

Hartman, Saidiya V. *Scenes of Subjection: Terror, Slavery, and Self-Making in Nineteenth-Century America*. New York: Oxford University Press, 1997.

Howison, John. *European Colonies, in Various Parts of the World: Viewed in Their Social, Moral, and Physical Condition, by John Howison, of the Honourable East India Company's Bombay Service, And Author of, "Sketches of Upper Canada," "Foreign Scenes and Traveling Recreations."* 2 vols. London: Bentley, 1834.

———. "The Florida Pirate." *Blackwoods Edinburgh Magazine*, August 1, 1821, 516–31.

———. *The Florida Pirate, Or, An Account of a Cruise in the Schooner Esperanza, with a Sketch of the Life of Her Commander*. 2 vols. New-York: W. Borradaile, 1823; Pittsburgh: Cook and Schoyer, 1834.

———. *Tales from the Colonies in Two Volumes*. London: Henry Colburn and Richard Bentley, 1830.

Hyde, Carrie. "Novelistic Evidence: The Denmark Vesey Conspiracy and Possibilistic History." *American Literary History* 27, no. 1 (2015): 26–55.

James, C. L. R. *The Black Jacobins: Toussaint L'Ouverture and the San Domingo Revolution*. New York: Dial Press, 1938.

Jay, Gregory. "Douglass, Melville, and the Lynching of Billy Budd." In *Frederick Douglass & Herman Melville: Essays in Relation*, edited by Robert S. Levine and Samuel Otter, 369–95. Chapel Hill: University of North Carolina Press, 2008.

Jay, William. *The Creole Case, and Mr. Webster's Despatch; With Comments of the N.Y. American*. New York: New York American, 1842.

Johnson, Michael P. "Denmark Vesey and His Co-Conspirators." *William and Mary Quarterly* 58, no. 4 (2001): 915–76.

Johnson, Sara E. *The Fear of French Negroes: Transcolonial Collaboration in the Revolutionary Americas*. Berkeley: University of California Press, 2012.

Johnson, Walter. "Possible Pasts: Some Speculations on Time, Temporality, and the History of Atlantic Slavery." *Amerikastudien / American Studies* 45, no. 4 (2000): 485–99.

Jones, Howard. *Mutiny on the Amistad: The Saga of a Slave Revolt and Its Impact on American Abolition, Law, and Diplomacy*. Rev. ed. New York: Oxford University Press, 1987.

Karcher, Carolyn L. "Melville and Revolution." In *Melville's Short Novels: Authoritative Texts, Contexts, Criticism*, edited by Dan McCall, 344–55. New York: Norton, 2002.

———. *Shadow Over the Promised Land: Slavery, Race, and Violence in Melville's America*. PhD diss., University of Maryland, 1980; Baton Rogue: Louisiana State University Press, 1980.

———. "White Fratricide, Black Liberation: Melville, Douglass, and Civil War Memory." In *Frederick Douglass & Herman Melville: Essays in Relation.*, edited by Robert S. Levine and Samuel Otter, 349–95. Chapel Hill: University of North Carolina Press, 2008.

Kennedy, Lionel Henry, and Thomas Parker. *An Official Report of the Trials of Sundry Negroes, Charged with an Attempt to Raise an Insurrection in the State of South-Carolina: Preceded by an Introduction and Narrative; and in an Appendix, a Report of the Trials of Four White Persons, on Indictments for Attempting to Excite the Slaves to Insurrection. by Lionel H. Kennedy & Thomas Parker, Members of the Charleston Bar, and the Presiding Magistrates of the Court*. Charleston, SC: James R. Schenck, 1822.

Kritzberg, Barry. "A Pre-Civil War Struggle Against Capital Punishment: Charles Spear, Concord, and the Case of Washington Goode." *Concord Saunterer* 2, no. 1 (1994): 102–16.

Lee, Maurice S. "Melville, Douglass, the Civil War, Pragmatism." In *Frederick Douglass & Herman Melville: Essays in Relation*, edited by Robert S. Levine and Samuel Otter, 396–415. Chapel Hill: University of North Carolina Press, 2008.

Lepore, Jill. *New York Burning: Liberty, Slavery, and Conspiracy in Eighteenth-Century Manhattan* New York: Vintage, 2006.

Levine, Robert S. *Dislocating Race and Nation: Episodes in Nineteenth-Century American Literary Nationalism*. Chapel Hill: University of North Carolina Press, 2008.

———. *The Lives of Frederick Douglass*. Cambridge, MA: Harvard University Press, 2016.

———. *Martin Delany, Frederick Douglass, and the Politics of Representative Identity*. Chapel Hill: University of North Carolina Press, 1997.

———. *Martin R. Delany: A Documentary Reader*. Chapel Hill: University of North Carolina Press, 2003.

Levine, Robert S., and Samuel Otter. "Introduction: Douglass and Melville in Relation." In *Frederick Douglass & Herman Melville: Essays in Relation*, edited by Robert S. Levine and Samuel Otter, 1–18. Chapel Hill: University of North Carolina Press, 2008.

Linebaugh, Peter, and Marcus Rediker. *The Many-Headed Hydra: Sailors, Slaves, Commoners, and the Hidden History of the Revolutionary Atlantic*. Boston: Beacon Press, 2000.

Locke, John. *Two Treatises of Government*. Edited by Peter Laslett. 2nd ed. Reprint with amendments. London: Cambridge University Press, 1970; 1988.

Long, Edward. *The History of Jamaica; Or, General Survey of the Antient and Modern State of That Island*. 3 vols. London: T. Lowndes, 1774.

Lovejoy, Paul E. "Autobiography and Memory: Gustavus Vassa, Alias Olaudah Equiano, the African." *Slavery & Abolition* 27, no. 3 (2006): 317–47.

———. "Olaudah Equiano Or Gustavus Vassa—What's in a Name?" *Atlantic Studies* 9, no. 2 (2012): 165–84.

Masur, Louis P. *Rites of Execution: Capital Punishment and the Transformation of American Culture, 1776–1865*. Oxford: Oxford University Press, 1989.

Maynard, Douglas H. "The World's Anti-Slavery Convention of 1840." *Mississippi Valley Historical Review* 47, no. 3 (1960): 452–71.

McMullen, Bonnie Shannon. Review of "The Florida Pirate." By John Howison, *Washington Gazette*, November 20, 1821.

Melville, Herman. *Battle-Pieces and Aspects of the War: Civil War Poems*. Amherst, NY: Prometheus, 2001.

———. Herman Melville Papers, 1761–1964, "Billy Budd. A.Ms.; [n.p., n.d.]." MS Am 188 (363). Houghton Library, Cambridge, MA, Harvard University.

———. *Melville's Short Novels: Authoritative Texts, Contexts, Criticism*. Edited by Dan McCall. New York: Norton, 2002.

———. *Redburn, His First Voyage; White-Jacket, Or, the World in a Man-of-War; Moby-Dick, Or The Whale*. Notes by G. Thomas Tanselle. New York: Literary Classics, 1983.

Nell, William Cooper. *The Colored Patriots of the American Revolution, with Sketches of several Distinguished Colored Persons: To which is Added a Brief Survey of the Condition and Prospects of Colored Americans . . . with an Introduction by Harriet Beecher Stowe*. Boston: Robert F. Wallcut, 1855.

Newman, Richard S. *The Transformation of American Abolitionism: Fighting Slavery in the Early Republic*. Chapel Hill: University of North Carolina Press, 2002.

Osagie, Iyunolu Folayan. *The Amistad Revolt: Memory, Slavery, and the Politics of Identity in the United States and Sierra Leone*. Athens: University of Georgia Press, 2000.

Otter, Samuel. *Melville's Anatomies*. Berkeley: University of California Press, 1999.

Paine, Thomas. *Rights of Man: Being an Answer to Mr. Burke's Attack on the French Revolution*. Buffalo, NY: Prometheus, 1987.

Parker, Hershel. *Herman Melville: A Biography, Volume 1, 1819–1851* Baltimore: Johns Hopkins University Press, 2005.

Poe, Edgar Allan. "The Philosophy of Composition." In *Edgar Allan Poe: Poetry, Tales, and Selected Essays*, 1373–85. New York: Library of America, 1996.

Powell, Richard J. "Cinque: Antislavery Portraiture and Patronage in Jacksonian America." *American Art* 11, no. 3 (1997): 49–73.

Rafferty, Matthew Taylor. *The Republic Afloat: Law, Honor, and Citizenship in Maritime America*. Chicago: University of Chicago Press, 2013.

Ragsdale, Bruce A. "Incited by the Love of Liberty: The *Amistad* Captives and the Federal Courts." *Prologue* 35, no. 1 (2003): 1–28.

Rasmussen, Daniel. *American Uprising: The Untold Story of America's Largest Slave Revolt*. New York: Harper Collins, 2011.

Ratcliffe, Donald J. "The Decline of Antislavery Politics, 1815–1840." In *Contesting Slavery: The Politics of Bondage and Freedom in the New American Nation*, edited by John Craig Hammond and Matthew Mason, 267–90. Charlottesville: University of Virginia Press. 2011.

Rediker, Marcus. *The Amistad Rebellion: An Atlantic Odyssey of Slavery and Freedom*. New York: Penguin, 2012.

———. *The Slave Ship: A Human History*. New York: Viking, 2007.

———. *Villains of All Nations: Atlantic Pirates in the Golden Age*. Boston: Beacon Press, 2004.

Reynolds, David S. *John Brown, Abolitionist: The Man Who Killed Slavery, Sparked the Civil War, and Seeded Civil Rights*. New York: Knopf Doubleday, 2006.

Richardson, David. "Shipboard Revolts, African Authority, and the Atlantic Slave Trade." *William and Mary Quarterly* 58, no. 1 (2001): 69–92.

Rogers, Alan. "'Under Sentence of Death': The Movement to Abolish Capital Punishment in Massachusetts, 1835–1849." *New England Quarterly* 66, no. 1 (1993): 27–46.

Rogin, Michael Paul. *Subversive Genealogy: The Politics and Art of Herman Melville*. New York: Alfred A. Knopf, 1983.

Ruttenburg, Nancy. "Melville's Handsome Sailor: The Anxiety of Innocence." *American Literature: A Journal of Literary History, Criticism, and Bibliography* 66, no. 1 (1994): 83–103.

Sale, Maggie Montesinos. *The Slumbering Volcano: American Slave Ship Revolts and the Production of Rebellious Masculinity*. Durham, NC: Duke University Press, 1997.

Sinha, Manisha. *A Slave's Cause: A History of Abolition*. New Haven, CT: Yale University Press, 2016.

Smith, Gerrit. *Gerrit Smith and the Vigilant Association of the City of New York*. New York: John A. Gray, 1860.

Spady, James O'Neil. "Power and Confession: On the Credibility of the Earliest Reports of the Denmark Vesey Slave Conspiracy." *William and Mary Quarterly* 68, no. 2 (2011): 287–304.

Spear, John Murray, and Charles S. Spear, eds. *Prisoner's Friend: A Monthly Magazine Devoted to Criminal Reform, Philosophy, Science, Literature, and Art*. Boston, 1849.

Stauffer, John. *The Black Hearts of Men: Radical Abolitionists and the Transformation of Race*. Cambridge, MA: Harvard University Press, 2002.

Stowe, Harriet Beecher. *Uncle Tom's Cabin: Authoritative Text, Backgrounds and Contexts, Criticism*. Edited by Elizabeth Ammons. New York: Norton, 1994.

Sundquist, Eric J. *Empire and Slavery in American Literature, 1820–1865*. Jackson: University Press of Mississippi, 2006.

———. *To Wake the Nations: Race in the Making of American Literature*. Cambridge, MA: Belknap Press of Harvard University Press, 1993.

Taylor, Eric Robert. *If We Must Die: Shipboard Insurrections in the Era of the Atlantic Slave Trade*. Baton Rouge: Louisiana State University Press, 2006.

Thomas, Brook. "The Legal Fictions of Herman Melville and Lemuel Shaw." *Critical Inquiry* 11, no. 1 (1984): 24–51.

Trouillot, Michel-Rolph. *Silencing the Past: Power and the Production of History*. Boston: Beacon Press, 1995.

Turner, Nat, and Thomas R. Gray. *The Confessions of Nat Turner, the Leader of the Late Insurrection in Southampton, Va.: As Fully and Voluntarily made to Thomas R. Gray, in the Prison Where He was Confined, and Acknowledged by Him to be such when Read before the Court of Southampton, With the Certificate, Under Seal of the Court Convened at Jerusalem, Nov. 5, 1831, for His Trial, Also, an Authentic Account of the Whole Insurrection, with Lists of the Whites Who were Murdered, and of the Negroes Brought before the Court of Southampton, and there Sentenced, &c*. Baltimore: Lucas & Deaver Print, 1831.

Walker, David. *David Walker's Appeal to the Coloured Citizens of the World* (1829). Edited by Peter Hinks. University Park: Pennsylvania State University Press, 2003.

Wallace, Robert K. "Fugitive Justice: Douglass, Shaw, Melville." In *Frederick Douglass & Herman Melville: Essays in Relation*, edited by Robert S. Levine and Samuel Otter, 39–68. Chapel Hill: University of North Carolina Press, 2008.

Woertendyke, Gretchen. "John Howison's New Gothic Nationalism and Transatlantic Exchange." *Early American Literature* 43, no. 2 (2008): 309–35.

Wong, Edlie L. *Neither Fugitive nor Free: Atlantic Slavery, Freedom Suits and the Legal Culture of Travel*. New York: New York University Press, 2009.

Yannielli, Joseph. "Cinqué the Slave Trader: Some New Evidence on an Old Controversy," *Common-Place* 10, no. 1 (2009), http://www.common-place-archives.org/vol-10/no-01/yannielli/.

Ziff, Jerrold. "John Langhorne and Turner's 'Fallacies of Hope.'" *Journal of the Warburg and Courtauld Institutes* 27 (1964): 340–42.

Page numbers in italics refer to illustrations.

Colonization Society. *See* African Colonization Society

Colored American (abolitionist newspaper), 82

Colored Mariners' Database, 33

Columbus, Christopher, 141n50

Committee for the Abolition of the Slave Trade, 5

competence, 38, 39–40, 94

conversion narratives, 94

Cooper, James Fenimore, *The Red Rover,* 72, 139n1

Cormantees, 16

cosmopolitanism, 35, 40, 55

Covey (fictional character), 88

Crane, Gregg, 112, 149n55

Creole mutiny, 3, 8, 85–88, 95, 143n7; abolitionist rhetoric and, 72–76; right to revolt and, 93

Cuba, 54, 86, 91–92, 97

Cuffe, Paul, 40

Cugoano, Ottobah, 33

Davidson, Cathy N., 9, 135n18, 136n12

Davis, David Brion, 7, 15, 135n12, 136n14, 139n89

Dean, John, 24, 99

death penalty. *See* capital punishment

de Cressé, Auguste Jean Baptiste, 18, 30, 137n27, 138n59

dehumanization, 14, 26, 31, 34, 57, 75

Delano, Amaso (fictional character), 119–123, 129

Delany, Martin Robison, 48, 85, 96, 146n59; *Blake,* 8, 72–77, 87, 89–93, 97, 146n60; *The Condition, Elevation, and Destiny of the Colored People of the United States,* 89, 146n59

Demerara uprising (1823), 56

demonization, 9, 106, 119, 125

Deputies of Color (St. Domingo), 29

Deslondes, Charles, 44

Devany (slave in Vesey conspiracy), 42

Dewey, Loring, 69

Dillwyn, William, 22

Dittersdorf, Mrs. (fictional character), 66–67

Douglass, Frederick, 48, 85–86, 129, 132, 145n46; escape from slavery, 6; Goode trial and, 103; Harper's Ferry raid and, 96; on John Brown, 147n78; militancy, 143n7, 146n50, 146n53

—WORKS: "A Slave's Right to Revolt," 88; *My Bondage and My Freedom,* 5, 88; *The Narrative of the Life of A Slave,* 88, 115; *Narrative of the Life of Frederick Douglass,* 73, 150n63; "The Heroic Slave," 8, 72–77, 87–89, 93–97, 122, 146n50; "West India Emancipation" speech, 88–89

Drescher, Seymour, 15, 136n14

Du Bois, W. E. B., 82, 144n30

Egerton, Douglas R., 48–49, 140n27

Elmer, Jonathan, 122, 150n82

emancipation, 58–60, 106–107. *See also* abolitionist movement; free blacks; freedom

Emerson, Ralph Waldo, 86, 103, 145n47

emigration, 69, 89, 92, 146n59

emotions, 23, 39, 118

Enlightenment, 7, 12

enslaved people: agency of, 14, 28, 39, 68, 73, 75, 111 (*see also* revolutionary possibility); as "good" or "happy," 57, 121, 125; rhetoric about (*see* abolitionist rhetoric; proslavery arguments; "usefulness" arguments); as sailors, 6, 33–37, 136n13 (*see also* black sailors; sailors); treatment of (*see* Middle Passage; slavery: brutality of); women, 27, 37, 58. *See also* fugitive slaves; slave trade; slave trafficking: illegal

equal protection, 129

Equiano, Olaudah, 2, 9, 13–15, 73, 80, 132; *Interesting Narrative,* 7, 11, 14–15, 19, 21, 28, 32–40, 108, 115

Esperanza (fictional ship), 55

evidence: on Atlantic Slave Trade, 23–28; in Vesey conspiracy, 48–51. *See also* sailor testimony

evil, absolute, 107

extralegal space, ocean as, 85

Ferdinand, King, 141n50

Fergus, Claudius K., 15

fighting, among sailors, 115–118

flogging, 34, 36, 101, 105, 148n26, 150n66, 150n72; Melville and, 113–118

Foy, Charles R., 33

Franklin, H. Bruce, 148n8

ABOUT THE AUTHOR

LENORA WARREN is Assistant Professor of English at Colgate University.